INCENTIVES FOR COUNTRYSIDE MANAGEMENT
The Case of Environmentally Sensitive Areas

D0144128

INCENTIVES FOR COUNTRYSIDE MANAGEMENT
The Case of Environmentally Sensitive Areas

Edited by

MARTIN WHITBY

Professor of Countryside Management
Centre for Rural Economy
University of Newcastle upon Tyne

CAB INTERNATIONAL

CAB International
Wallingford
Oxon OX10 8DE
UK

Tel: Wallingford (0491) 832111
Telex: 847964 (COMAGG G)
Telecom Gold/Dialcom: 84: CAU001
Fax: (0491) 833508

A catalogue entry for this book is available from the British Library.

ISBN 0 85198 897 0

Typeset by Solidus (Bristol) Limited
Printed and bound in the UK at the University Press, Cambridge

CONTENTS

v

CONTRIBUTORS

David Colman is the Professor of Agricultural Economics at the University of Manchester.

Julie Froud is a Research Associate in the Department of Accounting and Finance at the University of Manchester.

Guy Garrod is a Research Associate in the Department of Agricultural Economics and Food Marketing at the University of Newcastle upon Tyne.

Garth Hughes is a Lecturer in Agricultural Economics at the University of Wales, Aberystwyth.

Philip Lowe is the Duke of Northumberland Professor of Rural Economy at the University of Newcastle upon Tyne.

Joan Moss is a Lecturer in the Department of Agricultural Economics at the Queen's University of Belfast.

Lucy O'Carroll is a Lecturer in the Department of Agricultural Economics at the University of Manchester.

Noel Russell is a Lecturer in Agricultural Economics at the University of Manchester.

Caroline Saunders is a Lecturer in Countryside Management at the University of Newcastle upon Tyne.

Sarah J. Skerratt is a Research Associate in the Department of Agricultural Economics at the Scottish Agricultural College, Edinburgh.

Martin Whitby is the Professor of Countryside Management at the University of Newcastle upon Tyne.

Ken Willis is a Reader in Environmental Economics in the Department of Town and Country Planning at the University of Newcastle upon Tyne.

Preface

Publication of this book requires acknowledgement of the many people and even institutions without whose efforts it would not have been possible. In particular it will be obvious to the reader that this work would not have seen the light of day had it not been for the series of events beginning in 1984 (or perhaps earlier) which led to the EC adoption of Regulation 797/85 and the subsequent passing of the UK Agriculture Act of 1986. Obviously the Ministry of Agriculture, Fisheries and Food was a major participant in those events, together with its counterparts in Scotland, Wales and Northern Ireland. I am grateful to those agencies for having generated the demand for this book, and also to many of their employees too numerous to mention separately for their generous advice during the preparation of the text.

Nearer home I freely acknowledge the contributions of the authors of this volume which have substantially exceeded responsibility for the words with which their names are associated. In particular all have commented constructively on the final chapter and several have advised me on particular aspects of the text. I also recognize the contribution of Paul Allanson, David Harvey and several other colleagues at Newcastle who have offered constructive comment on various parts of the text.

The production of this text has been made both more effective and more pleasurable by the work of two student assistants, Abby Tyler and Sue Pries, whose contribution to the preparation of tables and indices will be recognized by all who use them. Finally the assembly and printing of many drafts as well as the final version of the text has benefited immeasurably from the cheerful competence of Ruchelle Everton.

Martin Whitby

1

THE POLITICAL AND ECONOMIC ROOTS OF ENVIRONMENTAL POLICY IN AGRICULTURE

Martin Whitby and Philip Lowe

Introduction

This book explores the first results of a substantive change in agricultural policy which occurred in the mid-1980s. This change was an important one for conservation in that it was the first positive recognition in policy of a connection between agricultural expansion and environmental damage. It has also been seen as part of an attempt by government to escape from the expensive agricultural policy dilemma resulting from over-production, by offering direct incentives to farmers to farm less intensively.

This chapter seeks to explain how the UK reached the point, in 1984, when it proposed an important modification of the Common Agricultural Policy (CAP) to allow the creation of Environmentally Sensitive Areas (ESAs). The radical nature of that proposal was that, within these areas, member states of the European Community (EC; now called the European Union) might foster and encourage the retention of traditional farming systems thought to be environmentally benign: a radical proposal indeed, compared with the previous several decades which are still widely, if somewhat indiscriminately, described as 'productivist', denoting an unquestioned search for further output from the farm land base. The policy era preceding the introduction of ESAs might more accurately be seen as dominated by a concern to increase productivity as a step towards prosperity.

For more than half a century agricultural production had been influenced by more or less strongly interventionist policies affecting the structure of its resource use and the pattern of its output. However, not all decisions made in or about agriculture are attributable to the political process; many other factors may be adduced. For example, during the same period, agriculture had been the focus of a major technical revolution which had greatly influenced the way it produces and hence its economic role in rural areas. Furthermore, British agriculture had never operated in isolation from foreign influences during that period: the wartime submarine blockade was a major reason for interventionist policies; in the 25 years following the war explicit 'cheap food' policies allowed the country to take advantage of expanding world supplies of food whilst supporting farm incomes through a system of deficiency payments; and from 1973 onwards the UK became increasingly involved in the EC's Common Agricultural Policy, which still mainly uses market intervention systems to address the farm income problem.

Ministers and their departments have had to respond to major shifts of advantage and disadvantage, some of them very sudden, throughout this period. A comprehensive explanation of the current policy environment must therefore address the underlying economic and social processes at work as well as the political factors. The remainder of this chapter therefore analyses the sequence of events which led up to the adoption of the relevant EC regulations and their implementation in the UK. The analysis will use both economic and political arguments in the search for explanation.

Agricultural Policy in Deadlock

The evolution of agricultural policy since the war has been dominated by the major objective of producing an appropriate level of farm output mainly by means of supporting farming income through price policy (Tracy, 1989). The appropriate level of output has proved an elusive concept and the farming interest has accused governments of interpreting it too restrictively from time to time. At other times, particularly during the 1970s and early 1980s, others have criticized the level of support for agriculture for leading to too rapid a rate of expansion of production.

To the farming interest the main criterion of policy success has been the level of farm income and, judged against this objective, it could be argued that the achievements of agricultural policy have been modest. Figure 1.1 presents the course of aggregate farming income in real terms (at 1987 prices) since 1971. Despite marked year-on-year fluctuations, due to the weather and to the volatility of world markets, the general trend of real farming income has been unambiguously downwards throughout this period, with perhaps some levelling off around an aggregate of £1 billion. By contrast real gross domestic product (GDP: a measure of national income) has increased by some 50% over this whole period.

This downward fluctuating level of farming income was mainly attributable to falling real prices and rising costs. But it raises the question of how farms survive as businesses in such circumstances. The answer to this question has several elements. First, for a number of reasons, the income situation of individual farms is better than the aggregate suggests. The

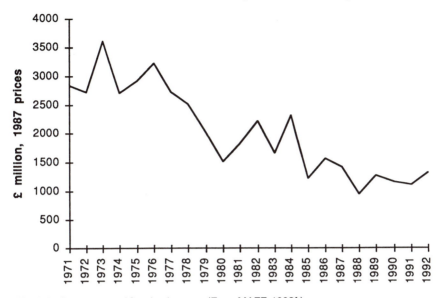

Fig. 1.1. Aggregate real farming income. (From MAFF, 1993f.)

number of farms is declining, if slowly, which allows aggregate income to be shared amongst fewer people. Farmers have many other potential sources of income and these will offset the loss due to the decline of farming income. Although the rate of increase in off-farm income is not known precisely, it will have helped make good the decline in real income of many businesses. Third, income is calculated net of depreciation, which is an accounting convention to allow for the replacement of capital goods. However, in times of economic recession farmers may cut back on capital replacement and indeed on new investment, in order to maintain household income. The fact that depreciation has become greater than new capital formation during the 1980s shows that they have chosen this response to some extent.

These reasons would suggest that a consequence of falling farm incomes has been a reduced rate of investment. Some farmers have managed to maintain their rate of investment by increasing their indebtedness during the last two decades. But the overall reduction in investment will have been further encouraged by the reduced rates of support for investment offered in successive farm investment grant schemes during the 1980s and by farmers' expectations changing in response to the uncertainties surrounding agricultural policy as it has been restructured. Although the evidence of investment falling below the industry's depreciation bill may seem symptomatic of a non-sustainable situation, this set of circumstances perhaps reflects a necessary moderation of the industry's planned rate of expansion. As such it may be welcomed as an appropriate response to over-supplied markets.

The problem of over-supply has long been familiar to farmers and their policy-makers. It arose as early as the 1950s, when the growth of world food supplies began to test the newly introduced deficiency payments system of farm support. Then the increasing abundance of supply was indicated, in the UK, by falling domestic food prices as world market prices fell and imports entered freely. Under the CAP, however, internal prices have been maintained at a level substantially higher than world market prices and EC policy-makers have been unable to reduce prices fast enough to check surplus production and encourage demand to achieve market balance. Under prevailing support mechanisms, production surplus to market demand is purchased into (intervention) storage and/or their export to the rest of the world is subsidized. A system better shaped to stimulate the continued growth of production, and hence of support costs, would be difficult to design!

During the 1970s and early 1980s the most costly surpluses to appear were in the dairy sector and their share of the CAP Market Regulation budget reached 29.6% in 1984, finally forcing the conclusion that quotas must be applied to milk production. Quotas were introduced, at short notice, in 1984 and the relative cost of dairy support has declined, from a peak of 32.1% of budget in 1985, to 16.2% in 1990 (EC, 1985a, 1990). Nevertheless dairy farm incomes have been comparatively buoyant since the introduction of quotas, prompting two related questions: who is now paying for the cost of supporting dairy farm incomes? and why could similar mechanisms not be applied to other sectors in surplus?

The answer to the first question must be partly that the consumer pays through higher prices and partly that some increase in efficiency has promoted income growth on dairy farms. The second question is one that has preoccupied the EC for some time, but no acceptable similar mechanisms operating at the level of the individual farm have so far been found. Discussions have centred on the possibility of introducing them for cereals and other production but the mechanisms introduced so far operate largely at the national level. Exceptions to that are the recently introduced beef and sheep quotas, which are not so much production quotas as support payments, and are not as effective in containing support costs whilst sustaining incomes. Another recent thrust of policy has been the attempt to decouple price support from income support in the hope of reducing the growth of policy costs induced by expansion, whilst maintaining incomes.

It may be concluded that buoyant farm incomes in the postwar period, combined with a generous system of tax allowances and capital grants and a rapid rate of technical innovation together fostered a high rate of investment in agriculture. A side-effect of that investment was the appearance of environmental damage which attracted the criticism of environmentalists. The industry's very success in expanding production has undermined market stability, and prices, followed by aggregate income, have trended downwards for two decades at least. This, in turn, has encouraged farmers to actively seek alternative means of income. One such opportunity, which arose from ⌐ recognition of the coincidence of interest between farmers and environmentalists, is in the payments now made to farmers for managing the countryside.

The Development of Environmental Policy in Relation to Agriculture

The roots of organized concern for the rural environment go back to the late 19th century. Then and throughout most of the 20th century the major threats were seen to arise from urban and industrial expansion. Concern for the countryside tended to be coloured by a highly romantic and idealized view of farming which, in a chronic state of depression until the 1940s, seemed to pose no threat to other rural interests and pursuits, but whose debilitated condition seemed to compound the countryside's vulnerability.

Farming, particularly the arable sector, had been in a depressed condition since the 1870s and few people anticipated the rapid transformation it would undergo in the postwar period under the auspices of state support. Even so, agricultural intensification, realized through the adoption of new technologies, the spread of mechanization and the consolidation of holdings, transformed the rural environment. As the scale of the postwar revolution in agriculture became apparent, there was a shift of emphasis of environmental concern from a focus on urban and industrial pressures as the main threat to landscape and wildlife, to a preoccupation with the destructive effects of changing farming and forestry practices and technologies. This shift involved profound changes in the popular image of agriculture. The sheer pace of development destroyed any illusions that it was intrinsically an unchanging or slowly evolving activity.

Gradually, various environmental implications of agricultural intensification came to be recognized. The appearance of industrialized farm buildings first aroused concern in the 1950s. Then the dramatic decline in the numbers of certain birds drew attention to the side-effects from some synthetic pesticides. Other issues followed, including the loss of hedgerows, moorland and heathland reclamation, the drainage of wetlands and the destruction of nature conservation sites. It was only in the 1970s, however, that an overall concept of agricultural change seems to have been fully grasped – that changes in agriculture could comprehensively alter 'the landscape' rather than just individual features of it (Countryside Commission, 1974). Opinions began to harden also as evidence accumulated that 'all changes due to [agricultural] modernization are harmful to wildlife except for a few species that are able to adapt to the new simplified habitats' (NCC, 1977). A survey of habitat losses conducted by the NCC and published in 1984 revealed the following grim chronicle: over the previous 35 years, the nation had lost 95%

of lowland herb-rich grasslands, 80% of chalk and limestone grasslands, 60% of lowland heaths, 45% of limestone pavements, 50% of ancient woodlands, 50% of lowland fells and marshes, over 60% of lowland raised bogs, and a third of all upland grasslands, heaths and mires.

With the growing appreciation of the totality of agricultural change, the whole system of agricultural support came under attack as the root cause of intensification, rather than the activities of individual farmers, and pressure built up for general powers to regulate the environmental impact of agricultural and forestry development. These issues have been vigorously pursued by a rural conservation movement which is particularly well organized and well established in Britain. There are several dozen national groups concerned with the conservation of the rural environment. Their combined membership roughly doubled during the 1980s to over 3 million. They have led the public campaign to protect the countryside and have usually operated in tandem with the statutory conservation agencies who act as advocates of the cause of rural conservation within government. In seeking to tackle the environmental impact of agriculture, these groups and agencies have had to confront powerful vested interests.

For their part, agricultural interests led by the National Farmers' Union (NFU) and the Country Landowners' Association (CLA) have been determined to preserve two cherished and related freedoms in responding to environmental criticisms of modern farming: *first* the autonomy of the Ministry of Agriculture Fisheries and Food (MAFF) and of the farming community in the administration and implementation of agricultural policy; and *second* the autonomy of the farmer and the rural landowner in making production and land-use decisions. Environmental regulations, by making farmers answerable to non-agricultural authorities and interests, would have the effect of diminishing the power of the farming lobby as well as the autonomy of the farmer: such regulations have therefore been stubbornly resisted.

Agriculture and food comprise the only industrial sector to have its own Ministry. This not only gives the sector crucial access to government decision-making and the allocation of resources, but it also underpins the exclusive relationship between the Ministry and agricultural interest groups. Defence of its administrative territory therefore has special significance for MAFF and its associated interests and the Ministry has assiduously opposed the imposition of constraints or responsibilities which might give outside groups or other departments leverage over its work. Thus it failed to pursue the requirement of the 1968 Countryside Act which provides that every Minister and government department must have regard to the natural beauty and amenity of the countryside. The Ministry also successfully blocked attempts to make this duty more specific in the passage of the 1981 Wildlife and Countryside Act.

In 1978 the Ministry's Advisory Council, in a report on Agriculture and the Countryside, proposed that the remit of the Ministry's extension arm, the

Agricultural Development and Advisory Service (ADAS), should be widened to include conservation as well as food production. In the event few of the Report's recommendations reached the statute book. Although ADAS had already begun to develop its conservation expertise, the need formally to broaden its remit became a repeated call, winning the support not only of environmental groups and parliamentarians, but also of agricultural interest groups. One of the hindrances to the adoption of environmental consider- ations in agricultural policy-making has been the reluctance of MAFF to collaborate with environmentalists or other agencies. MAFF's reputation for intransigence was apparent in a survey of the leaders of national environmen- tal groups conducted in 1980 in which the Ministry was voted the least accessible government department and the most unreceptive one (Lowe and Goyder, 1983). The Countryside Commission, the government's own statu- tory adviser on countryside matters, was led to complain in 1979 that: 'Over the years we have regularly had cause to regret a lack of regard for conservation and recreation in Ministry policy and practice: we have tended to make more progress dealing with the private farming and landowning organisations directly' (Countryside Commission, 1979).

The farming lobby, much more than the Ministry has, indeed, sought to actively influence the terms and nature of the conservation debate. Being challenged, perhaps more than any other economic interest, by environmen- tal criticism, the NFU and the CLA have actively engaged in discussion with environmental groups. Throughout they have stressed the need to foster and maintain the voluntary cooperation and goodwill of the farming community if practical remedies are to be found in response to conservation problems. Together the NFU and CLA have responded to the charges of conservationists by presenting farmers and landowners as stewards of the countryside.

In practical terms this has meant considerable effort by the two organizations to nurture a conservation ethic and sense of moral responsibil- ity among their members. When confronted by specific environmental problems, the farming lobby has typically responded by promulgating schemes of voluntary self-regulation (Cox *et al.*, 1990). Agriculture's excep- tional freedom from any statutory environmental regulations and the reliance placed instead upon informal or voluntary safeguards is an indication of the skill with which agricultural autonomy has been defended and the sig- nificance of the postwar policy commitment to increased food production. Implicit, and often explicit, in much of the NFU's and CLA's argument against controls is the claim that these would be unworkable because farmers and landowners would not cooperate in their implementation, even though agrarian lawlessness is not a noted feature of British society.

In 1978 an inter-departmental Countryside Review Committee (1978) examined the possibilities for more integrated management of the country- side. On the premise that 'any new policy must have the broad support of the farming community', the Committee roundly rejected the imposition of controls over agriculture, arguing that they would be cumbersome, costly and unconstructive. Instead, it called for a 'voluntary and flexible policy, based on advice, encouragement, education and financial inducements.' It is this approach that has been largely pursued by government, and there has been a marked reluctance to introduce controls over agriculture.

With respect to nature conservation sites, however, powers were introduced by the 1981 Wildlife and Countryside Act specifically to regulate changing farming practices. Since 1949 there has been a provision to designate wildlife habitats as Sites of Special Scientific Interest (SSSIs). The designation assumed the continuation of traditional land management, and the areas enjoyed no protection from shifts in agricultural or forestry practices. By the mid-1970s it was evident that many were being damaged or destroyed by agricultural intensification or afforestation, and a survey conducted by the NCC in 1980 suggested that the annual rate of damage to SSSIs was 4%. Since 1981, therefore, farmers whose land is within an SSSI must notify the official Nature Conservancy Council of their intention to carry out any potentially damaging operation. Depending on the nature of the site and its wildlife significance the list of potentially damaging operations might include ploughing or draining or pesticide or fertilizer application or an increase in stocking density.

The period of notification was initially three months, but was extended to four in 1985. The intention was to give the Nature Conservancy Council an opportunity, if necessary, to persuade farmers to modify their plans or to negotiate a management agreement. If agreement is not reached, there are powers to extend the notification period: negotiating a satisfactory management agreement can take many months, years even. There are also back-up powers to apply a nature conservation order if a farmer proves uncooperative. The vast majority, though, do cooperate not least because the principle of payment to farmers is that they should be fully compensated, usually on an annual basis, for not proceeding to improve their land and intensify their production. Pressures to extend these procedures to the wider countryside or to protect landscapes as well as habitats have been resisted by the government, which regards the SSSI safeguards as cumbersome and expensive, even though it devised them.

A commonly noted shortcoming of countryside management and the conservation regulation of farming practices was that they typically involved the conservation agencies swimming against the tide of agricultural support. Compensation to farmers for not destroying a wildlife habitat, for example, was paid by these agencies rather than by MAFF, whose promotion of agricultural productivity and new farming methods had helped create the problem. By the mid-1980s, despite the efforts of the farming lobby to contain the issue, a considerable tide of opinion was building towards the environmental reform of agricultural policy. In the summer of 1984 more than 170 MPs signed a motion expressing alarm at the continuing threats to Britain's heritage of landscape and wildlife and calling on the government 'to ensure that agricultural policy, and the structure of public funding, is widened so as to take full account of the need to protect and enhance the environment.'

In 1985 the Parliamentary Environment Committee published a review of the working of the Wildlife and Countryside Act and had this to say about the practice of compensating farmers for not destroying the environment:

> The illogicality of one part of government (MAFF) offering financial inducement to someone to do something which another part of government (DOE and related bodies) then has to pay him not to, is clear. The primary reason for the negative character of management agreements is thus the conflict which the CLA describe: management agreements arise in order to control a farmer subsidised to damage the environment. They are there to prevent and not to promote. The argument stated so baldly may seem crude; we obviously need food and MAFF is not a nature devouring monster. However, the underlying logic is inescapable: to prevent the conflict the farmer should not be encouraged to damage the environment in the first place.
>
> (House of Commons Papers, 1984–85, para. 46)

Government Ministers became receptive to arguments concerning the reform of agricultural support as other problems mounted for the support system, including over-production and rising budgetary costs.

One of the first fruits of the new direction was the introduction of Environmentally Sensitive Areas (ESAs) to cover parts of the country whose landscape and ecology were threatened by widespread agricultural change and where farmers would be paid to continue farming in a traditional manner. This was the first specifically environmental measure to be supported directly from the agricultural budget. In 1985, also, MAFF launched a new Agricultural Improvement Scheme of grants to replace those which had been so roundly condemned for encouraging environmental degradation. New grants were to be available for planting hedges, repairing traditional walls, planting broadleaved shelter belts and even for employing the services of specialist consultants to provide landscaping advice for farm development schemes.

The 1986 Agriculture Act set the seal on this new emphasis in agricultural policy. Unlike the many earlier Acts of the same title, this one contained measures which positively tackled matters of central importance to conservation. The Act also placed a statutory duty on Agriculture Ministers to balance the conservation and promotion of the enjoyment of the countryside, the support of a stable and efficient agricultural industry, and the economic and social interests of rural areas. Forestry had acquired similar obligations under the Wildlife and Countryside (Amendment) Act of 1985.

A working party on Alternative Land Use and the Rural Enterprise (ALURE) was set up in Whitehall and an unprecedented package of policies was presented to the House of Commons jointly by the Minister of Agriculture and the Secretary of State for the Environment. A central part of that package was the announcement of the second round of ESAs (MAFF (and the Secretaries of State for Northern Ireland and for Scotland), 1987b).

How do we explain this emphatic U-turn? First, it represented a triumph for the steady attrition by the environmental lobby which had built up broad parliamentary support for the reform. But it also marked a major shift in strategy by the Ministry which, as we have seen, had a reputation for being inward-looking and defensive in protecting its own departmental territory and the interests of the agricultural sector. No longer was this a tenable strategy, with so much critical debate surrounding agricultural policy, with Thatcherite pressures to commercialize, privatize and reduce many of its traditional functions, and with speculation in the farming press extending even to the Ministry's possible demise. Agricultural policy-makers have been propelled into attempting means of curbing over-production and the public cost of farm supports. In so doing, they have tended to embrace environmental concerns, not necessarily through any deep convictions, but because most environmental improvements reduce agricultural output, thereby contributing to the alleviation of surplus and budgetary problems. With the change in its responsibilities, the Ministry adopted a much more active and promotional stance, generating a flow of policy initiatives and assuming a more positive and prominent role in the promotion of conservation in the farmed countryside. Its own internal logic might be that this offered a means of continuing to support farm incomes, albeit in selected areas, whilst reducing the incentives to expand production.

Major policy initiatives involving grant aid to farmers included set-aside and the farm woodland scheme, as well as an even more pronounced shift in the Ministry's capital grant scheme towards environmental requirements and pollution control. In 1989 the new Farm and Conservation Grant Scheme stipulated that plans should take into account the impact on the countryside of farm improvements. For the first time the Ministry was formally empowered to refuse grants if proposals were considered environmentally detrimental.

By and large, environmental groups have welcomed the Ministry's new outlook and the increased attention paid by ADAS staff to environmental issues. However, some scepticism remains amidst a feeling that rural conservation is still a secondary matter for the Ministry. All too often, especially with controversial schemes such as set-aside and farm woodlands, the Ministry uses conservation arguments to justify policy change but the details of policy pay little heed to ensuring tangible and enduring conservation benefits. Nevertheless, it is no longer possible for the Ministry to treat conservation opinion with the indifference of the past.

The Flagship of Agri-Environmental Policy

Undoubtedly, the flagship policy in the Ministry's new found commitment to conservation is ESAs. The authorization for them comes from a modification promoted by the British Government to the EC's New Structures Directive, which was under discussion in 1984. This was duly passed by the Council of Ministers and became Article 19 of Council Regulation 797/85 on Improving the Efficiency of Agricultural Structures (EC, 1985a). Under Article 19 member states were authorized to introduce 'special national schemes in environmentally sensitive areas'. These were to be areas of high conservation value where schemes would encourage farming practices favourable to the environment. Initially, it was not agreed that such initiatives could receive support from the Community budget, but this point was conceded in 1987 with agreement on Regulation 1760/87 which provided a maximum of 25% reimbursement from the European Agricultural Guidance and Guarantee Fund (EAGGF = FEOGA). Article 19 was implemented in the UK by the Agriculture Act 1986 (Section 18).

MAFF formulated criteria to the effect that ESAs should cover areas whose national environmental significance was threatened by agricultural change, but which could be conserved through the adoption or maintenance of a particular form of farming practice. The areas should also represent a discrete and coherent unit of environmental interest to permit the economical administration of appropriate conservation aids.

The Agriculture Act was followed by a period of consultation between MAFF and other agencies (those concerned with conservation, countryside and heritage) who had to choose areas from the very long list of possible candidates, including 46 in England and Wales, and ten in Scotland (Friends of the Earth, 1992). The full list of areas designated and the sites from which they were chosen are listed in Table 1.1 and the course of designation since 1987 is summarized in Table 1.2.

The so-called 'first round' of ESAs were launched in 1987 to be followed by a second round in 1988. At the end of their first five years all of the first-round schemes were renewed and in 1993 a further third round of schemes was presented and a fourth round, to be introduced in 1994, was also indicated. The designation of the first-round schemes was followed by semi-public discussions with the Farmers' Unions over the terms and rates of compensation.

The areas that have been designated are very different in character, ranging from the lowland heaths and grassland of Breckland to the wet pastures, reedbeds and willow-lined rivers of the Suffolk valleys; from the intricate patterns of small fields and stone-faced boundary banks, lying between rocky heather-covered hills of the Lleyn Peninsula to the steep, wooded valleys and rounded hills of the Shropshire borders and from the open moors of peat and heather of the North Peak to the Black Wood of Rannoch

Table 1.1. Proposed Environmentally Sensitive Areas 1985.

Area	Date (if) designated	Area	Date (if) designated
Shetland		North Downs	
Orkney		Ashdown Forest	
Central Deeside		Pevensey Levels	
Caithness and NW		South Downs	1987/88
Sutherland Coast		Surrey Heaths	
Uists and Benbecula	1988*	Itchen Valley	
Inner Hebrides Coastal		Test Valley	1988
Nithsdale		New Forest Grazings	
Breadalbane	1987	North Wessex Downs	
Strathallan		South Wiltshire Downs	
Whitlaw/Eildon	1988	Mendips	
Northumberland National		Somerset Levels and	
Park Moorland		Moors	1987
South Solway		Exmoor	1993
North Pennines	1987*	Dartmoor	
Lake District	1993	Bodmin Moor	
Arnside and Silverdale		West Penwith Moors	1987*
Yorkshire Dales		Anglesey	1993
North York Moors		Lleyn	1988*
Lower Derwent Valley		Southern Snowdonia	
Peak District	1988*	East Montgomeryshire and	
Shropshire Hills		East Radnorshire	
Clun Valley	1988*	Mynydd Elenydd	
Wyre Forests		Radnor Forest and South	
Nene Washes and Valley		Radnorshire Upland	1993*
Ouse Washes and Valley		Black Mountains	
Breckland	1988	Black Mountain, West	
The Broads	1987	Brecon Beacons	
Suffolk Coast and Heaths	1988*	Gower	
Dedham Vale		Teifi	
North Kent Marshes	1993	Pembrokeshire	

*Areas may not coincide with designated ESAs.
Source: Friends of the Earth (1992).

on the lower mountain slopes in Breadalbane (Fig. 1.2). What they have in common, though, is a landscape and ecology critically dependent on the continuation of agricultural systems which are, typically, extensive and livestock based, though some are threatened more by decline and others more by improvement and intensification.

Farmers in the first and second round of ESAs (see Table 1.2) were offered a five-year agreement awarding them an annual payment in return for

Table 1.2. Current ESAs by designation and renewal dates and type of habitat: August 1993.

Name	Year first designated	Initial area	Renewal year	Renewed area	Type of habitat
England					
The Broads	1987	29,870	1992	36,000	Drained marshland, marsh/dyke, fen/carr woodland
Somerset Levels and Moors	1987	26,970	1992	27,000	Wetland
Pennine Dales	1987	15,960	1992	46,000	Wet pasture, haymeadows, woodlands
West Penwith	1987	7176	1992	7176	Coastal heathland, inland heathland, sods and wetland
South Downs	1987/88	61,000	1992	69,000	Species-rich chalk turf
Breckland	1988	94,032	1993	94,032	Grazed heath, calcareous grassland, wetlands
North Peak	1988	49,600	1993	54,800	Peat moorland, grasslands, heather heath
Shrops Border (Clun)	1988	21,000	1993	21,000	Rough grazing, valley woodlands, hedgerows
Suffolk River Valleys	1988	32,149	1993	44,000	Reedbeds, wet grassland, rivers and ditches
Test Valley	1988	2600	1993	4800	Chalk stream communities, chalk grassland
Avon Valley	1993	5200			Water meadow systems, grassland, small woods, scrub and willow carr
Exmoor	1993	81,000			Open moorland, coastal heath, grassland, wooded river valleys
Lake District	1993	245,200			Fells and valleys, lakes, woodland, grassland, ancient field systems
North Kent Marshes	1993	14,700			Coastal marshes, ditches, dykes, ancient field systems
South Wessex Downs	1993	45,900			Small stream valleys, wet pastures, grassland, archaeological remains

Table 1.2. *continued*

Name	Year first designated	Initial area	Renewal year	Renewed area	Type of habitat
South West Peak	1993	33,900			Open moorland, blanket bog, enclosed grassland
Scotland					
Breadalbane	1987	120,000	1992	181,207	Arctic/alpine uplands, woodland, open water
Loch Lomond	1987	42,000	1992	49,687	Upland moors and heaths, grasslands, blanket bogs, open water
Machair Uists etc.	1988	7000	1993	18,110	Dry plain, sandy dunes
Stewartry	1988	42,000	1993	60,312	Coastal marshes, wetland, unimproved grassland, semi-natural woodland
Eildon/Whitlaw	1988	8000	1993	35,125	Unimproved grassland, wet basin mires, heath
Wales					
Cambrian Mountains	1987/88	153,000	1993	153,000	Rough grazing, oak woodland, haymeadows
Lleyn Peninsula	1988	39,750	1993	39,750	Coastland, headlands, valley wetlands
Isle of Anglesey (Ynys Môn)	1993	72,000			Rough grazing, woodland, wetland
Radnor	1993	100,500			Rough grazing, woodland, wetland
Clwydian Range	1993	28,000			
Preseli	1993	115,000			
Northern Ireland					
Mourne/Slieve Croob	1988	33,000	1993	33,000	Coastal features, blanket and peaty bogs, archaeological sites
Glens of Antrim	1989	7400	1993	38,000	Coastal cliffs, peaty bogs

					Wetland, woodland and scrub, blanket bog, moorland, mountains
West Fermanagh and Erne Lakeland	1993	60,000			
Total Areas	1988/89	792,507	1992/93	1,687,958	
Proposed Areas					
England					
Cotswold Hills	1994	84,700			
Dartmoor	1994	100,500			
Blackdown Hills	1994	39,900			
Essex Coast	1994	26,300			
Shropshire Hills	1994	3800			
Upper Thames Tributaries	1994	29,500			
Northern Ireland					
The Sperrins	1994	90,000			
Slieve Gullion	1994	18,000			
Grand Total, all ESAs	1994	2,206,099			

Derived from Baldock *et al.*, *Journal of Rural Studies*, Vol. 6, No. 2, 1990; MAFF News Releases 13/92, 15/92, 17/92, 29/92, 73/93, 75/93, 77/93; and DANI ESA/2 booklets.

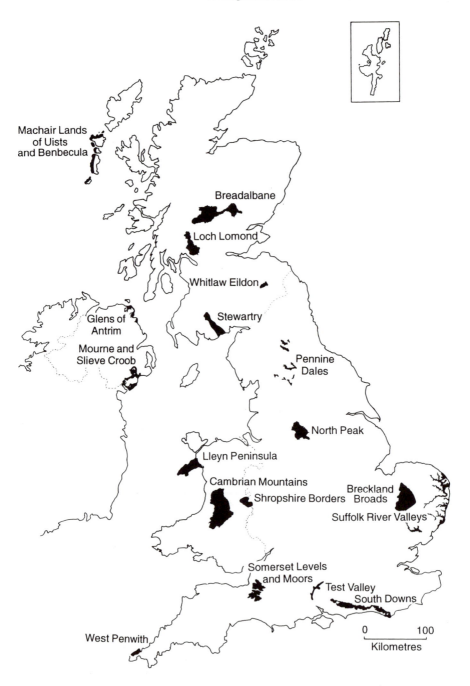

Machair Lands
of Uists
and Benbecula

Breadalbane

Loch Lomond

Whitlaw Eildon

Glens of
Antrim

Stewartry

Mourne and
Slieve Croob

Pennine
Dales

North Peak

Lleyn Peninsula

Cambrian Mountains

Shropshire Borders

Breckland
Broads

Suffolk River Valleys

Somerset Levels
and Moors

Test Valley

South Downs

West Penwith

0   100
Kilometres

Fig. 1.2. UK ESAs, 1988. Crown copyright.

following a prescribed set of farming practices. Typically the prescriptions cover a range of daily and seasonal farming activities. They vary according to the physical and farming circumstances of each ESA. Most include restrictions on fertilizer use and stocking densities, prohibitions on the use of herbicides and pesticides and on the installation of new drainage or fencing. Farmers also agreed to manage appropriately features such as hedges, ditches, woods, walls and barns, and to protect historic features. Both the practices and the rates of payment are standard within areas, but highly diverse from one ESA to another.

In many ESAs participants are required to complete a plan identifying the features of the farm to which the prescriptions will apply. The plan enables the standard prescriptions to be applied to the specific circumstances of each farm. The rates of payment take account of the actual and potential profits which a farmer forgoes by following the prescribed management practices. Allowance is also made for such factors as the financial security which the agreement will provide, the typical size of farms in the area, as well as their existing cropping patterns. The payment made to individual farmers is the standard rate per hectare multiplied by the area included in the scheme. In some areas, the complexity of landscape types and habitats necessitated a second, higher tier of area payments, associated with additional constraints, e.g. a more restrictive grassland management regime or, in the case of the South Downs and other ESAs, to induce farmers to reinstate ploughed-up pastures.

The response of farmers has been enthusiastic and contrasts sharply with the early reaction to the SSSI regulations. Initial progress was most advanced

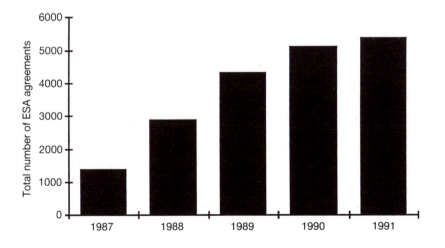

Fig. 1.3. Total number of ESA agreements. (Source: MAFF.)

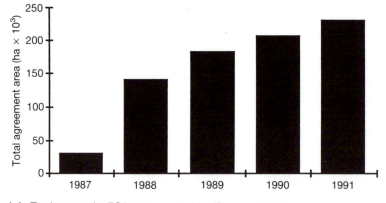

Fig. 1.4. Total area under ESA agreements: UK. (Source: MAFF.)

with the ESAs in England, where, by the end of the first year, some 100,000 hectares had been entered into the scheme, representing 87% of the total targeted area of land seen as eligible for agreements. Figures 1.3 and 1.4 show the pace of uptake of the agreements in the first and second rounds of designation in the UK.

The attraction of the ESA scheme to farmers compared with the SSSI regulations is that it is entirely voluntary, it is typically less restrictive, it is much simpler to enter and is administered by agricultural officials rather than conservation officials. The attraction to the government is that it is simpler and apparently cheaper to administer. This is mainly because of its use of flat rate subsidies for traditional husbandry rather than the individual 'profits foregone' compensation in the case of SSSIs, which involves complex negotiations and assessments for each and every farmer.

The ESA programme, with its direct and tangible commitment to conservationist farming, marks a significant departure for agricultural policy in the UK. For the first time farmers are being paid by MAFF to 'produce' countryside, and they seem to be responding to this challenge as keenly as they once did to past encouragements to produce more milk or barley. Unlike any other form of protected area, ESAs are the responsibility of Agricultural rather than Environment Ministries. It has thus created important precedents in the deployment of agricultural funds and personnel representing a potentially important first step in transforming MAFF into a Rural Ministry and helping to perpetuate its existence in a period of liberalizing and deregulating agricultural policy.

In overcoming one sectional division it has leapfrogged a second – that between landscape protection and nature conservation. This increasingly anachronistic feature of British conservation has been blurred by describing the new areas as 'of national environmental significance'. Archaeological concerns are also catered for. However, ESAs fall short of a fully integrated approach to environmental management.

Nevertheless, ESAs have won warm support from farming and environmental groups alike. Indeed bodies as diverse as the Royal Society for the Protection of Birds (RSPB), Friends of the Earth and the Farmers' Union of Wales have pressed for the ESA approach to be applied much more widely across the countryside. MAFF has rejected the notion of a blanket approach and, although it has expanded the ESA programme, it remains a minor though well publicized aspect of policy. This has led some environmentalists to regard it as a distraction from the main task of reforming agricultural policy more generally. Even the Countryside Commission has argued that altering the administration of Hill Livestock Compensatory Allowance payments, so that they no longer encourage overstocking and grassland improvements, would greatly diminish the need for ESAs in the uplands. Another legitimate criticism lies with the voluntary nature of farmer participation. While it is quite appropriate that such a novel scheme should seek to foster the confidence and cooperation of farmers and not alienate them, it could be argued that this is being taken to excessive lengths. For example, a farmer can enter just parts of his farm and be paid accordingly, but still be free to intensify production on the rest – paradoxically, perhaps, using part of the ESA payments to finance such change. Likewise, those farmers who choose not to participate in the ESA programme can undertake environmentally damaging improvements for which they may even remain eligible for MAFF grants.

Such features prompt more general reflections on this episode in the development of agricultural and environmental policy. For the stark contrast between the farming community's often vociferous opposition to SSSI designations in the early 1980s and its evident enthusiasm for the ESA concept cannot wholly be accounted for in terms of the politics of attrition or the changed policy context of the later period. In the aftermath of milk quotas and amongst incessant discussion of ways of curbing production across a broad spectrum of commodities, ESAs have enabled a renovation of the 'permissive corporatism' which has, in the postwar period, been the approach to state involvement in the regulation of agriculture preferred by farming and landowning interests (Cox *et al.*, 1988).

Corporatism, a style of interest intermediation in which producer groups play an important role in regulating their own constituencies by reaching bargained agreements with state agencies, may range from highly bureaucratic and state-directed 'controlling' forms to 'permissive' kinds more reliant on market mechanisms and incentives. The latter clearly allow higher degrees of autonomy and discretion for producer groups and their representative organizations. Indeed, where control has been necessary within agriculture, the farming and landowning community has been anxious both that it take a permissive form and that the control remain within the industry. In terms of such long-cherished priorities the attractions of the ESA arrangements are plain enough.

Hence, whilst SSSI designation and its associated mechanism of the management agreement is an often protracted and highly bureaucratic procedure, entailing elements of compulsion and administration by a conservation agency and including the possibility of criminal liability, the ESA scheme is both voluntary and administered by MAFF through the advisory service with which farmers are familiar and at ease. As such the scheme, with its flat rate payments set at 'reasonable' levels, bears the familiar stamp of British incrementalism. The difficulties apparent in the operation of the Wildlife and Countryside Act 1981 thus elicited a policy response embodying neither a radical shift nor a new institution but, rather, yet another addition to the already lengthy list of designated areas in the countryside. How enduring this innovation will prove may be judged in the light of the evidence presented in the following chapters.

The trajectory of the issue in political terms is also not dissimilar from many other environmental conflicts. The running in the initial phase, from the late 1970s through to the mid-1980s, was made very much by the conservation movement highlighting cases of environmental damage from agricultural intensification. The conservation agencies also played a key role in the early development of the policy response – the NCC with the Wildlife and Countryside Act and the Countryside Commission in devising the Broads Grazing Marshes Scheme (the forerunner of ESAs, specifically designed to halt the drainage and ploughing up of the Halvergate Marshes). With the formulation of ESAs, the initiative passed firmly back to MAFF, and conservation pressure groups became marginal to the further development of policy. What many saw as a fundamental attack on the agricultural policy community has thus been deflected. A new support policy for farmers has been devised, but as yet, the environmental benefits remain uncertain, although the criteria against which this policy must be judged eventually are environmental. The policy also provides a new source of income for farmers in areas of conservation interest without obliging them to negotiate individual management agreements.

ESAs in Practice

After the first and second rounds of ESAs in 1987 and 1988, these schemes were all renewed in 1992 and 1993, at the end of their first five years. The implementation of successive schemes has been increasingly smooth. In May 1993, in response to the EC 'Agri-Environment Directive' (EC, 1992a), MAFF published a set of proposals regarding a further round of six new ESAs to be designated in 1994 (MAFF, 1993i). These include ESAs in the Cotswold Hills, Dartmoor, the Blackdown Hills, the Essex Coast, the Shropshire Hills and the

Fig. 1.5. UK ESAs, 1994. Crown copyright.

Upper Thames Tributaries. There will also be further ESAs designated in Scotland, Wales and Northern Ireland before this book appears. Their designation will bring the total designated area to over 2 million hectares, more than doubling the areas designated in the first and second rounds in 1987/88. The drastically changed map of ESAs is presented in Fig. 1.5 for comparison with Fig. 1.2.

The May 1993 proposals also carry an interesting further idea for combining access with ESA agreements by promoting access where none is currently provided for. This will be brought about by enhancing the payments to farmers who provide extra access on their ESA land, as long as it is subject to an agreement with at least five years to run. The land selected for such arrangements will be non-arable and must not have existing rights of way across it. This option will meet some of the conservationists' objections to the earlier rounds of ESAs which did not explicitly make any provision for access. However, given the legal complexities of access and the problems of changing arrangements, once they have been established in use, one may wonder how well such proposals will be received by landowners and farmers.

An interesting feature of the 1986 Act is that it contains a requirement that:

> Where agreements have been made . . . with persons having an interest
> in land in a designated area the minister shall arrange for the effect on
> the area as a whole of the performance of the agreements to be kept
> under review and shall from time to time publish such information as he
> considers appropriate about those effects.
>
> (Section 18, sub-section 8)

Such a requirement is novel within the mores of British government but is in keeping with proposals for policy monitoring and evaluation in the handbook recently published by the Department of the Environment (DOE, 1991b) and with the longer-standing series of handbooks issued by the Treasury (HM Treasury, 1991). The pronouncements on environmental policy which have become a regular autumn event (DOE, 1990, 1991a, 1992) have also contributed to a commitment to evaluation of policies and to an aura of openness in government which Whitehall-watchers will welcome.

This requirement has been met by a programme of monitoring undertaken by MAFF. Two types of monitoring are undertaken at the ESA level. These include an internal programme which is 'designed to identify any significant changes to wildlife, landscape or historic features which occur after designation' (Hooper, 1992, p. 53). In addition MAFF has instigated a number of socioeconomic evaluations, funded through its Chief Scientist's Group, most of which have now been completed. No single guideline exists for the evaluation of policies, which may account for the variation in methodological styles adopted for the ESA evaluation studies reported in later chapters.

MAFF has now published ten of its internal monitoring studies (MAFF, 1992a–e, 1993a–e) and some are referred to in the chapters which follow. The monitoring studies have tended to emphasize the measurement of physical change which can be detected, both from aerial photographic data and from field surveys. An example of the field survey material is presented by MAFF (1992a), showing the impact of the Pennine Dales ESA on hay-cutting dates. In particular, it demonstrates the divergence of practice between those with and those without management agreements within the ESA, showing the impact of the prescription. That none of those with agreements had undertaken cutting before the prescribed date, whilst nearly half the non-agreement fields had been cut, indicates complete compliance with this element of the management prescription during the three years reported. It is notable that the period covered refers to 1988–90, ending substantially before the first ESA programme in the Pennine Dales. This underlines a major problem with the monitoring programme, that it was originally intended to produce results for a Ministerial review of the programme to consider a redesignation of the first-round ESAs before the end of that round. In order for the analysis of results to be completed in time, this meant that most of the published studies were unable to make firm assessments of the trend of events within the ESAs.

Typically the socioeconomic studies were commissioned shortly after the ESA programme was launched and ran for two or three years. They were all undertaken by universities or consultants, to a precise brief. The objectives of these studies were to investigate the economic and financial impact of the ESA on participating farms, on the regional economy and on the national exchequer; to assess the impact of the ESA on farmer attitudes and perceptions; and to develop a methodological approach to the assessment, evaluation and performance review of ESAs.

The socioeconomic studies reflect the same problem of timing as the monitoring studies, namely that in a short period trends cannot be convincingly identified. Indeed, the socioeconomic studies exhibit a more extreme form of this problem, especially where they present data such as farm incomes which rely on the collection and manipulation of information by third parties (in this case usually accountants) and may well be some years out of date as they become available.

An Outline of the Book

Most of the work reported in this book relates to the first and second rounds of designated ESAs. So far the socioeconomic studies have not been published elsewhere. Their existence is a necessary condition for the production of this volume, which draws substantially upon them, particularly in the next seven chapters. These chapters present vignettes of seven ESAs based on surveys of practice. After that, Chapter 9 reviews the complex question of measuring the benefits of such policies using the most appropriate economic technique available. Then the main alternative policy options which might have been applied to achieve similar objectives are compared in Chapter 10, mainly in economic terms. A final chapter then summarizes the material presented and discusses the future of the policies reviewed here.

2

GRASSLAND CONSERVATION IN AN ARABLE AREA
The Case of the Suffolk River Valleys

Noel Russell

Introduction

East Anglia and Suffolk have always been part of an agricultural area dominated by the production of arable crops. Responding to signals generated by postwar agricultural policies this area of arable cropland has tended to increase at the expense of grassland. This arable encroachment has been a particular problem in the Suffolk River Valleys even when compared with other similar areas (e.g. the Norfolk Broads). However, unlike the Brecklands (Chapter 4) a core area of grassland remains. The Suffolk River Valleys ESA scheme was introduced to protect, enhance and expand this core grassland.

The scheme is based around seven discontinuous areas of grassland located in valley bottoms along the southern and eastern coast of Suffolk. Approximately three-quarters of the scheme area lies within two Areas of Outstanding Natural Beauty (AONBs) – the Dedham Vale and the Suffolk Coasts and Heaths. This scheme area encompasses roughly 32,000 hectares of mostly grade II arable and grassland prone to winter flooding.

Since the 1940s there has been a programme of drainage, usually as a prelude to further conversion from grassland to arable. Barritt (1983) reports reductions in grassland area of 32% in the Coasts and Heaths AONB between 1970 and 1981, and a reduction of 13% is reported for the Deben Valley over a similar period. In the mid-1980s ADAS estimated that at least one quarter of the remaining grassland could be converted to arable use within existing technological and economic constraints. This has had three key effects: firstly the role of grassland in the landscape of eastern Suffolk has been greatly diminished; secondly the ecological value of the grassland areas has been reduced by fragmentation; and thirdly grazing livestock enterprises have become marginalized, as output decreases below the minimum critical mass to support necessary infrastructure in some areas, leading to problems of undergrazing and partial abandonment.

The Suffolk River Valleys ESA Scheme

It is against this background, of continuing pressure for arable encroachment on the remaining grassland area, that the Suffolk River Valleys scheme was introduced in 1988 (to run for five years) as part of the second round of ESA designations. The scheme objectives may be summarized as follows (MAFF, 1993a):

1. to support livestock farming on existing areas of grassland;
2. to encourage conversion of arable to grassland and extend areas of wet grassland;
3. to conserve landscape, wildlife and historic features.

In setting out to achieve these objectives, three sets of management prescriptions and associated levels of payment were offered to farmers. *Tier I prescriptions* restricted pesticide use, encouraged appropriate management of grazing and prohibited reseeding and increased fertilizer use; payment level, £70 per hectare. *Tier II prescriptions* required compliance with Tier I and also restricted grazing, cultivation and mowing; the use of lime, slag and organic manure was prohibited; high water levels were to be maintained in wet meadow dykes during the summer period; payment level, £180 per hectare. *Tier III prescriptions* promoted the conversion of arable land to grassland for subsequent management under Tier I or Tier II prescriptions; payment level, £200 per hectare.

Participation in the Scheme

Agreements under each tier (see Box 2.1) also included clauses relating to management and maintenance of hedges, trees, woodland, scrub, ponds and reedbeds, the construction of buildings, roads and other infrastructure and the safeguarding of features of historical interest. Areas of grassland may be entered into any of the three tiers but participating farmers must enter all their permanent grassland within the scheme boundary.

In the first four years of the scheme (up to the end of 1991) a total of 8335 hectares was entered into the scheme. This included 5880 hectares of grassland (Tiers I and II) comprising 76% of the estimated eligible area and 2455 hectares converted from arable (Tier III) amounting to around 16% of eligible area (MAFF, 1993a). These compare favourably with target uptakes of 5800 hectares of grassland and 1500 hectares of arable reconversion. Russell and Froud (1991) estimate that a further 65 hectares of grassland and 100 hectares of arable reconversion will have entered the scheme in 1992.

Box 2.1. Management guidelines: Suffolk River Valleys ESA

Tier I (all land covered by agreement):

- Cultivate grassland only with a chain harrow or roller.
- Graze so as to avoid poaching; graze any aftermath of hay or silage.
- Maintain or decrease existing fertilizer application rates.
- Restrict the use of herbicides to weed wiper or spot treatments of named species.
- Maintain existing drainage systems, ditches and dykes without improvements, additions, modifications, or the use of chemicals.
- Maintain ponds, reedbeds, hedges and trees in a traditional manner; avoid causing damage to historic and landscape features.
- Obtain written advice before starting any construction or engineering work not requiring planning permission; and early in the agreement on the management of woodland, scrub and reedbeds.

Tier II:

Compliance with Tier I, and in addition:
- Maintain specified water levels in dykes, ditches and on water meadows.
- Avoid cultivations between 1 April and 15 July inclusive; avoid grazing between 1 April and 15 May inclusive; avoid cutting for hay/silage before 16 July.
- Avoid the use of inorganic fertilizers, slurry, pig or poultry manure, sewage sludge, lime and slag; do not fill low areas with river or ditch dredgings.

Tier III:

Conversion of arable land to grassland for management under Tiers I or II.
- Cease arable production and establish grassland within the first 12 months of the agreement.
- Consult Project Officer regarding the use of fertilizers, lime, slag, etc. and after the first 12-month period follow remaining guidelines in selected tier.

Survey of Participants and Non-Participants

The impact of the scheme on agricultural output, input use and farm incomes was assessed using detailed questionnaire interviews with farmers. The potential exchequer savings arising from reductions in agricultural support costs were also assessed and the attitudes of both participants and non-participants towards the scheme were also investigated. The results of this investigation are reported in detail in Russell and Froud (1991) and summarized in MAFF (1993a).

These results are based on random samples of participating and non-participating farmers. The survey of participants covered 227 holdings with 5221 hectares under agreement. Non-participants on 25 holdings covering 1103 eligible hectares were also interviewed. Interviewing was initiated in

November and December 1989 with some selective re-interviewing in November to January 1990/91. A mixture of personal and telephone interviews was used.

Characteristics of Participants

Only 37% of the participant sample farms lie entirely within the ESA boundary. With an average size of 150 hectares, approximately 16% of this land is entered into the scheme, a further 13% is eligible but not entered while around 43% is outside the scheme boundary. Just over 75% of the land is owner occupied, around 15% is let on full tenancy and 10% on annual or other licence.

Around 12% of these farmers have no agricultural enterprise, their land being grazed by horses or let out on annual licence; 14% specialize in arable crops, another 24% carry only livestock or dairy enterprises; while 50% operate as mixed livestock and arable farms. Twenty per cent of this sample can be considered to be farming part-time (i.e. employing less than one full-time worker) and roughly three-quarters have significant non-farm sources of income.

The Principal Effects of the Scheme

In estimating the impact on output, input use and farm incomes it is recognized that the scheme has been initiated within the context of an ongoing and changing policy environment. This raises issues surrounding the extent to which observed change, as estimated from participant interviews, might have occurred if the scheme had not been implemented. Background changes in input use, crop areas and livestock, which would have occurred in the scheme's absence, are therefore assessed as a starting point and this information is used to estimate the net additional impact of the scheme.

Background Changes on Participating Farms

Trends at national and regional level of a number of key variables are examined in relation to the particular characteristics of the Suffolk scheme area. The general pattern portrayed is one of national trends adjusting to policy signals such as the introduction of milk quotas in 1984 and the first-round ESA programme in 1987. The increase in arable area in the early 1980s, the rapid decline following 1984 and the slower decline in recent years is consistent with this interpretation. Beef cow and sheep numbers have also responded to these signals, with a particularly rapid expansion of sheep numbers up to 1991.

Recognizing first of all, that the scheme area may encompass more

Table 2.1. Estimated background annual changes in output levels and input use in the Suffolk River Valleys scheme area. (From Russell and Froud, 1991.)

Factor	Annual percentage change
Cereals area	−2.0
Sheep numbers	+7.5
Beef cattle	+6.0
Fertilizer and chemical use	0
Labour	−3.5
Grazing rentals	−3.0

marginal arable land than other parts of Suffolk or East Anglia, and secondly that farmers may initially over-react to signalled change in the policy environment, national and regional trends are adjusted in reaching the estimates of background 'policy-off' changes presented in Table 2.1.

Scheme-Induced Changes in Agricultural Output and Input Use

Table 2.2 presents a summary of the net effect of the scheme on crop area and livestock numbers. Changes in crop production arise in the Tier III arable conversion component of the scheme. The numbers in Table 2.2 are the estimated gross changes on the sample farms expressed at scheme level and adjusted for the background changes presented in Table 2.1. There have been changes in livestock numbers in all three components of the scheme with significant reductions on Tier I and Tier II land offsetting substantial increases on Tier III land leaving a net increase in both cattle and sheep in all years of the scheme. Again this information is based on estimated changes on the sample farms expressed at scheme level and adjusted for background changes.

Fertilizer use was reduced from 52 kg N to 44 kg N per hectare on Tier I land, from an overall average of 10 kg N per hectare to zero on Tier II land and from 72 kg N to 44 kg N per hectare (both well below the prescribed limit of 125 kg N per hectare) on Tier III land. These changes may all be attributed to the scheme since a background stable level of fertilizer use is assumed. A saving in fertilizer costs is therefore estimated. Similarly, the proscription of lime application on Tier II land leads to additional saving.

Increases in costs are associated with the conversion of arable land to grass under Tier III (mostly comprising fencing costs) and with the

Table 2.2. Estimated changes in crop area and livestock numbers 1989–92. (From Russell and Froud, 1991.)

Acreage/ numbers	Net change				Estimated yield (t/ha)
	1989	1990	1991*	1992*	
Wheat (ha)	−405	−690	−856	−940	5.51
Barley (ha)	−334	−565	−698	−766	4.04
Oilseed (ha)	−18	−38	−50	−56	3.23
Other (ha)	−77	−173	−227	−254	–
Sheep (nos.)	2406	4114	5075	5515	–
Cattle (nos.)	221	477	617	678	–

*Forecasts.

Table 2.3. Net overall effect of the scheme on incomes of participating farmers 1989–92. (From Russell and Froud, 1991.)

Income component	Net change (£000)					Total impact 1988–92
	1988	1989	1990	1991*	1992*	
Income gains:						
Scheme payments	725.8	904.3	993.1	1036.7	1062.9	4722.8
Livestock margins	0	110.7	210.0	263.8	287.9	872.5
Fertilizer/lime savings	48.9	54.3	55.8	56.5	57.1	272.6
Income losses:						
Crop margins	0	−314.1	−556.6	−697.3	−768.2	−2336.3
Compliance costs	−300.1	−152.3	−87.2	−43.1	−24.1	−606.9
Machinery costs	0	−5.9	−5.9	−5.9	−5.9	−23.5
Net change	474.6	596.6	609.3	610.8	609.7	2901.3

Note: Totals may not add due to rounding.
*Forecasts.

maintenance of water levels on some Tier II land. These once-off compliance costs were estimated at £238 and £24 per hectare respectively. Increases in costs also arise due to the need to extend the machinery stock to cope with expanded grassland under Tier III of the scheme. It is assumed there would have been no change in the absence of the scheme.

Scheme-Induced Changes in Farm Incomes

The aggregate net effect of changes in income induced by the scheme are presented in Table 2.3. These are positive for each year and increase from around £374,000 in 1980 to just over £600,000 in 1992. The aggregate effect is to increase farm incomes in the Suffolk River Valleys by around £2.9 million over the first five years of the scheme above what they would have been if the scheme had not been introduced. However, these aggregate changes conceal some important variations. In particular, differences between components of the scheme and between categories of participant are totally masked in Table 2.3. These differences are highlighted in Tables 2.4 and 2.5 respectively.

Income changes by scheme component

Table 2.4 shows that the Tier I component of the scheme generates an increase in income of £316 per hectare over the first five years. This is equivalent to around 90% of the payments made. On Tier II land the corresponding figure of £955 per hectare is around 106% of scheme payments. This means that, whereas 10% of payments were absorbed by compliance costs on Tier I farms, the scheme actually generated additional savings amounting to 6% of scheme payments on Tier II land. The higher costs of arable conversion on Tier III land, in relation to payment level, are also reflected here. The increase in income generated by the scheme amounts to only £73 over the five years, some 8% of payments made. These figures are arrived at after taking account of the measured total change on scheme farms

Table 2.4. Net effect on farm incomes by scheme component.

	Net change in income per hectare (£)					
Component	1988	1989	1990	1991*	1992*	1988–92
Tier I	75	61	61	60	59	316
Tier II	180	193	194	194	194	955
Tier III	−38	36	29	23	23	73

*Forecasts.

as well as the estimated background changes which would have occurred in the absence of the scheme.

Income changes by category of participant

In looking at variation in income effects by category of participant the principal concern is with the possibility of scheme-induced adjustments in the market for short-term and long-term agricultural tenancies. The effect of the scheme on owner/landlord income *vis-à-vis* that of graziers/tenants will depend on how rentals change in response to scheme payments and prescriptions. Since not all tenants and graziers are in the scheme these rental adjustments provide a mechanism for transfers between participants and non-participants as well as between category of participant.

There was no clear indication of any effect of the scheme on rents for long-term agricultural tenancies though there was a general assumption that if the scheme increased farm incomes then rents would eventually rise. This did not provide a basis for further analysis.

Table 2.5. Net effect on incomes for landowners and graziers. (From Russell and Froud, 1991.)

| | Net effect on income (£) per hectare 1988–92 | | | | | |
| | Tier I | | Tier II | | Tier III | |
Income component	Owner	Grazier	Owner	Grazier	Owner	Grazier
Income gains:						
Increase in gross margin						645.0
Scheme payment	350.0		900.0		1000.0	
Fertilizer/lime saving		41.9		121.2		
Change in rent		165.6		165.6	172.0	
Income losses:						
Reduction in gross margin		−57.8		−38.0	−1464.0	
Compliance cost			−24.0		−238.0	
Change in rent	−165.6		−165.6			−172.0
Net effect	184.4	149.7	710.4	248.5	−530.0	473.0

The market for short-term grazing, however, showed more marked changes, with a reduction of 39% during the first two years of the scheme. This can be attributed to the substantial increase in grassland available to rent both as a means to avoid undergrazing and as a result of arable conversion under Tier III of the scheme. The effects of these adjustments on a landowner who rents out all scheme land and the grazier who rents it are shown in Table 2.5 for Tier I, Tier II and Tier III.

For Tier I and Tier II it is assumed that the owner and grazier have participated in the rental market prior to the scheme being implemented. Thus reductions in rents reduce the owner's income and increase that of the grazier. The net effect of these and other changes is to increase incomes on Tier I land by £184 and £150 per hectare respectively for owners and graziers. The higher payment on Tier II land mean that owners' incomes increase by £710 per hectare and those for graziers by nearly £250.

On Tier III land any rental of grassland represents a new entry to the market. The rental is an increase in income for the owner and a cost for the grazier. These and other adjustments generate a net decrease of £530 in owners' incomes and a net increase of £473 in those of graziers.

Impact of the Scheme on Budgetary Costs

The costs of a scheme to the UK exchequer are an important consideration in policy decision-making. For the scheme examined here these costs are related,

Table 2.6. Impact of the scheme on UK exchequer costs. (From Russell and Froud, 1991.)

Year	Net cost of payments* (£000)	Savings on crop support[†] (£000)		Additional livestock support (£000)	Net savings as % of payments	
		Min.	Max.		Min.	Max.
1988	621	–	–	–	–	–
1989	777	80	80	57	7	7
1990	822	143	466	48	12	51
1991	858	180	581	60	14	61
1992	881	199	638	65	15	65
1988–92	3959	602	1765	230	10	40

*Gross payments less EAGGF reimbursements which amount to around 16% overall.
[†]After 1989 the minimum estimate assumes a UK contribution to CAP support of £20 per tonne for wheat and £25 per tonne for barley. The maximum estimate is £75 per tonne for both crops.

first of all, to the costs of administering the scheme and the payments made to participants. In addition to these direct effects there are indirect effects arising from changes in the costs of agricultural support due to scheme-induced changes in agricultural output. The extent to which these savings might finance scheme payments is of particular interest.

Table 2.6 presents information on scheme payments (net of the European Agricultural Guidance and Guarantee Fund (EAGGF = FEOGA) reimbursements) and changes in the UK's contribution to agricultural support. Net payments amount to nearly £4 million while support cost savings from reduced crop production range from around £0.6 million to nearly £1.8 million. There is an offsetting increase in livestock support costs of around £0.2 million; scheme administration costs have not been included.

The net support cost savings generated by the scheme build up over the five years to a maximum of between 65% and 15% of scheme payments. These savings provide finance for no more than 40% of net payments over the whole five-year period.

Long-Term and Indirect Effects of the Scheme

Potential Effects of the Scheme on Productivity

It was accepted from the outset that any adjustment which has been observed in this study is only the initial part of a longer-term dynamic process which will continue to influence output, input use and incomes as farmers learn more about how compliance with scheme guidelines affects their farming system. Only when the full impact of the scheme has manifested itself, and farmers have completed their adjustment process, will the long-run equilibrium be reached. The extent to which this long-run equilibrium position might differ from what has been observed in this study, has important implications for the future management of policies for agriculture and the rural environment.

Changes in fertilizer, lime and chemicals

An important feature of farmers' response concerns the changes in fertilizer levels on land converted from arable to grassland under Tier III of the scheme. The guidelines in this case required that no more than 125 kg N per hectare be applied for conversion. However, even before the scheme, average usage was less than 60% of this amount and further reductions to about 35% of this level were observed after the land had been converted, giving a reduction from the pre-scheme application rate of 39%.

This would seem to indicate that guideline levels of fertilizer application were not in any sense restrictive on farming activities in the scheme area. In fact it seems clear that much lower levels might have been accommodated within the existing system of farming with the possibility of enhancing scheme achievement. At the same time some farmers expressed concern that reducing fertilizers and lime and strict controls on the use of herbicide may seriously impair productivity as soil acidity rises and the weed 'seed bank' builds up.

These changes, together with those arising from the prohibition on reseeding and the requirement to raise water levels on Tier II land, are geared towards encouraging the maintenance of traditional vegetation cover. This has been made clear right from the start of the scheme but the productivity of this vegetation for livestock production will only be apparent when farmers have a number of years of experience with this system. The general expectation is that productivity will be lower than under the more intensive management systems which are no longer practised, but much uncertainty remains here. The possibility of declining productivity over time is, however, a major concern of farmers in the scheme which has important implications for the longer-term effectiveness of future policies for agriculture and the rural environment.

Changes in stocking levels

The scheme guidelines address the problems of undergrazing as well as overgrazing, and there is some evidence that the reduction in stocking rates on Tier I and Tier II grassland and the low initial stocking rates on the newly converted grassland in Tier III, may represent only the first part of a longer-term process of adjustment. The livestock farming system has, as a result of the scheme, been expanded to include both the additional grassland made available under Tier III and a proportion of existing grassland which had previously not been an integral part of the livestock economy. In many cases existing stocking rates are so low that they are well within the capacity of this land even with reduced fertilizer and lime applications. This has created an additional demand for grazing animals which can only be met in the longer-term due to natural lags in livestock production response. Much of the observed changes in stocking rates will therefore likely represent participants' attempts to comply with scheme guidelines by 'spreading' available livestock over all their grassland. Much of this land can carry additional livestock so it is reasonable to expect that stocking rates will increase back towards guideline levels as more grazing livestock become available.

Longer-term implications for the scheme

Much will depend on whether farmers discover that their initial adjustments over- or under-estimate the changes ultimately needed. The possibility that output and income might be increased towards previous levels, while remaining within scheme guidelines, could emerge as farmers gained experience in the management of environmentally friendly systems, allowing productivity increases against the additional constraints imposed by, or arising from, scheme guidelines. This type of response might be possible as more grazing livestock become available in Suffolk. This would effectively reduce the costs of future participation in similar schemes, allowing the possibility of reduced scheme payments (in real terms) or, alternatively, encouraging more widespread uptake.

On the other hand, continued reductions in output and increases in production costs may come about as the delayed effects of compliance with guidelines, on underlying agricultural productivity, are made manifest. There is some evidence that this may arise from the restriction on application of lime and herbicides as soil acidity and the weed seed bank build up over time.

These potential problems, together with the prohibition of reseeding and the requirement to raise water levels on some land, have led a number of participants to suggest that they might adopt a 'stop-go' policy with respect to future schemes. Their intended strategy would involve withholding some land from immediate participation in any renewed scheme while they set about liming and reseeding, so as to re-establish 'normal' productivity levels. The land may then be re-entered into a scheme for environmentally sensitive management for a further limited period. It is not clear that this strategy would allow the objectives of this type of scheme to be achieved. In any case, under this scenario, the costs of scheme participation would be expected to increase over time raising the possibility of reduced scheme participation and/ or the need for increased payment levels.

Impact of the Scheme on Non-Scheme Land

The impact of the scheme on output and input use on non-scheme land is an additional knock-on effect which needs careful consideration. The importance of this factor has been underlined by farmers' well-known response to set-aside policies in the USA where much of the direct effect on output was cancelled out by an increased intensification of production on other land. Fears that British farmers may respond in a similar manner to the ESA scheme and other policies for agriculture and the rural environment, have been widely voiced.

This phenomenon, sometimes referred to as a 'halo effect', might be motivated by a wide variety of circumstances. For example, it can be seen primarily as a possible response to falling income from agriculture, as output on scheme land is reduced in complying with the guidelines, encouraging participants to make up for these reductions by intensifying production on other land. Since income for most participants will have increased under the scheme investigated here, this is unlikely to provide strong motivation. The increase in liquidity, associated with the receipt of scheme payments, might also encourage intensification on non-scheme land. This is seen as most likely to happen when farm operations are constrained by a cash shortage. In these circumstances, payments under the scheme enable the farmer to increase his input use to a level more consistent with what he regards as optimum but which could not have been achieved without the extra liquidity. An alternative view of this process suggests that, when working capital is scarce, restricting the use of inputs on part of the farm reduces their opportunity cost thus making it economically sensible to increase their use on other parts of the farm. In any case, what is being suggested here is that any scheme which restricts input use on part of the farm can provide incentives to increase input use on the remainder; i.e. intra-farm halo effects might be encouraged by the ESA.

Conversely incentives towards extensification on non-scheme land might also arise here, due to a type of 'demonstration' effect of the scheme. This could occur when farmers have become locked into intensive techniques and are not willing to face the uncertainty associated with switching to extensive methods of production. In these circumstances, the implementation of the scheme, on participant farms, may demonstrate that the impact of extensification on output and income has been popularly overestimated, and may encourage both participants and non-participants to reduce input use on non-scheme land.

Despite the various incentives for changes on non-scheme land, discussed in the previous paragraphs, almost no evidence for any type of halo effect emerged from the present study. Some few farmers suggested that they had reduced fertilizer levels on non-scheme parts of the farm but it was not possible to clarify whether these reductions could be attributed to the scheme or whether they were part of other background changes on the farm. Any scheme-related component of this change would not, however, have been significant.

Looking Towards the Future

Characteristics of Non-Participants

The study estimated that approximately 200 holdings with around 1800 hectares of grassland and 12,500 hectares of arable area (a total of 14,300 hectares eligible land) had not participated in the scheme. On average, holding size was 109 hectares, somewhat less than that of the participants. Of the average area of cropland per farm (91 hectares) approximately 68% was estimated to be within the scheme boundary. Ninety per cent of all grassland on these holdings is estimated to be eligible for the ESA. The remaining 15% of land lying inside the designated area on the non-participating holdings is accounted for by woodlands, orchards, gardens and set-aside.

The predominant reason for not entering arable land into Tier III is that, given the value of payments (£200 per hectare), it was felt to be not worth converting reasonably good-quality cropland to grass. The high cost of fencing and the uncertainty over the future of livestock economics are further deterrents to the conversion of cropland which is not particularly wet. Some of the grassland, although within the boundaries, is not technically eligible because it may be used for non-agricultural purposes such as campsites and airfields. Anticipated problems with weed control, and the inability to ensure that the land could be adequately grazed, were other reasons given. Some grassland is also used fairly intensively for dairying and hence because of the specification that all eligible grassland should be entered some holdings have chosen not to participate at all. Other holdings have individual reasons for not joining; the land may be put up for sale in the near future and there are fears that being in the ESA may reduce its value; disagreement between family members over whether the land should be entered; and concern that the ESA may lead to increased public access.

Changes which Might Improve the Scheme

The foregoing analyses clearly indicate that, in the Suffolk River Valleys, the ESA Scheme has been successful. Targets for uptake have been exceeded (especially for arable conversion under Tier III), there has been the start of a general resurgence in the livestock economy, and there have been many other significant achievements. However, there are a number of areas where further improvements might be made through changes in specific elements of the scheme.

For example, some attention might be focused on achieving greater conservation benefits within the structure of the existing scheme. This might be accomplished by a closer matching of the guidelines to existing farming operations so as to avoid having targets which are already being exceeded as part of existing practices. Tier I guidelines were particularly notable here, to the extent that reductions in fertilizer rates and stocking levels were being observed where no such reductions were mandated.

Changes to the structure of the scheme might also be contemplated. For example, the provision of grants for specific conservation investment activities such as dam construction and many others, would improve the structure of incentives within the scheme, by making the relationship between payments and conservation activities more transparent. At the same time a broader-based selection of management options and payment levels would enhance the ability of farmers to match conservation activities to the potential of their land and to their farming aspirations. In this way it might be possible to take advantage of changing attitudes among farmers and the availability of more experienced personnel to include more site-specific components in the scheme which focus more on the enhancement of wildlife habitats.

Changes in payment levels will also need to be considered in the near future. There is, however, ambiguous evidence emerging from this study as to what changes might be necessary or desirable. As the longer-term effects of following guidelines become apparent, there is a high probability that the costs of participation being borne by farmers will increase, as productivity declines under increasing soil acidity and weed problems. This would indicate a need for increased payments to encourage continued participation by farmers. On the other hand the possibility of increasing stocking levels, within scheme guidelines, might lead to a reduction in participation costs and hence alleviate the need to increase payments.

As the scheme evolves, further changes in structure, to improve conservation benefits and reduce costs, might prove feasible and desirable. For example, the cost of basic protection of the rural environment over wide areas could be reduced using a suitably based cross-compliance option (Russell and Fraser, 1993). At the same time, detailed and site-specific enhancement of wildlife habitats would be achieved in a more cost-effective manner by carefully targeting the use of subsidized land purchase.

Changes which might involve extending the ESA programme over a wider area should be approached cautiously. It is not clear that there is, as yet, a large enough cadre of experienced personnel available for this task though no evidence on this has been sought in this study. Our investigation did, however, uncover some evidence that a whole range of special circumstances may have been operating in the Suffolk River Valleys which may have had a significant bearing on the success of the scheme. In particular, it was noted that conservation efforts have had a long history involving a wide range of organizations (Colman *et al.*, 1992). These efforts have undoubtedly been significant in ensuring that a base area worth including in the ESA Scheme was maintained in these areas and very likely had an influence in the changes which were observed in our study.

3

SINGLE-TIER SYSTEM WITH MANY FARMS PARTLY OUTSIDE THE ESA
The Case of the Pennine Dales

Caroline Saunders

Introduction

The Pennine Dales area is a complex system of glaciated river valleys in Yorkshire, Durham and Cumbria. The first ESA, designated in 1987, was nearly 16,000 hectares consisting of mainly enclosed valley bottom land in eight separate areas in parts of ten Dales: Weardale, Dentdale, Rookhope, Deepdale, Teesdale, Langstrothdale, Arkengarthdale, Wharfedale, Swaledale and Waldendale. Their locations in Great Britain are recorded on Fig. 1.5 (see p. 21).

The Pennine Dales were selected as an ESA in the first round of designation because they exhibited a number of the appropriate features. These include archaeological and historical interest with, for example, field patterns dating from the Iron Age and the existence of lead mining in the 18th and 19th centuries. It is the latter which has contributed to the typical small-scale farm found in the Dales.

Farming in the Dales is almost entirely based upon grass, with mainly sheep and some cattle and dairy, especially in the more favourable lower parts of the Dales. The traditional system of farming in the Dales is based upon the management of 'in bye' land for the production of hay. The stock are removed from the hay meadows in spring and the hay cut in July and August, frequently over a long period; the hay is stored in the field barns for winter fodder, and stock are then allowed back on the land. This low-intensity system of agriculture with few, if any, additional inputs has led to botanical diversity

The Author gratefully acknowledges the contribution of Dr Mary Walsh who undertook the fieldwork from which this chapter draws.

41

and associated wildlife in the meadows, with late-flowering species allowed to mature and survive.

The Dales therefore have a distinctive landscape with fields bounded by stone walls and dispersed field barns. This and the biological diversity of the hay meadows have been recognized in a number of designations. The lower part of the ESA is in the Yorkshire Dales National Park and the upper part in the North Pennines Area of Outstanding Natural Beauty; the ESA also contains National Nature Reserves and a number of Sites of Special Scientific Interest. However, these were not seen as sufficient to offset the potential threats to the Dales, especially from agriculture.

Since World War II there have been rapid increases in agricultural productivity brought about by technological change and improved management practices, encouraged by agricultural policy. These changes did not initially have such a great impact on the Dales due to a variety of factors, not least their location and physical limitations. However, pressures for agricultural intensification in the Dales have grown not least due to Hill Livestock Compensatory Allowances (HLCAs), i.e. headage payments, and from 1980 the introduction of the EC sheep policy, both of which encouraged an increase in stocking. In response some farmers intensified their land use – by using inorganic fertilizer; by reseeding meadows and pastures with high-yielding varieties; by draining land; and by switching from hay to silage making.

Despite these changes and agricultural support farm incomes have continued to decline relative to other sectors, contributing to the decline in agricultural population and encouraging the amalgamation of farms. As a result many familiar features fell into disrepair and the traditional farming system threatened to disappear. It is these factors which led to the designation of the Pennine Dales as an ESA.

The ESA Scheme in the Pennine Dales

The original ESA Scheme came into operation on 1 March 1987 for five years; it was reviewed and revised in 1992 (MAFF, 1993i) with a new scheme introduced. The objectives of ESA are:

(1) to conserve and enhance the natural beauty of the area;
(2) to conserve the flora and fauna and geological and physiographical features of that area; and
(3) to protect buildings and other objects of historic interest in that area.

(Statutory Instrument 2253 (1986))

The original management prescriptions are summarized in Box 3.1.

The ESA is voluntary but all participants must enter all their land within the boundary and comply with the management prescriptions in return for £100 per hectare per annum.

Box 3.1. Management prescriptions in the Pennine Dales ESA.

- The maintenance of grassland without ploughing, levelling, reseeding or new drainage.
- The exclusion of stock from meadows at least seven weeks before the first cut for hay or silage.
- Not to cut hay or silage grass before the following dates:
  - Dentdale with Deepdale, 1 July;
  - Wharfedale, Langstrothdale and Waldendale, 8 July;
  - Swaledale with Arkengarthdale, Teesdale and Weardale with Rookhope, 15 July.
  - ... and in any case not before the herbage has flowered and seeded.
  - [In fact in the early years of the ESA the cutting date was relaxed in some Dales]
- Cut silage to be wilted and turned before removal.
- Strict limits on the use of artificial fertilizer, farmyard manure, lime, slag, and herbicides: no applications of pesticides or slurry.
- The maintenance of stockproof stone walls and weatherproof field barns using traditional materials.
- Avoiding damage to features of historic interest.
- Obtain written advice on any constructions not requiring planning permission and on the management of woodland or scrub within the agreement area.

The impact of the Pennine Dales ESA has been evaluated in two studies commissioned by MAFF, an internal one concerned with environmental impacts, including landscape, management, biological and historical monitoring (MAFF, 1992a) and another concerned with the socioeconomic impacts, the Newcastle study (Whitby *et al.*, 1992). It is the results of these which provide most of the information regarding the operation of the ESA reported here.

The MAFF (1992a) study used a number of techniques to assess the impact of the ESA, including aerial photography, field survey and farmer questionnaire, at two main periods – 1987, when the ESA was established, and 1990. The socioeconomic study at Newcastle (Whitby *et al.*, 1992) was based upon questionnaire survey conducted among farmers between late 1989 and mid-1990. Both studies included three types of farmers – agreement, non-agreement and control, i.e. farms outside the ESA in the Dales which were similar to those designated[1]. The samples differ, with the socioeconomic study interviewing slightly more farmers and covering a third of agreement and a fifth of non-agreement farmers.

Both studies establish a reference situation with which the policy can be compared. In the MAFF (1992a) study this was through the collection of

---

[1]Control Dales in the Newcastle study were Upper Allendale and Littondale, and in the MAFF study Coverdale and Littondale.

information in the base period, 1987. In the socioeconomic study farmers were asked how they would have behaved in the absence of the policy. Both studies also used a control group as a comparator for assessing change on ESA farms.

A distinguishing feature of the Pennine Dales ESA, compared to other ESAs, is that it is not a discrete block of land but made up of eight small separate parts. Therefore many farmers had land outside the boundary, giving rise to the concern that participating farmers would offset the constraints of the ESA by intensifying the use of land outside the boundary. This so-called 'halo effect' was examined by both the MAFF and socioeconomic studies. In the MAFF study an actual halo area was defined and changes within it were examined. In the socioeconomic study farmers were asked to separate changes in farming practice on land inside and outside the boundary.

The uptake in ESA has been high, with 295 agreements in 1991 covering 9793 hectares; that represented nearly all the area MAFF expected to be under agreement and nearly two-thirds of the total area. Uptake was greater in the higher parts of the Dales, covering 76% of farms compared with 69% in the lower parts of the Dales, reflecting the different potential for agricultural intensification (MAFF, 1992a).

Land Cover and Use in the Pennine Dales ESA

The land cover of the ESA was estimated at 62% meadow pasture, 9% rough grazing, 14% acid grass moor and 6% woodland, with the remaining 9% made up of urban area, rock, scrub, bracken and water (MAFF, 1992a). The same study found no significant changes in land cover from 1987 to 1990.

The pattern of land use on ESA farms is illustrated in Table 3.1. Rough grazing accounts for the greatest proportion of area on all ESA farms at 57%, followed by improved pasture at 23%, then meadow at 19%. The proportion of rough grazing is higher on agreement farms, covering 59% of the area compared to both of the other groups. The importance of meadow land, which is the main protected area under the ESA, varies between the groups, with the non-agreement farms having the highest percentage followed by the area under agreement and then the control.

The Newcastle study estimated the area of land farmed within and outside the boundary on agreement and non-agreement farms as shown in Table 3.2. Fifty-five per cent of the agreement farmers and 80% of non-agreement farmers had land outside the boundary. However, most of this land is rough grazing with only 26% of agreement farmers and 32% of non-agreement farmers having land outside the ESA capable of improvement. Moreover, the area of land outside the boundary is small with agreement farmers only having 505 hectares of meadow land altogether.

The Newcastle study found non-agreement farmers had the smallest sized

Table 3.1. Land use by sample category: Pennine Dales Survey. (From Whitby *et al.*, 1992.)

Land use category	Agreement area	Non-agreement area	Control* area
Area (ha)			
Meadow[†]	3538	2991	599
Improved pasture	4261	3017	1273
Rough grazing	11,584	7516	2383
Woodland	275	115	102
Totals	19,658	13,639	4357
Per cent of total agricultural area			
Meadow	18	22	14
Improved pasture	22	22	29
Rough grazing	59	55	55

*Area of land sampled.
[†]Permanent grassland was broken down into meadow and improved pasture to represent the use of land in the Dales more accurately, with the former being used for hay and silage and the latter for better grazing.

Table 3.2. Agricultural area within and outside ESA boundary. (From Whitby *et al.*, 1992.)

	Agreement area (ha)	Non-agreement area (ha)
Inside boundary	9557	6556
Outside boundary	9825	6971
Total	19,382	13,527

farms, the average total farm area being 61.6 hectares. Agreement holdings were larger, with an average of 109.0 hectares. The control group had the largest holdings, with 137.1 hectares per farm.

The Newcastle study confirmed the predominance of extensive grazing farming systems, showing that 98% of non-agreement farmers carried sheep and, whilst all carried cattle, 22% had commercial dairy units. Eighty per cent of all agreement farms carried sheep and 78% cattle, with 10% running dairy units. Thirteen per cent of the control farmers had commercial dairy units, the

C. Saunders

Table 3.3. Total stock numbers by farm category, 1989. (From Whitby *et al.*, 1992.)

	Agreement	Non-agreement	Control
Breeding ewes	55,747	39,274	12,328
Other sheep	17,368	10,519	3085
Suckler cows	3365	3325	589
Dairy	823	1029	149
Other cattle	5424	5816	988
Total area of holdings (ha)	19,695	13,638	4357

remainder being mainly sheep and suckler cow enterprises.

Table 3.3 reports the number of stock by farm category. This shows clearly that sheep are the most important stock, followed by suckler cows, with the followers to breeding cows also being important. Whilst there are

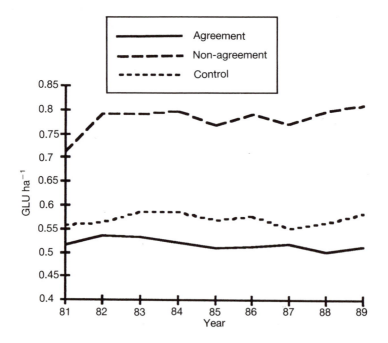

Fig. 3.1. Grazing Livestock Units (GLU) per hectare and type of farm. (Source: MAFF Agricultural Census.)

fewer non-agreement farms in the ESA Dales, they carry more dairy cattle than the agreement farms.

Converting the livestock data into grazing livestock units (GLU[2]) gives an average for the Dales of 0.66 per hectare. On agreement farms the GLU per hectare was 0.60 compared to 0.78 per hectare on non-agreement farms, again reflecting the lower intensity of land use on agreement farms. The GLU per hectare on control farms was 0.53; lower than both other groups.

Changes in stocking rate are identified by the Agricultural Census[3] as shown in Fig. 3.1. This illustrates that differences between ESA farms existed prior to the inception of the ESA in 1987. Moreover, since the ESA was introduced the GLUs per hectare on non-agreement and control farms have risen compared to a decline on agreement farms.

Impact of the Pennine Dales ESA

The MAFF study of the ESA covered landscape, historical and biological features. Due to the nature of these features the evaluation period of 1987 to 1990 was recognized as too short to reach conclusions about the environmental impact of the scheme but could give indications of possible future trends. The MAFF study found no significant changes, with some indication of improvement in biological diversity on agreement land.

The socioeconomic impact of the ESA at Newcastle examined the impact of the ESA on a number of factors including farming practice, stocking rates, yields, employment and income. Where possible these effects are separated into those inside and those outside the boundary to assess the importance of the 'halo' effect referred to above.

Farm Practices

To estimate the impact of the ESA, farmers were asked to indicate any changes over the last three years, i.e. before and after the ESA was introduced; these were then compared between the groups of farms to assess the impact of the ESA. Table 3.4 outlines the major changes in annual or regular farm practices since the inception of the Scheme on ESA farms inside and outside of the boundary, and for the control group.

The main recorded change in annual farm practices has been in the amount of artificial fertilizer used. On agreement farms 42% reduced their

---

[2]Grazing livestock units allow expression of livestock in units equivalent to one dairy cow.

[3]For the Newcastle study a special analysis of the agricultural census data was done to allow comparison over time. This aggregated farms according to their status in the Dales, that is agreement, non-agreement or control farms in 1989, and it is these data which are used in this chapter. Due to the different ways data are collected some differences occur between the census and survey data, particularly in the case of the control.

Table 3.4. Impact of main items in ESA management package on annual farm practices. (From Whitby *et al.*, 1992.)

| | % of ESA farms | | | | | | % of sample control farms | | |
| | Agreement | | | Non-agreement | | | | | |
	No change	Increase	Decrease	No change	Increase	Decrease	No change	Increase	Decrease
Inside boundary:									
Fertilizer	32	–	42	81	12	4	63	12	5
FYM	65	2	8	88	7	6	89	11	–
Bought-in hay	38	29	3	75	2	3	80	7	10
Outside boundary:									
Fertilizer	10	4	1	72	15	–			
FYM	49	3	–	68	4	–			

Note: Percentages will not total 100% as not all farmers undertake all farm practices.

Table 3.5. Fertilizer use on Dales farms, 1989. (From Whitby *et al.*, 1992.)

	Agreement	Non-agreement	Control
Fertilizer use (kg/ha on meadow land)	13.7	47.3	44.3

artificial fertilizer use compared to 4 and 5% on the non-agreement and control farms. Moreover, no agreement farm increased its use of fertilizer, compared with an increase of 12% on both non-agreement and control farms. This indicates the ESA's impact in reducing fertilizer use. Quantifying this change, there has been an average reduction of 8.75 kg per ha applied on meadow land affected by the ESA amounting to an overall reduction of 31 tonnes on all land affected.

The MAFF study found that on 55% of meadows and 21% of pastures there had been a reduction in fertilizer use, with the amount of nitrogen applied being halved on the fields sampled. On land outside the boundary there seemed little evidence of any halo effect, with only 15% of agreement farmers who had land outside the boundary using fertilizer and three-quarters of these reporting no change in its use; thus supporting the conclusion from the MAFF study that there was no significant halo effect.

The MAFF study found that 44% of fields received farmyard manure (FYM) with the average application being 8 tonnes per hectare, below the permitted maximum of 10 tonnes. No significant changes in practice could be found as a result of the ESA, substantiating the findings of the Newcastle study as shown in Table 3.4.

Another change in farm practices reported by both studies was the increase in buying-in of hay. According to the results of the Newcastle study the buying-in of hay has increased by 29% on agreement farms in contrast with an increase of 2 and 7% on non-agreement and control farms respectively. This increase may offset hay yield losses resulting from adherence to the ESA prescription. It was calculated that on these 29% of agreement farms the average increase was 16.5 tonnes per farm of bought-in hay. Across the ESA this amounted to an estimated increase of 1221 tonnes[4].

The level of fertilizer use on agreement farms is notably lower than that of non-agreement and control farms; Table 3.5 shows that agreement farms are applying under a third of that on both non-agreement and control farms.

No agreement farms were identified as cutting before the dates prescribed, which compares with half the non-agreement meadows being cut before these dates. However, an unintended consequence of the ESA is that on agreement

---

[4]This implies imports of plant nutrients into the area roughly equivalent to the estimated reduction in fertilizer.

farms haymaking when started was generally completed in a much shorter period, with 60% of fields being cut in the first two weeks and haymaking complete after six weeks, compared to ten weeks on non-agreement farms. This paradox was confirmed by the MAFF study which found that some fields were actually being cut earlier due to the ESA with some resulting deterioration in biological diversity. In fact other research in the Pennine Dales suggests that allowing farmers to cut as previously, that is when the weather is most suitable, does little to damage the floral diversity of the hay meadows (Smith and Jones, 1991).

Another unintended consequence of the ESA may be the shift from hay to big bale silage. The MAFF study found an increase from 31% of farms making silage in 1987 to 38% in 1990 although they suggest that this may underestimate the trend given the wet summer in 1987. This change was also identified by the Newcastle study, with some evidence that farmers were shifting to silage to reduce the risks associated with the prescribed cutting dates; the size of this effect was not quantified.

The impact of the ESA on occasional farm practices, such as drainage, liming, reseeding and walling, was more difficult to determine as not many farms had undertaken these since the inception of the ESA. Results from the Newcastle study showed a lower level of reseeding, drainage, liming and herbicide use on agreement farms, when compared to the other two groups, which does indicate that the ESA has reduced the rate of intensification of land use in the ESA. A main impact of the ESA on such practices has been the increase in walling on agreement farms, with 38% reporting an increase compared to 11% on non-agreement farms and 30% of the control. There was little discernible impact of the ESA on maintenance of traditional buildings between the agreement and non-agreement groups. A few agreement farms reported an increase in the maintenance of woodland within the boundary compared to both non-agreement farms and agreement farm land outside the boundary. However, this increase was lower than that for the control.

Changes in Yields

Table 3.6 gives the results of the Newcastle study on changes in yields on ESA farms with land inside and outside of the ESA boundary, and the controls. This shows that there has been a fall in hay and silage yields on 43 and 22% of agreement farms respectively; this is a substantial decline, especially when compared to non-agreement and control farms. The fall in yields may reflect the restriction on fertilizer use which prevents second-cut hay or silage. Lack of 'fog' or the aftermath following the first cut was a further reported consequence of the fertilizer restriction. There was little evidence of changes outside the boundary in agreement farms to support the idea of a halo effect, apart from an increase in silage making on 10% of farms.

In physical terms the average loss in hay yields was 67 square bales or

Table 3.6. Changes in fodder yield since inception of the ESA for all farm categories inside the ESA boundary. (From Whitby et al., 1992.)

	% of ESA farms						% of sample control farms		
	Agreement			Non-agreement					
	No change	Increase	Decrease	No change	Increase	Decrease	No change	Increase	Decrease
Inside boundary:									
Hay	38	–	43	80	11	7	70	25	5
Silage	11	–	22	64	8	8	71	24	5
Outside boundary:									
Hay	10	7	16	12	13				
Silage	4	10	17	3					

0.54 tonnes per hectare, a reduction of 30%. In the case of silage, the average reduction was calculated to be 7.09 big bales or 3.5 tonnes per hectare, a reduction of 31%. These results are consistent with experience of yields measured in other studies of the area (e.g. Smith and Jones, 1991). Farmers did expect that yields would decrease further in the future with the continuing reversion of formerly fertilized land.

Changes in Stock Numbers

The Newcastle study showed some movement away from the more intensive dairy and cattle to sheep production on agreement land. On two-thirds of agreement farms there had been no change in sheep numbers. There was a decline in numbers on 3% (on average 22 per farm) and an increase on 10% (on average 30 ewes per farm) of farms. There was a decrease in cow numbers on 14% of agreement farms (on average 11 per farm) with no change on 64%, the remainder not carrying cattle. This change was equivalent to a rise of 0.03 ewes per hectare and fall of −0.02 suckler cows per hectare.

This change from dairy and cattle to sheep is supported by farm type classification from the Agricultural Census, which shows the past trends for farms classified by their status in relation to the ESA in 1989. This is illustrated in Fig. 3.2, which shows, for farms which were in the ESA in 1989, the fall in the proportion of sheep and cattle farms, from 58% in 1985 to 48% in 1989 and the rise in proportion of sheep-only farms from 34 to 43% over the same period. This is in contrast with non-agreement farms where only 26% were sheep only and 54% sheep and cattle with no change from 1985 to 1989.

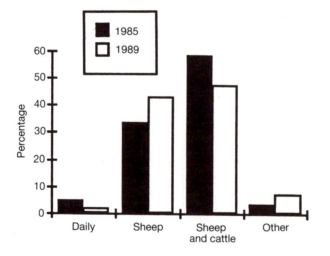

Fig. 3.2. Percentage of agreement farms by farm type, 1989. (Source: MAFF Agricultural Census.)

To place these changes in farming type into context and to allow comparisons to be made, the increase in sheep numbers and the fall in cattle numbers were converted into grazing livestock units. The results of this showed a very slight change on agreement farms, equivalent to an overall net fall of 0.01 GLUs per hectare.

Farm Employment

According to the Newcastle study the level of employment including part-time employees by type of farm was approximately 1.4 workers per agreement farm and 1.9 on non-agreement farms and one per farm on the control. No changes in employment were found due to the ESA. Most of the labour on farms was accounted for by the farmer; i.e. 71% on agreement farms and 52% and 58% on non-agreement and control farms. Family labour is next most important followed by hired labour. Agreement farms had the lowest proportion of full-time farmers at 68% compared to 88% on non-agreement farms and 79% on control farms.

Seasonal/casual employment is important on Dales farms, with 30% of agreement farms using family casual seasonal workers and 43% hired casual/seasonal compared to 44 and 37% respectively on non-agreement farms, and 37 and 27% on control farms.

Sixty-one per cent of the agreement farms had some form of contract work carried out, silage making and walling work being the major tasks. The percentages for the non-agreement and control were higher, at 80% and 86% respectively. Again the major tasks were baling and walling, though over one third of the control also hired contractors for sheep shearing. It is in contracting that the main change in employment occurred from 1987 to 1990, with half of agreement farms reporting an increase compared to only 12.5% on non-agreement farms and a 56% increase on control farms.

Farm Incomes in the Pennine Dales

The Newcastle survey contained several questions regarding the financial results of farming from a sub-sample of 33% of those interviewed. Due to the small control sample for income, the source of control information was the Northern Region Farm Business Survey (FBS) (Johnson, 1991), which regularly reports income data for groups of hill farms in the Northern Region. The FBS results were converted to the same temporal basis as the Dales sample and indexed using the same sources.

Farmers were asked to give their latest available accounts and accounts for three years previously, to enable a comparison before and after the introduction of the ESA. However, that expedient introduced some lack of precision as to the year to which sample averages relate. The years '1984' and '1987' reported relate to the latest three years available on the relevant farms.

Many of the accounts had either recorded no payments or only partial ESA payments thus understating their potential impact on farm income. The data do provide a comparison between agreement and non-agreement farms in the early years of the ESA compared to their respective income situation three years previously. The accounts were indexed to convert them to 1989 prices and are averaged per hectare.

Table 3.7 shows that agreement farm output (which includes ESA payments) had risen by 42% over the period. This increase was largely due to the rise in sheep sales and subsidies, including the ESA payments, which were equivalent to 12% of income. Sheep revenue remained a fairly constant 40% of output, whereas output from cattle fell as a proportion of the total from 30% in '1984' to 24% in '1987', possibly reflecting the impact of the Scheme identified earlier in this chapter. Variable costs on agreement farms only rose slightly with a fall in the cost of feed, fertilizer and seed again reflecting the impact of the Scheme. Fixed costs also rose mainly due to increases in rent, rates and insurance, all changes generating a rise in gross margins by 56%

Table 3.7. Comparison of sub-sample aggregates: Dales Survey. (From Whitby *et al.*, 1992.)

Item	Agreement farms		Non-agreement farms		FBS	
	'1984'	'1987'	'1984'	'1987'	'1984'	'1987'*
Average per farm (£ per total hectare in 1989 prices)						
Total output	79.1	112.4	143.1	223.0	87.31	114.35
Total variable costs	25.3	28.5	55.9	62.6	24.84	30.96
Gross margin	53.8	83.9	87.2	160.4	62.47	83.40
Fixed costs	29.4	42.9	63.1	96.5	38.5	55.87
Management and investment income	24.4	41.0	24.1	63.9	23.97	27.51
Per cent changes						
Total output		+42.2		+55.9		+31.0
Total variable costs		+12.5		+11.9		+24.6
Gross margin		+56.1		+84.0		+33.5
Management and investment income		+68.4		+164.1		+14.8

*The years '1984' and '1987' relate to the latest three years for which financial data were available.

and in management and investment income by 68%.

The level of output on non-agreement farms was approximately twice that on agreement farms and output increased at a greater rate over the period. The proportion of output from cattle and other livestock sales (mainly milk) was also higher than on agreement farms although the former fell from 37 to 30% of output whereas output from other livestock sales rose from 16 to 20%. These findings for non-agreement farms confirm that these farms were more intensive producers with higher proportions of beef and dairy production.

Variable costs on non-agreement farms are a slightly higher proportion of output than on agreement farms; however, they have risen at a slower rate, which is surprising given that these farmers are not constrained in input use. Although the costs of feed/fertilizer and seed on these farms have risen, compared to a fall on agreement farms, the main reason for the difference is a rise in sundry costs on agreement farms and a fall in these costs on non-agreement farms.

Fixed costs on non-agreement farms have risen by 53%, the main increase being due to a doubling of rent, rates and insurance. Therefore although gross margins rose by 84%, which is more than on agreement farms, management and investment income rose by 164% compared to 68% on agreement farms.

The agreement group compares closely with the per hectare results for the FBS Northern Hill Farms in '1984'. Over the following three years output per hectare rose faster on agreement farms and variable costs increased more slowly, with the result that gross margins, gross or net of fixed costs, increased substantially more on the ESA agreement farms than on the FBS sample. However, this was due to ESA payments: when they were excluded actual output on agreement farms rose at a slower rate than on FBS farms.

An estimate was made of the impact of ESA on the total level of farm income in the Dales. This involved estimating the total account for the ESA and then calculating agreement farm income in the absence of the ESA. The impact of ESA on income was assessed by applying the change in the FBS account from '1984' to '1987' to the '1984' agreement account on the grounds that in absence of the ESA agreement output and expenditure would have changed at the same rate as the FBS. The results of this are presented in Table 3.8 and compared to the actual '1987' account for agreement farms.

Table 3.8 shows that over the period output increased by 8.5% or £173,800. Variable costs fell by 11% mainly due to the fall in feed, fertilizer and seed (the fall in purchased fertilizer offsetting the rise in bought-in feed). Gross margins therefore increased by £234,300 or 16% on agreement farms due to the ESA. The change in fixed costs was an increase of £5500 or 2.5% leading to a rise in management and investment income of £228,800 or 40%.

The total value of ESA payments estimated from the survey data is

Table 3.8. Aggregate estimate of the impact of the Scheme on agreement income compared to '1987' actual income with and without ESA payments. (From Whitby *et al.*, 1992.)

Item (£000, 1989 prices)	Agreement farms (1)	Estimated agreement farms without ESA (2)	Aggregate net impact of ESA (1 − 2)
Total output	2214.1	2040.3	173.8
Variable costs	560.9	621.3	−60.4
Gross margin	1653.2	1418.9	234.3
Fixed costs	845.1	839.6	5.5
Management and investment income	808.1	579.3	228.8

£267,000, which is considerably lower than the total payments implied by multiplying the payment of £100 per hectare by the area under agreement in '1987', of 8071 hectares, giving total payment of £807,100 in a full year. This is an underestimate, due to a number of farms not having received all their ESA payments at the time of the survey.

The rise in output, gross margins and management and investment income on both ESA and FBS farms reflects the general rise in Less Favoured Area (LFA) farm income over the period. Real incomes on LFA livestock farms in the UK rose by 28% from 1984/87 to 1988/89; however, since then *real* incomes have fallen (MAFF, 1993f) which would be reflected in the ESA farm accounts.

Cost of the ESA

As stated above the ESA payment cost £100 per hectare. If this is multiplied by the uptake rate it gives a cost of payments of £979,300 in 1991–92 or, excluding the contribution from the EC, £734,500. However, the ESA also provides exchequer savings through the reduction in output as discussed earlier. Estimated savings in exchequer cost were obtained from MAFF by commodity and these were applied to the changes in output estimated from the Newcastle study. The main savings related to changes in livestock numbers as well as other impacts of the ESA, i.e. the increase in bought-in fodder, mainly hay, and the switch out of dairying to less intensive livestock production. Whilst no attempt was made to estimate the exchequer savings from the diverted milk quota an estimate was made of the increase in hay bought in by agreement farmers due to the ESA and the exchequer savings calculated using barley equivalent. The average exchequer savings amounted to £87,000 per year in 1987/88 and £120,000 in 1991/92 – just over 10% of the cost of the ESA to the UK exchequer in 1991–92.

Attitudes of Farmers

The success of the ESA depends upon the willingness of farms to participate in the ESA and comply with the management prescriptions. Therefore the Newcastle study examined the attitudes and perceptions of farmers towards the ESA.

Of the agreement farmers surveyed nearly 30% found the ESA sufficiently attractive, with 39% stating that they would have joined for lower payments. This proportion is consistent with the third of farmers who did not have to alter farming practice to comply with the ESA or the 39% who would not have altered farm practice if the ESA did not exist.

A quarter of agreement farmers thought that the ESA could be made more attractive by increasing payments; relaxing (a quarter of farmers) or removing constraints (a fifth) was also suggested, particularly the cutting date and fertilizer application, with some farmers arguing, as reported earlier in this chapter, that earlier cutting dates would not reduce the diversity of the meadows. For all groups of farmers interviewed, maintenance of walls and barns was not seen as major disadvantage of the ESA, although some agreement farmers did report difficulty in finding contract labour for walling and lack of time for repairs themselves.

A source of discontent was the boundary, particularly with farmers who had a small area of meadow land in the ESA, compared to others who had areas of rough grazing inside the boundary. In fact 36% of non-agreement farmers indicated that changes in the boundary would make the ESA more attractive. However, over half the non-agreement farmers had no interest in the ESA and 70% stated it would cause a fall in income, presumably reflecting the more intensive land use on these farms and the change in farm practice required to comply with the management prescriptions. Thus, not surprisingly, the main way to make the ESA more attractive to non-agreement farmers was relaxation or removal of the constraints, with 89 and 39% respectively stating that elimination and relaxation of constraints would make the ESA more attractive.

Problems occurred in obtaining attitudes to the ESA from control farmers as they were unfamiliar with the ESA or its prescriptions. The attractiveness of the scheme to them largely depended upon the amount and type of land which would be eligible, with many giving a negative response if the scheme only included meadow land.

Review of the ESA

The ESA has been effective in terms of uptake rate and compliance with the prescriptions. However, there remained some criticism of the ESA with the MAFF study highlighting potential problems, for example the shorter cutting periods. Other potential problems included the switch to silage and some evidence of farmers no longer using hay meadows for forage production. Farmers' criticisms of the ESA include the drawing of the boundary; preference for more flexibility over cutting dates; and payments tiered according to the agricultural potential of the land rather than tighter constraints as in other ESAs.

Some of these factors were addressed in the new ESA introduced in 1992, which embodied a number of important changes on the original ESA and trebled the original area. The most significant change was an increase in the ESA area to include more Dales, with the boundary expanded in some of the original ESA Dales.

The other changes relate to the management prescriptions, expanding the agreement time to ten years, with an opt-out after five, and two separate tiers of agreement. The changes to the management prescriptions generally increase the management constraints. Tier I has similar management prescriptions to the original ESA but offers a higher payment for meadow land at £125 per hectare and a lower payment for other land of £90 per hectare. Farmers must identify their meadow land and manage it as such. A common cutting date, 8 July, has been introduced across all Dales with all meadows having their first cut in August once every five years. This reduces the problem of the reduced cutting period on some agreement farms.

A further restriction compared to the original ESA is the reduction in the application of inorganic fertilizer to once per year. This is unlikely to be attractive to farmers who complained under the original ESA that aftermath grazing was reduced and this will now be reduced further as a second application of fertilizer in early autumn is not allowed. There is also a reduction in FYM application from 10 to 5 tonnes per hectare. This is likely to be a constraint given the average application is 8 tonnes per hectare, although the problem of estimating this amount and monitoring the constraint was raised by farmers in the Newcastle study.

Under Tier II, in return for higher payments of £210 per hectare, farmers must, in addition to the constraints under Tier I, apply no inorganic fertilizer; remove stock from the meadows by 15 May; observe a hay cutting date of 15 July and not cut for silage until August. Under the new ESA farmers may adopt a conservation plan which offers grants for capital expenditure of an environmentally friendly nature.

It is difficult to predict the attractiveness of the new ESA. Whilst it addresses many of the environmental concerns of the original ESA it does not deal with many of the criticisms of farmers. However, given the fall in farm incomes since 1987 the new ESA may well prove to be as attractive if not more so than the old one.

Conclusions

The Pennine Dales ESA has been successful if measured in terms of uptake and compliance with the prescriptions. Its impact upon the landscape, historical and biological features cannot yet be estimated although there are some positive indications of improvement. However, the fact that 42% of agreement farmers have reduced their fertilizer and are cutting later does suggest that there will be some improvement in biological diversity. Likewise the increase in walling on agreement farms suggests that the landscape is being maintained or enhanced. It has been successful in maintaining agreement farmers' incomes; some of these farmers might have intensified their land use without the ESA. Evidence of the 'halo effect' was slight, with small changes in fertilizer use on land outside the area increasing yields.

The new ESA does emphasize the conservation objectives of designation by increasing the constraints, many of which seemed to be of major concern to farmers. Whether uptake will be as great has yet to be seen but given the fall in agricultural incomes over the last few years alternative forms of agricultural support like the ESA will retain their attraction.

4

COMPETITION WITH OTHER ENVIRONMENTAL DESIGNATIONS ON A LOWLAND HEATH
The Case of the Breckland

Lucy O'Carroll

Introduction

The Breckland area of East Anglia, covering 94,032 hectares, contains three main landscape types of conservation interest: heathland, woodlands and wetlands.

The importance of the heathland sites in the Breckland was recognized by Ratcliffe (1977), who listed 19 in the area considered to be of Nature Conservation Review Status. In terms of wildlife interest, the heaths support a rich variety of flower species, some of which are not found elsewhere in Britain, as well as rare heathland birds (including the stone curlew, which has its main population in the Breckland), moths and other species.

Traditionally the Breckland has been an open, virtually treeless area, although the mature Scots pine of the shelter belts are of interest. In addition, the coniferous plantations which were begun in the early 1920s are now being felled and replanted. This has introduced new forms of wildlife habitat to the area, of which more will be discussed below.

The area also incorporates a range of wetland features (meres, fens and pingoes) which are of great ecological value, and a significant number of sites of archaeological interest. The combination of the Breckland's landscape and wildlife value with these factors led to it being designated an Environmentally Sensitive Area (ESA) in 1988.

In order to assess the value and effectiveness of ESA designation of the Breckland, several important issues must be addressed. First, is the area's ESA status justified? Given the financial costs of the instrument, a positive answer to this question requires not only that the Breckland has high landscape and wildlife value, but also that designation has protected and enhanced the conservation interest more effectively than, or in different ways from, alternative existing approaches. Second, and of equal importance, is whether the ESA is the most efficient and effective approach to dealing with the specific problems of the Breckland area; are there any significant deficiencies or problems with its current use? Third, will any of these be overcome with the revised ESA guidelines introduced in 1993, or could alternative instruments prove more effective? These issues are addressed in the discussion which follows.

Recent Changes Affecting the Conservation Interest

The basic conservation interest of the Breckland has been outlined above; the reasons for its designation as an ESA may also be traced to a number of significant changes to the landscape (and hence to its value for wildlife) which have taken place this century, as a result of pressures generated by an ever-growing need for land in the district.

Heathland

Taking the case of heathland first, one of the most obvious changes in the area has been the massive loss of this type of land cover, from an estimated 29,000 hectares in 1900 to only 7000 hectares at present. In fact it was this landscape type which originally gave the area its name; 'brecks' are areas of marginal interest in farming terms, ploughed only every 12 or 15 years, resulting in a topography of sandy heaths.

One of the most important reasons for the loss of heathland is arable farming. Agriculture in the Brecks has always in the past been dominated by the physical constraints associated with its sandy, drought-prone soils. Thus it has traditionally been classed as 'marginal' farmland, useful for cereal production during times of high grain prices, but otherwise of very limited agricultural potential. In fact there have been periods when rabbit grazing rather than arable cropping was the main activity.

In the late 1920s, however, government subsidies encouraged an increase in the area of wheat and the planting of sugarbeet. The success of the latter crop in particular led to more general improvements in mechanization, reclamation and the development of profitable specialist crops. By 1941/42, 75% of farms in the Stanford area of the Breckland were classified as Grade A (Sheail, 1979).

Following World War II, farmers in the Brecks (as elsewhere) were encouraged to produce more crops more efficiently. To fulfil this aim much of the heathland was ploughed up and converted to arable production during this period. Furthermore, over the past 20 years the widespread availability of irrigation has had a significant impact on Breckland agriculture, accelerating the process of change. Given an adequate supply of water, sandy soils are now capable of growing a very wide range of high value crops such as vegetables.

The modern agricultural landscapes born out of these developments tend to be open, in contrast to the traditional arable landscape which was characterized by pine lines and 'belts'. Some of these remain, but have also altered due to lack of proper management. They are now frequently old and gappy, and in many areas the historical landscape appears derelict.

Thus while physical constraints have traditionally kept agricultural practice in harmony with the conservation interest of the area, and indeed have been instrumental in the development of this interest, technological advances and increased profitability have not only overcome these constraints but have also altered the relationship between agriculture and the conservation interest of the land.

Loss of heathland has also occurred as a result of a reduction in grazing. In particular, in the 18th and 19th centuries the rabbit population of Breckland was vital in maintaining the heath vegetation and patches of bare soil so characteristic of the heath landscape. Thus the effects of myxomatosis and the reduction in sheep numbers (due to changing agricultural requirements) have profoundly altered the overall landscape of the Brecks, with scrub woodland now dominating over heath.

River Valleys and Wetlands

Turning to the river valleys and wet landscapes, some of these (such as Market Weston and Hopton Valley) retain much of their former intricate landscape of water meadows, reed beds, fens and carrs. However, developments which have impacted upon arable land have also had an effect here. In particular, technological advances have resulted in many stream courses being altered to allow better drainage. This has permitted floodplain meadows to be ploughed.

The Military Presence

The third significant change to take place has been the military presence. In 1942 the War Office decided that designation of an area in the Breckland for military training purposes was desirable; thus 6700 hectares were requisitioned in the Stanford area, accompanied by subsequent purchases of Bridgham Heath, land at Barnham, and airfields at Lakenheath, Mildenhall and Honington.

The impact of this development has been mixed. Army camps have been constructed with little screening, making virtually no concession to the Breck landscape. The story has been similar for the airfields, which have obliterated heaths, arable areas, woods, tracks and the archaeological features of former landscapes.

On the other hand, the military presence has had a positive impact at Stanford, where coniferous forests are gradually being reverted to heath, or are being replaced by deciduous plantings. Further, about 4800 hectares are farmed, largely by sheep grazing. Thus the grass heaths have not only been retained but, in parts, extended. This point will be returned to later, in an overview of the ESA; for the present it should be noted that Ratcliffe (1977) judged military use likely to cause less harm to the traditional landscape and wildlife of the Breckland than modern agriculture.

Effects of these Changes

The changes described above have had a profound effect on the conservation interest of both the heathland and wetland of the Brecks. On the heathland, the lack of grazing management due to the decline in the rabbit population has resulted in the invasion of heaths by birch and scrub, with grassland becoming rank in many areas. Since Breckland plants tend to require open, disturbed soils in which to germinate and become established, their populations have suffered.

It is not only the *absolute* loss of this habitat which is of concern, but also its fragmentation into between 50 and 60 separate parts, resulting in smaller sites which are more vulnerable to destruction and subject to invasion. There is a particular problem with woodland, for although recent large-scale afforestation has introduced new wildlife habitats to the Breckland, these are themselves likely to cause problems for the remaining traditional habitats through invasion and competition.

All of this has resulted in the decline of most rare Brecks species, some to the point of extinction, a marked fall in the populations of rare heathland birds, and extinction of a number of moths.

As for wetland, the desire to improve the arable potential of the area has seen destruction and damage of wetland and valley fens by drainage and abstraction schemes. This has resulted in the loss of meres, fens and pingoes, all features of great ecological value. Valuable wildlife areas of unimproved grassland are also under threat of improvement by fertilizing and the application of weedkillers.

In addition, pressures on the conservation interest of the area can be traced to increased urbanization, and to the enrichment of traditionally sandy soils by increased nutrients in rainfall. This has accelerated the process of change in vegetation from being sparse and patchy to relatively lush cover.

Sites of Special Scientific Interest (SSSIs) in the Breckland

Prior to ESA designation, the system of SSSIs in the Breckland played a significant role in protecting the conservation interest of the area. Farmers could be offered individually negotiated management agreements (MAs) to prevent them from undertaking activities which might threaten the environmental value of SSSIs, for which they would be compensated on the basis of profit foregone.

The first of 42 SSSIs in the Breckland was notified in 1952, at Cavenham Heath. The total area now covered by this designation amounts to 8361 hectares, or 8.6% of the Breckland as a whole. Four of these sites are also National Nature Reserves. It is therefore important to examine why this system was not considered to be fully effective in protecting the area before 1988, and why ESA designation was thought likely to compensate for some of these deficiencies.

The major advantage of management agreements on SSSIs over other mechanisms for protecting land is their flexibility. This arises from the fact that they are negotiated on an individual basis. On the other hand, the flexible nature of MAs tends to increase the time spent in their negotiation and hence their costs. This can be a problem in cases such as the Breckland where the Countryside Commission (in its initial submission for ESA status for the area) considered that the greatest threat to its conservation interest arose out of possible changes in ownership, where a quick return is generally required on the initial investment, resulting in a heightened threat from arable conversion, drainage and so forth. In such situations a rapid response to threats is required.

The serious problem of heathland fragmentation in the Breckland could in part be dealt with by positive payments to encourage arable reversion. However, the emphasis of the system of management agreements on SSSIs has been on responding to threats; scarcity of resources (and the need to base payments on full profit foregone) has left little opportunity for such positive agreements. With the introduction of positive payments on a small number of SSSIs through the Wildlife Enhancement Scheme, however, movement in this direction may have begun.

Management agreements are not fully effective in preventing damage to SSSIs, since neglect and undergrazing cannot be specified as 'threatening' activities, and yet may cause the degeneration of a site. In an analysis of 34 of the Breckland SSSIs, the Brecks Study Group (1991) listed lack of management or undergrazing as the main threat on 16 of the sites. Dolman and Sutherland (1991) have argued that lack of management has exacerbated the problems of nutrient enrichment of the soil in the area, leading to a reduction in the numbers of birds and plants so severe that on some sites protected as SSSIs or National Nature Reserves, many of the original rarities have disappeared. The authors even question whether the continuation of SSSI status on certain sites is justified.

Finally, the SSSI system provides no protection for areas which fall below the quality required for notification, but which make an important contribution to the overall conservation interest. In the Breckland such areas may be viewed as acting as 'buffers' for high-quality, fragmented sites, under threat from woodland encroachment or arable reversion, and hence having a valuable role to play in protecting the conservation interest of the area.

The ESA Mechanism in the Breckland

The 1988 ESA Guidelines

The prescriptions set out in the ESA guidelines for the Breckland in 1988 involved grazing, control of scrub and restrictions on fertilizers, herbicides and lime, to allow maintenance of the heathland and dry grassland, and indeed some arable reversion (all under Tier I of the policy, with a payment level set at £100/hectare/annum). As for wet grassland, covered by Tier II of the policy with payment at £125/hectare/annum, additional restrictions were placed on drainage and on the dates after which hay and silage could be cut.

Under Tier III, the environmental value of arable field margins could be increased by restricting spray applications to create conservation headlands, hence encouraging insect populations, for payments of £100/hectare/annum. Wildlife strips of uncropped, unsprayed fallow could also be introduced in arable fields for a higher rate of £300/hectare/annum.

Thus the ESA was introduced to provide more *comprehensive* protection for the area than the existing SSSI system. In relation to this, all land covered by ESA agreements has also had to meet several additional standards. Hedges and hedgerow trees have had to be maintained in a traditional manner; features of geomorphological interest (such as meres and pingoes) are not to be damaged or destroyed, and farmers have had to obtain advice on the management of woodland, Scots pine belts, copses and trees (see Box 4.1).

By basing payments on standard amounts for stipulated practices within Tiers, it was hoped that the ESA would be less costly (in terms of time and resources) to implement than management agreements. Furthermore, these payments are for *positive* actions by farmers; thus it was hoped that there would be a beneficial effect on heathland management after (in many cases) a long period of decline.

A considerable amount of monitoring and consultation has been carried out to assess the impact of the ESA guidelines introduced in 1988, and this can be drawn on to determine the level of success the mechanism has had in protecting and enhancing the landscape and wildlife value of the Breckland. One of the most important indicators is uptake. Where a large number of farmers are unwilling to enter the ESA, this obviously reduces its ability to play a positive role in conservation. In the extreme case of the Test Valley, for example, uptake has been poor (only around 21% of its expected level). Once land is entered into the scheme, however, it is the effect of the guidelines on the wildlife and landscape of the area which is of concern. Thus the success of the Breckland ESA, and its 1993 revisions, will be judged on these criteria.

Box 4.1. Management guidelines: Breckland ESA.

Heathland and dry grassland

- Maintain without ploughing, levelling, rolling, or reseeding.
- Graze hard but avoid poaching; where possible remove stock between 15 March and 16 May to allow the establishment of nesting birds.
- Restrict supplementary feeding to areas agreed with Project Officer.
- Avoid irrigation and the application of fertilizers, manures, lime, slag and pesticides.
- Restrict use of herbicides to weed wiper or spot treatments, and to named species; control bracken and scrub by agreement with Project Officer.
- On *arable reversion to heathland* crop the land for two years under special restrictions to reduce nutrient levels in the soil; then after harvesting the second crop manage the land according to the heathland and dry grassland guidelines.

Wet grassland

- Cultivation only with chain harrow or roller; avoid between 31 March and 1 July.
- Avoid cutting for hay or silage before 1 July, under- or overgrazing, or poaching.
- Restrict use of fertilizers to specified levels; avoid use of slurry, pig or poultry manure, sewage sludge, lime, slag and pesticides; restrict herbicides to weed wiper or spot treatments of named species.
- Maintain existing drainage systems without improvements, additions or modifications.
- Restrict supplementary feeding to areas agreed with Project Officer.

Headlands

- Cease cropping at least 6 metres in from the existing field edge.
- Create a seedbed in the headland between 31 July and 1 January according to specified restrictions.
- Avoid mechanical damage and the use of fertilizers, manures, lime, slag, pesticides and irrigation; restrict herbicides to weed wiper and spot treatments of named species.
- On *uncropped* headlands avoid the use of unapproved herbicides; and the use of insecticides between 31 August and 1 January.

All land covered by agreement

- Maintain historic and landscape features; and hedges, hedgerow trees, ponds and ditches without the use of chemicals.
- Obtain written advice before starting any construction or engineering work not requiring planning permission; and early in the agreement on the management of woodland and individual trees.

Measuring Success on the Basis of Uptake

Since non-agricultural land (including woodland) is not included in the scheme, this leaves a total of 51,600 hectares of the Breckland eligible to enter. The target considered to be a measure of initial success of the scheme was an uptake of 75% of heath/dry grassland and 1000 hectares of valley grassland (MAFF, 1993c). The overall annual uptake under these precriptions since the beginning of the scheme is given in Table 4.1.

Table 4.1 shows that while more than twice the target area has been entered into wet grassland agreements (2220 hectares in total), there has been less than 35% uptake on heath and dry grassland[1]. A large proportion of the grassland that has not entered the scheme is managed relatively intensively; for example, while 82% of the land in which heather is a major component was under agreement by the end of 1991, only 22% of semi-improved dry grassland was protected in this way. This implies that payments were not set at a high enough level to encourage the more productive land into the scheme.

This important point is also reflected in the low level of arable reversion which has taken place under the ESA scheme. Although no target uptake figure was set in this case, the fact that only 10 hectares of arable land has been reverted to dry grassland is generally acknowledged to be disappointing. On the other hand, the total area of fields which contain uncropped wildlife strips and conservation headlands has amounted to approximately 3000 hectares and 1800 hectares respectively. Thus around 12% of arable land in the Breckland is covered by such agreements, which exceeds the target of 10% adopted for the arable field margin options.

Table 4.1. ESA uptake – heathland/dry grassland and wet grassland. (From MAFF, 1993c.)

Year	Area entering agreement (ha)			% of ESA heathland and grassland	No. of agreements
	Heathland/ dry grass	Wet grassland	Total		
1988	920	1610	2530	24	53
1989	370	360	730	7	14
1990	105	190	295	3	21
1991	30	60	90	1	5
Total	1425	2220	3645	35	93

[1]The figure given in Table 4.1 includes wet grassland.

Thus the picture on uptake is rather mixed. Although most of the valuable riverside margins are now covered by ESA agreements and there has been some creation of new environmental value through the arable field margins, the response to several important elements of the scheme in the Breckland has been disappointing. The main reason given by farmers for non-participation was financial; low uptake appears to be the result of the opportunity cost of entering the relevant Tier being high relative to payment levels, so deterring a significant number of potential entrants. This issue is returned to below.

Measuring Success on the Basis of Wildlife Impacts

The grazing management stipulations of the ESA scheme were intended to restore heathlands to their former condition and prevent scrub invasion. Thus it was anticipated that there would be a reduction in coarse grasses and competitive plant species, along with an increase in the species adapted to the specialized conditions of the Breckland, such as Spanish catchfly and spiked speedwell. In areas of heather cover, the grazing regime was also expected to increase the diversity of its age and structure.

Botanical monitoring of sites in the Breckland (MAFF, 1993c), based on a comparison of ESA-entered with 'control' (i.e. non-participant) plots, found that vegetation height was reduced in both types of plot, for both heather and grassland sites. This was thought to be due in part to activity by wild animals and to unusually dry weather over the period. However, the reduction in height was noticeably greater on ESA plots, due to the grazing regime introduced. Although the recommended threshold vegetation height for stone curlews has not yet been reached, the overall reduction should have improved the habitat for these important birds. Further, although livestock grazing on ESA plots has not prevented the establishment of woody plants, growth of younger plants has been checked. By contrast, such plants in the control plots have tended to increase in height each year.

However, the findings have been less favourable for scrub encroachment. Although the ESA guidelines encourage landowners to fully graze heathland and dry grassland and to control gorse, broom and Scots pine where it persists, the area of scrub was found to have increased on the two 'typical' heaths entered into the ESA and examined under the monitoring scheme. Furthermore, the *rate* of spread does not appear to be falling in response to the increased stocking levels introduced under the ESA. This implies that more positive action needs to be taken to remove scrub where it threatens the visual and ecological value of heaths.

In addition, although monitoring of the uncropped wildlife strips has shown that the numbers of plant species and the biomass of vegetation is significantly greater on the strips than on conventionally managed heath-lands, potentially problematic arable weeds were recorded at some sites.

Dealing with this problem will require sensitive management, however, since some weedy sites also have reasonable proportions of valuable species.

Measuring Success on the Basis of Landscape Impacts

Changes to landscape are usually much more gradual than wildlife impacts; thus only initial trends can be identified in the relatively short space of time since the designation of the Breckland as an ESA. Having said this, arable reversion to grassland or heathland provides a rapid change in land cover, restoring the traditional pastoral character of the river valley landscape and providing potential for expansion of heaths to reduce the threats posed by fragmentation. As already noted, however, uptake of the arable reversion option has been very limited and hence any landscape effects have been modest.

In addition to worries over the effects of continued scrub encroachment on the traditional 'openness' of the Breckland, concern has been expressed over the management of the historic pine treelines which characterize the landscape. Since the narrowness of the belts severely limits the opportunity for natural regeneration of the trees, positive management and replanting are required. As yet, the impact of the ESA on this problem has been small. In addition, there is evidence of gappy treelines on land *not* entered into ESA agreements being replanted with broadleaved species; by its nature, the ESA cannot influence actions being carried out on non-participant land, even where their overall impact may be significant.

Furthermore, the lowering of water levels (due to climatic conditions over the period and increasing demands for water abstraction) is posing a major threat to the landscape and environmental value of the ponds, meres and associated wetlands of the Breckland. The results of monitoring have shown a drop in water levels at 85% of sites, with over a third of these losing more than 66% of their 1987 surface water area (MAFF, 1993c). No direct relationship has been found between water level change and adjacent land cover or the presence of an agreement boundary. Thus although the condition of these areas is an important environmental issue, it appears to be outside the realms of the ESA.

Conclusions on the ESA Mechanism

The designation of the Breckland as an Environmentally Sensitive Area appears to have checked the long-term trend of a net loss of grassland and heathland to arable production and other land uses. Monitoring also suggests that there is no evidence of major disturbance or significant change to historic sites on agricultural land. However, there are evidently a number of important problems which the ESA has not overcome. These have arisen in part because of the inability of the mechanism to control activities on land which is not subject to ESA agreements. The replacing of pines with broadleaved species in historic treelines has already been noted. There is also evidence of losses of grassland on non-agreement land which have largely offset some of the small gains to arable reversion on land which *is* under agreement. Outdoor pig rearing, which has a notable detrimental effect on landscape quality as a result of the construction of buildings and radial fencing, has increased on non-agreement land. Finally, there is evidence that participants in the scheme have intensified their arable cropping and stocking regimes on their non-agreement land, in response to commercial pressures.

Thus although it is a more comprehensive designation than the SSSI system, the ESA fails to provide *integrated* management for the area as a whole. While 94,032 hectares of land may be designated as being of high environmental quality, only a relatively small proportion is entered into the scheme and hence is currently being protected by the designation. This is partly a problem of ineligibility; the drying out of meres, fens and pingoes, for example, will have important detrimental landscape and wildlife impacts, but cannot be addressed by the ESA mechanism. Since it is administered by the Ministry of Agriculture, the scheme applies to agricultural land only. In this sense ESA designation is similar to SSSI notification in that it is useful for protecting the conservation interest on areas to which it applies; as it currently operates, however, it may not be effective in preventing loss of valuable wetland or heathland fragmentation.

A related issue is that the ESA scheme has aims other than those of providing environmental protection and enhancement. It is hoped that it will reduce agricultural output. It is also designed to maintain farm incomes. These additional aims have influenced the design of the scheme and are reflected in the fact that the payment made for any one agreement has been determined more by the size of the holding rather than by the conservation value of the land or the actions taken to protect that value. Thus although it has greater emphasis on positive actions than the management agreement system, insufficient incentives have been provided to encourage effective removal of gorse or maintenance of pine lines. However, attached to the revised ESA guidelines for the Breckland are a set of activities (such as hedge planting and pine belt restoration) which are directly eligible for cost-sharing grants, as part of an optional conservation plan.

The lack of integrated management is also in part a problem of uptake. In particular, there has been a very small response to the arable reversion option, designed to encourage traditional river valley landscapes and to protect heathland. It seems that payments were not pitched high enough to compensate farmers for the reduction in gross margins that they would have experienced by joining the scheme. This failure is an important one, since the need for reversion was one of the major reasons why the SSSI system was felt to be inadequate. As a result, more attractive grants were called for, and have been introduced as part of the revised ESA guidelines in 1993. Specifically, for arable or improved grassland a Tier II heathland reversion option has been introduced, with payments set at £300/hectare/annum, while payments for uncropped wildlife strips and conservation headlands (now under Tier IV) have been increased to £350/hectare/annum and £110/hectare/annum, respectively.

Choosing the appropriate level of payments is one of the major problems with the ESA mechanism. Standard contracts and flat-rate payments within Tiers reduce the time spent on, and consequent costs of, negotiation compared with management agreements, and streamline the necessary administration. However, since flat-rate payments are not individually tailored, the marginal cost of increasing payments to encourage uptake is high, as additional payment has to be made on *all* hectares entering the relevant Tier, including those owned by farmers whose opportunity costs would have been covered at lower payment levels. Finding the correct balance between the desired level of uptake and making the best use of available resources will require some careful calculations, since introducing higher payments evidently increases the number of farmers who are receiving more than they would need in order to be persuaded into the ESA scheme.

The Countryside Commission has been particularly critical of the fact that farmers can choose which of their land to enter into the scheme, leaving their non-participant land unrestricted. They argue that it makes no sense for the ESA to pay a farmer to revert a piece of arable land to grass, only to have them plough a neighbouring pasture (Countryside Commission, 1992). They believe that the knock-on effects of ESA entry could be prevented if applicants were required to offer the *whole* of their eligible land for management within the relevant Tier I (i.e. the most basic Tier), while entry into higher Tiers should remain optional. The Royal Society for the Protection of Birds has also called for the setting of a basic standard of good farming practice for entrants (RSPB, 1991). Although this is already common practice in some ESAs (West Penwith and the Pennine Dales, for example), it was not introduced for the Breckland in the 1993 changes.

Finally, although the Breckland's designation as an ESA is indefinite, the agreements entered into by MAFF and willing farmers are of fixed duration. Under the original scheme they lasted for a period of five years; this has now been extended to ten years (with a 'break clause' incorporated, allowing either party the option to terminate the agreement after five years). Thus, in common with management agreements, there is no guarantee of protection of the heathland, wet grassland or arable strips beyond the length of the agreement. If the priorities of policy-makers change, or if the farmers decide that it no longer suits them to be tied to the ESA stipulations, any positive conservation benefits provided by the mechanism may well decline or disappear after the existing agreement has ended.

The Role of Public and Voluntary Body (VB)
Land Ownership in the Breckland

So far, the nature and effectiveness of ESA designation of the Breckland has been examined in comparison with the system of SSSI designation and management agreements. These are not, however, the only means employed to protect the landscape and wildlife value of the area. A range of local-level designations will be discussed in the next section; of greater significance, though, is public and voluntary body land ownership. This is of interest not only because of its current contribution to protecting the area, but also because of its historical influence on the conservation value (and hence subsequent environmental designations) of the Breckland.

Of the total area of 94,032 hectares, 32,488 hectares (approximately 35%) is currently in public or voluntary organization hands, as Table 4.2 shows. Further, 22 out of the 42 Breckland SSSIs are wholly or partly owned or leased by public or voluntary organizations. These 22 sites cover 6203.2 hectares, almost 80% of the total SSSI area.

These statistics suggest that there may be a relationship between SSSI notification, arising as a result of the conservation interest of sites being protected at a level sufficient to merit this designation, and public and voluntary land ownership. They do not, however, establish the *direction* of causality. In other words, it has yet to be determined whether SSSI notification encouraged the relevant organizations to purchase or lease these sites, or whether public or voluntary ownership itself led to later designation.

Table 4.2. Public/voluntary body ownership and leasing of land in Breckland.

Organization	Approximate area (ha)
County Wildlife Trusts	607
English Heritage	65
English Nature	438
Forestry Commission	20,000
Local Authorities	246
Ministry of Defence	11,000
National Trust	7
Water Companies	125
Total	32,488

Table 4.3. Sample of Breckland SSSIs owned/leased by public and voluntary bodies.

SSSI	Organization	Date involved	Date notified
Brettenham Heath	English Nature	1982	1970
Cavenham Heath	English Nature	1952	1952
Cranberry Rough	Norfolk Naturalists' Trust	1962	1961
East Wretham	Norfolk Naturalists' Trust	1938	1954
Knettishall Heath	Suffolk County Council	1974	1984
Maidscross Hill	Anglian Water	1964	1975
Stanford PTA	Ministry of Defence	1940s/50s	1971
Thetford Heath	Norfolk Naturalists' Trust	1948	1954
Wangford Warren	Suffolk Wildlife Trust	1973	1954
Weeting Heath	Norfolk Naturalists' Trust	1942	1958

For the sample of ten Breckland SSSIs shown in Table 4.3, in six cases the relevant organizations became involved a significant amount of time before SSSI notification took place, and in one involvement was in the same year as designation. This suggests that public and voluntary ownership *has* played a role in protecting the conservation interest sufficiently to allow subsequent SSSI notification.

Moreover, there are cases where, without such ownership, SSSI designation would not have taken place at all. One of the best illustrations of this is at Stanford Practical Training Area, already referred to above. As a result of Ministry of Defence ownership, areas of long-established heath have been preserved and, more importantly, land has been allowed to revert back from arable cropping to heath. The latter is of particular significance, given the failure of both management agreements and the original ESA in this regard. Protection and enhancement of the conservation interest of Stanford has been accomplished because public access to the site is necessarily limited, the grass is kept sufficiently grazed by sheep, no trees are planted and, other than on peripheral areas, no pesticides, herbicides or fungicides are used. In addition, many wetlands, springs, streams and areas of standing water benefit from the fact that such a large area of land is under public ownership. This is because they are virtually unaffected by problems of drainage, pollution, eutrophication or water abstraction and therefore tend to be species-rich.

This case highlights a point raised earlier. Public or VB land ownership has an advantage over alternatives such as ESA payments and management agreements, since it is not limited by designation or eligibility. It can therefore be used to provide protection for 'buffer' areas which fall below the quality required for SSSI notification or those (such as the meres, fens and pingoes of the Breckland) which are crucial to the environmental interest but are not ESA-eligible.

Other cases are perhaps not as striking as that of Stanford, but are still of interest. Designation of part of the SSSI at Maidscross Hill for its typical Breckland flora, for example, was the direct result of Anglian Water's policy of not applying pesticides near areas of water supply. Thus it may be argued that the ownership (and leasing) of land by public and voluntary organizations has not only protected sites but, in certain cases, has enhanced them to such a degree as to justify subsequent SSSI notification.

In addition, ESA designation can to an extent be traced to the importance of the SSSI presence and the inability of the system of SSSIs to protect or enhance the conservation interest in a fully satisfactory manner. The existence of a significant amount of land in public and voluntary hands that is not of SSSI standard but *is* of sufficient interest to be included within the ESA boundary (indicated in Table 4.2) also provides evidence to suggest that the case for ESA designation was made stronger by such ownership.

It must be said, however, that the influence of this type of ownership has not always been a positive one. In the case of the Ministry of Defence, the detrimental effects of its presence in some parts of the Breckland have already been noted. Ownership by the Forestry Commission has also been highlighted as having a negative impact, although the Commission is currently introducing more conservation-oriented management on its sites. On those adjacent to public roads, for example, an effort is being made to plant a mixture of species, rather than conifers alone.

Furthermore, it is not being suggested that public and voluntary ownership is the only kind to have had a positive influence on subsequent designations. While 64% of the remaining heathland lies within the Stanford area, 17% (including some heaths of the highest conservation value) is privately owned and protected by the Elveden Estate. Nonetheless, the influence of public and VB ownership on the Breckland has been profound. It would be interesting to examine the historical development of the other ESAs to see whether this is illustrative of a general pattern. Certainly Colman *et al.* (1992) have found such ownership to be significant in the development of the Suffolk River Valleys and the North Peak ESAs.

Of course it should not be forgotten that this process of layering and interaction of mechanisms is ongoing. As is evident from Table 4.3, purchases by public and voluntary organizations have been continuing up to the present. The National Trust, for example, is concerned to acquire more land to protect the setting of Oxburgh Hall (near Swaffham), its only property in the Breckland. Purchase is considered necessary in such cases because of its advantages over the alternative mechanisms; in particular, its long-term nature and the flexibility and firm hold over management practices that it gives the new owner.

With a significant amount of land in public or voluntary body hands, in addition to the ESA and the system of SSSIs, this inevitably raises the question of whether there are any problems with double-funding of conservation-oriented activities. For example, tenants on land owned and protected by public organizations or VBs may also, where relevant, claim ESA payments. However, the rationale for this is that purchase provides long-term, 'baseline' protection, with the ESA ensuring appropriate detailed, short-term management of sites. If different organizations give grants for strictly different purposes, this avoids the danger of double funding. It is also worth noting that this form of interaction is adding to the success of the ESA scheme, as judged by uptake, where the public or voluntary body encourages tenants to enter.

Overview of the Breckland ESA

While there may not be a significant problem with double-funding of conservation-oriented activities, this does not prevent possible confusion or conflicts. This is particularly important given the large number of organizations involved in the Breckland. These are not only owners of land or administrators of the ESA (MAFF) and SSSI system (English Nature). For example, the RSPB is involved in the protection of the stone curlew through its important wardening and research activities in the area, although it is not a landowner.

Furthermore, as discussed briefly earlier, the ESA and the system of SSSIs are not the only designations which acknowledge the conservation value of the Breckland. The area lies within two Counties and four District Council areas. The Norfolk Structure Plan has designated the whole of the Norfolk Brecks as an Area of Important Wildlife Quality, while under the Suffolk Structure Plan much of the southern part of the Breckland is a Special Landscape Area. Both designations imply strict control of development. The County Councils also have powers to declare and manage Local Nature Reserves; this designation has been placed on Barnham Cross Common. In addition, both Councils have set up various initiatives to give advice and promote positive conservation work.

The District Councils have also formulated Local Plans which, through their statutory policies, give country landscape designations to much of the Brecks. These designations and the Conservation Areas designated by the Borough Councils in various towns and villages are concerned with the safeguarding of public access and promotion of development sympathetic to the conservation interest of the area.

Even with these layers of instruments and designations, however, there is a feeling that not all aspects of the conservation interest of the Breckland are being fully protected. The impacts of grassland losses, outdoor pig rearing and intensification on non-participant land have already been discussed. In particular, the Brecks Study Group (1991), a consultation body made up of the local authorities, statutory conservation bodies and various voluntary organizations in the area, has felt strongly that designation as an Area of Outstanding Natural Beauty is required. While this would increase the ability of the local authorities to control unsuitable development, the main benefit from this additional form of protection would be to facilitate coordination of conservation strategies.

The roots of this lack of coordination may to some extent be traced to the extensive public ownership of land in the area, in particular by the Forestry Commission. This is perhaps ironic, in view of the largely positive role of such ownership. The Hobhouse Report (Hobhouse, 1947) did not recommend Breckland for designation as a National Park for the specific reason that its intensive land use (forestry) would not allow sufficient public access to justify it. However, it is perhaps unfortunate that the means suggested for achieving this coordination is to place yet another designation on the land. It is not clear whether this approach would actually solve the inherent problem; it may be time for coordinated discussion by the different organizations involved (at national and regional level), both to define their individual roles and to produce a more coherent strategy for the area in the future.

The current extent of liaison between MAFF and the other organizations involved in the ESA areas varies from regular meetings with scheme participants and certain conservation bodies to little, if any, contact. Where liaison has been good, the RSPB points out that specific adjustments to the working of the ESA have been possible, and there is a clear understanding of the specific problems of the areas involved (RSPB, 1991). These considerations are particularly important for cases like the Breckland, where some elements of management may have to be more flexible than the basic ESA stipulations suggest; for example, cutting dates for hay or the ways in which weeds in arable field margins should be dealt with. Both the Countryside Commission and the RSPB support the setting up of a formal liaison panel for each ESA, although this has not been introduced under the 1993 reforms.

In addition, it has been suggested (Countryside Commission, 1992) that a more coordinated approach to conservation could be facilitated if Agricultural Development and Advisory Service (ADAS) officers were briefed, when approaching farmers about ESA agreements, to inform them of any supplementary grant systems available from the County Councils or other bodies. Farmers undertaking the new farm conservation plan option could be obliged to show draft plans to other grant-giving bodies. Again these suggestions have not been introduced, but would be a useful way of avoiding confusion and the danger of double-funding of conservation activities. They might also reduce the likelihood of actions which have a negative impact on the overall landscape or wildlife value being carried out on land which provides a 'buffer' for sites which have a major (SSSI) designation or which are ESA-entered.

Conclusions

The continental climate and sandy soils of the Breckland have provided a landscape and wildlife habitat which is not only considered to be of high environmental value, but is unique in the United Kingdom. In spite of the large number of Sites of Special Scientific Interest designated, the management agreement system has been too cumbersome and too 'negative' in nature to be fully effective in protecting the area. Furthermore, its concentration on only the most highly valued sites has not prevented heathland fragmentation. The designation of the Environmentally Sensitive Area in 1988 has addressed some of these issues. It was designed to protect a larger area, with payments for positive actions on the part of landowners or tenants. Enhancement of the existing conservation value or the creation of new interest have also been possible through the arable reversion and field margin options.

However, payment levels have clearly been pitched at an insufficiently high level to provide more than a token amount of reversion. Since the scheme is administered by the Agriculture Departments, only agricultural land is eligible. Thus the important meres, fens and other wetland features have not been protected, and their drying out is causing increasing concern. In addition, payments have been more for the size of the holding than for the environmental value of activities carried out on it. As a result, there has been insufficient emphasis on positive conservation management to deal effectively with scrub encroachment and 'gappy' pine lines. Finally, since landowners are not obliged to enter all of their land into the scheme, there has been a failure to achieve any feeling of integrated management for the area as a whole.

While some of these issues have been addressed in the 1993 revisions to the Breckland ESA guidelines, gaps still remain. Options such as increasing payments to encourage more farmers to enter the scheme, or providing consistent management by guaranteeing Tier I payments to all entrants, may prove to be a relatively expensive means of providing environmental benefits. Further, the provision of those benefits is only guaranteed for the length of the existing ESA agreement.

At the same time, examination of the record of public and voluntary body land ownership shows not only that it has had a striking influence on the area's historical development, but also that it is continuing to provide flexible, long-term protection and significant enhancement and creation of new environmental value, in ways that the other mechanisms have patently failed to do to any great degree. Thus the provision of grants to enable voluntary bodies to continue to acquire and manage land in the area in the future merits serious consideration, particularly as purchase can then be 'targeted' at sites considered to be under threat. The budgetary implications of this compared to the flat rate, standard payment ESA approach are explored in more depth in Chapter 10.

However, since it seems that no single mechanism can deal with all of the problems of the Breckland, the area is currently subject to a plethora of designations, overseen by a range of grant-awarding bodies. Therefore to prevent duplication and double-funding of activities, or confusions leading to oversights and 'gaps' in the system of protection, enhancement and creation of conservation interest, consultation between organizations and greater coordination of their activities and strategies is recommended. This is an essential step if the unique value of the Breckland is to be preserved and enhanced into the next century.

5

UPLAND MOORLAND WITH COMPLEX PROPERTY RIGHTS
The Case of the North Peak

Julie Froud

Introduction

Characteristics of the North Peak

The North Peak ESA, designated as part of the second round of English ESAs in 1988, encompasses the northern part of the Peak District National Park in Derbyshire, West Yorkshire, Lancashire and parts of Greater Manchester. The ESA stretches from the Hope valley in the south to Marsden in the north, straddling the block of gritstone moor which forms the southern end of the Pennines. The total area of the original scheme is 49,607 hectares, of which some 45,692 hectares were eligible. The ESA lies entirely within a Less Favoured Area (LFA).

Landscape and wildlife interest

The main landscape type, accounting for around three-quarters of the eligible area (MAFF, 1993e), is the upland plateau comprising heather, shrub and grass-covered peat moorland. These moors are mostly unfenced, emphasizing the characteristic open landscape. The moorland plateaux support a diverse flora and fauna. Much of the wildlife interest is related to the heather and its associated plant communities. In addition, the blanket peat supports various mosses and wetland grasses and the cloughs provide a suitable habitat for a number of important ferns. The ornithological value of these moors has been recognized in their designation as a Special Protection Area (SPA) under the EC Birds Directive and in a number of SSSIs, including Kinder-Bleaklow, a Grade One SSSI covering 11,750 hectares. The moors support birds such as the merlin, dunlin, curlew and golden plover as well as the red grouse, which is the focus of commercial interest.

The second landscape type is the enclosed and often improved pasture, or inbye, in the valleys and on the moorland fringes. These fields are enclosed by the traditional drystone walls which have helped to create the upland landscape valued by both the local population and the many visitors who use the area. The 1988 baseline survey of the North Peak (MAFF, 1993e) estimated that cultivated land on the lower slopes accounted for 12% of the ESA area, with derelict farmland (i.e. relict land on the upper fringes of the inbye) a further 4%. These meadows and pastures can again support a wide variety of plant, insect and bird life, although improvement through levelling, draining, reseeding and liming will significantly reduce the botanical variety.

The remainder of the designated area is accounted for by woodland, commercial forestry and a number of reservoirs, all such land being ineligible for ESA payments.

Farming characteristics

The main agricultural enterprise within the ESA is the rearing and selling of lambs and, to a lesser extent, calves. Most holdings comprise both inbye and moorland and run separate flocks on each. There is a limited amount of dairying, usually on the lower pastures and often on land lying just outside the ESA boundary. The inbye is also important for the production of winter fodder – traditionally hay but, increasingly, silage. Although the enclosed land usually accounts for only a small part of the total holding it is an essential element of the hill farm since it can support a much higher stocking rate and can be used to house animals from the moor during winter, lambing or tupping.

The institutional structure

The ownership structure of the North Peak is one of the interesting features of this area and, as will be seen in the proceeding discussion, plays a significant role in the way that the ESA scheme operates. Much of the moorland is owned by large private estates, the water utilities and increasingly the National Trust. The National Trust has been targeting the North Peak in recent years and consolidating its High Peak Estate so that it now owns some 14,300 hectares. As can be seen in Table 5.1, these public or quasi-public institutions account for 46% of the area and thus represent a significant local interest. Both these moors and those owned by the private estates are generally let out to graziers on one-year or shorter licences or gaits. These take the form of the right to graze a particular number of sheep (usually counted as one ewe plus lamb and one quarter follower where hill ewes are

Table 5.1. Institutional ownership in the North Peak.

Organization	Area owned (ha)	Proportion of total ESA (%)
National Trust	14,325	28.9
Water Companies	7414	14.9
Local Authorities	706	1.4
Peak Park National Park Authority	520	1.0

kept for four years) over a particular stretch of moorland. There is no common land in the North Peak although a number of individuals may have grazing rights on adjacent parts of the same moor. As the moorland is generally not fenced problems of trespass do arise in some areas, compounding the effects of overgrazing on particular pieces of land. Graziers have no formal security of tenure although in practice most moors tend to be let to the same licensee in consecutive years.

As well as grazing rights, these estates may also let out separate sporting rights where the main interest is the shooting of red grouse. In many cases the private estates keep these rights in hand with the shoots run on the basis of syndicates rather than commercial enterprises. These syndicates are managed by a gamekeeper on behalf of approximately eight members, each of whom have the right to provide one gun on each of the days upon which shooting occurs. The existence of actively used sporting rights alongside the grazing rights has implications for the way in which the moors have traditionally been managed. Grouse require a good coverage of heather, which should ideally be burnt regularly in small patches in order to provide feeding grounds at the edges of the burnt areas and cover in the older sections of heather. Although some grazing of the moor is beneficial to the grouse habitat, the presence of the shooting interest generally leads to a lower stocking rate than if the sporting rights were not used. The inbye land is mostly tenanted (in some cases under the same landlord as the moorland), or owner-occupied with the institutional landowners as significant actors.

Threats to the environmental value of the North Peak

The main threats to the North Peak, which were instrumental in its designation as an ESA, come from intensification of agriculture through land improvements facilitating a higher stocking rate and, on the inbye, allowing for silage production. On the moorland the critical factors are the winter stocking rates and the extent to which concentrated overgrazing can occur, often precipitated by the use of static winter feeding or foddering points. Where the moorland is burnt only irregularly then the problem of overgrazing will be exacerbated since the sheep will tend to avoid the areas where the heather has become old and leggy. Considerable damage to the vegetation can result from accidental fires with the peat continuing to burn underground for several weeks and leaving large sunken areas which quickly become eroded and, without being fenced off from sheep, are slow to revegetate or may remain bare. At the time the ESA was introduced, eroding moorland and encroaching bracken each accounted for 4.5% of the designated area. In particular areas erosion resulting from recreational pressures is acute. The North Peak contains the start of the Pennine Way and is in addition within a fairly short drive from the urban centres of Manchester, Sheffield and West Yorkshire. Atmospheric pollution has also taken its toll upon the vegetative quality.[1]

The North Peak ESA Scheme

Objectives of the North Peak ESA

In common with all the ESAs the North Peak ESA has the central aims of safeguarding the wildlife, historic and landscape interest implied by its designation and, where appropriate, encouraging landowners and managers to take steps to build upon these existing elements. More specifically, MAFF cites the following four objectives of the North Peak (MAFF, 1993e): (i) to support low intensity sheep grazing of the existing heather and shrub vegetation of the moorlands and to maintain their landscape, wildlife and archaeological value and to prevent erosion of the peat; (ii) to encourage long-term improvement in the quality and extent of the heather and mixed shrubby vegetation of the moorland; (iii) to maintain the open, unfenced character of the moorland; and (iv) to maintain the inbye landscape and its associated broadleaved woodlands.

Structure of the ESA

Unlike many of the other ESAs, if an individual intends to join the scheme they must enter all land over which they have control. Hence in theory a farmer is not able to enter only selected parts of the holding and exclude other, for instance more intensively used, parts. Participants can, however, elect which areas to enter into each tier. In the lowest tier, Tier I, land receives an annual payment of £10 per hectare essentially in return for undertaking not

---

[1]Phillips *et al.* (1981) give a comprehensive background to the problems of environmental degradation in the Peak District.

Box 5.1. Management guidelines: North Peak ESA.

Tier I (All moorland that is covered by agreement):

- Remove 25% of sheep flock from moorland between 31 December and 1 April.
- Rotate supplementary feeding on moorland to avoid poaching.
- Avoid ploughing, levelling, reseeding and fencing across the moorland.
- Avoid the use of fertilizers, manures, lime, slag and pesticides; restrict herbicide use to weed wiper or spot treatments of named species.
- Agree a programme of heather, grass or scrub burning or cutting.

Inbye land (including enclosed rough grazing):
- Obtain written approval before increasing existing fertilizer/manure rates; applying lime or slag; ploughing, levelling, or reseeding; or installing any new drainage or modifying existing systems.
- Avoid the use of pesticides and herbicides on land that has not previously been treated, unless to control named species as weed wiper or spot treatments; chemically control bracken using only Asulam.

All land under agreement:
- Avoid damaging any historic or landscape features; maintain existing features such as drystone walls and traditional field barns.
- Obtain written advice before constructing any new buildings or roads, etc. which do not require planning permission; and early in the agreement on the management of woodland.

Tier II:

Inbye and enclosed grazing:
- Remove stock from hay/silage field at least seven weeks prior to cutting.
- Avoid cutting grass for hay or silage before 16 July – and in any event not before wildflowers have set seed; graze the aftermath.
- Graze with sheep at a stocking rate equal to two ewes and followers per hectare per year; avoid the creation of muddy areas in wet conditions.
- Avoid the use of fertilizers, manures and pesticides; restrict herbicides to weed wiper and spot treatments of named species; chemically control bracken using only Asulam.
- Avoid any areas where nesting birds are present, marking the sites and abandoning cultivation between 31 March and 16 July.
- Obtain written advice regarding the restoration of derelict or damaged field walls.

Moorland:
- Agree a stock management programme with the Project Officer to improve vegetation, and do not exceed a stocking rate equal to one ewe and follower per hectare.
- Ensure that recently burned areas of heather are only lightly grazed.
- Begin a programme of moorland regeneration over at least one hectare of land within the first year of the agreement.

to intensify farming practices or alter the landscape character. In Tier II a payment of £20 per hectare is given in return for more restrictions on farming practices and some positive conservation actions. The guidelines associated with each tier are set out in MAFF (1988a); however, some of the key parts are mentioned briefly below (see also Box 5.1).

On the Tier I inbye land participants undertake not to increase their existing fertilizer application and not to take any action which would change the character of the sward, for instance liming, draining or reseeding. In addition, existing stockproof walls and traditional weatherproof buildings must be maintained. For Tier I moorland the guidelines of particular importance are those that stipulate that a quarter of the normal over-wintering flock must be removed from the moor, to carry out supplementary feeding in rotation and to agree a programme of heather, grass and scrub burning in advance.

On Tier II inbye the additional prescriptions include the proscription of mowing before mid-July, a maximum stocking rate of two ewes and followers per hectare, no applications of fertilizer and the avoidance of cultivations between April and mid-July if there are ground-nesting birds. On Tier II moorland a stock management programme must be agreed with stocking rates not in excess of one ewe per hectare and shepherding to ensure that newly burnt areas are grazed only lightly. In addition a programme of moorland regeneration on at least one hectare of land must be undertaken.

Scheme uptake

Uptake into the original North Peak ESA was high from the first year. In 1988, 79% of the eligible area was entered; by 1991 this had risen to 86%, some 39,130 hectares. For the inbye there has been a roughly even split between the two tiers. In the case of the moorland, however, virtually all of the eligible area has been entered into Tier II. There were 75 agreements signed under the original scheme, with a slightly smaller number of participants since some farms have separate ESA agreements for their moorland and inbye. It is estimated that on holdings which have joined the ESA scheme 20% of the inbye and 4% of the moorland lies outside the boundary and hence is ineligible. Approximately 52% of holdings have some non-eligible land, with the remainder lying entirely within the designated area.

The Participation Decision

For many farmers contemplating joining the ESA the idea of a guaranteed annual payment of on average £6650 was obviously an appealing one. Most were able to participate in the ESA without having to reduce their stocking levels, which for many farmers was the critical factor. Many had worries about the longer term implications of reducing the level of variable inputs, but since the ESA was running for only five years initially this was considered to be manageable. At the time the interviews were carried out there was increased uncertainty over the future of farming. The variable premium was being phased out and there was widespread discussion over 'reform' of the Hill Livestock Compensatory Allowance (HLCA) system as well as falling gross margins. Hence for many farmers the ESA offered a lifeline.

An explicit income objective was not the most-cited factor, although those that were cited, such as the availability of funds for maintaining the holding, rebuilding drystone walls and the opportunity to increase employment on the farm, particularly for family members, are related financial issues. Because many of the farmers have no security of tenure on their moorland they are effectively obliged to join the ESA if that is the wish of their landlord. In most cases the licensee was a willing participant (although not always in favour of the way the payments were divided), but in a small number of cases the landowner's decision to put such moorland into the scheme was the predominant reason for the farmer's compliance so as to avoid forfeiting the grazing rights. Hence it seems that the institutional structure certainly enhanced the level of participation. Certainly both landowners and shooting tenants could anticipate substantial funds as a result of joining the ESA, affording them the opportunity to improve the quality of the moorland.

Tier II Moorland Management Agreements

Because of the property rights structure within the North Peak, management agreements were signed between all parties with an interest on Tier II moorland. Generally this has involved the landowner, the grazier and, where the sporting rights are not kept in hand, the shooting tenant. Agreements outlined the overall management plan for the moor, the responsibilities of each of the signatories and how the scheme payments were to be divided. In general, the landowner had responsibility for undertaking moorland regeneration work, the sporting tenant for managing the heather-burning programme and the grazier for reducing stocking rates and carrying out shepherding. In addition, a feature of many of the agreements which did not constitute part of the original guidelines has been a schedule of bracken spraying for moors where its encroachment has become a particular problem. This has been the responsibility of the landowner, although the other two parties have also taken a share of the costs in many cases. There was no fixed formula for allocating payments between the parties but a typical division of the £20 per hectare annual payment would be 50, 35 and 15% to the grazier, landowner and sporting tenant respectively. The impact of the scheme on the incomes of all three types of participant is discussed later.

The Socioeconomic Monitoring of the North Peak ESA

The University of Manchester undertook the socioeconomic monitoring of the North Peak over a 2½-year period, starting in Autumn 1988 (Russell and Froud, 1991). All known participants were surveyed during 1989, mostly by personal interview. These surveys sought information on the farm, its enterprises and practices and then attempted to ascertain the extent to which compliance with the ESA had had an impact upon input use, output levels, farm incomes, employment and rents amongst other factors. Information was also sought on how farmers had decided whether to join the scheme, their attitudes towards its effectiveness and the extent to which they would like to see changes in the way in which it operated. In addition, because landowners and sporting estates were also party to agreements, approximately half of the participants in these two categories were also the subject of personal interviews in order to elicit similar types of information. A selective re-surveying was carried out in 1990 to try to identify further changes in farming practices since it was recognized that the full impact of the scheme would not become evident until it had run for a number of years. Finally, an attempt was made to identify those with land eligible for the scheme but who had decided not to enter any land. A telephone survey of these farmers was then undertaken to determine the reasons for not participating and also to see if there were any conclusions that could be drawn about inherent differences between the types of farmers that had joined and those that had not joined the North Peak ESA.

Characteristics of the Participating Farms

The average holding size is 668 hectares, of which 134 hectares is inbye and 534 hectares moorland. Of the inbye, 34% is owner-occupied and 58% tenanted. The moorland, however, is 67% grazed under licence, 15% owner-occupied and 15% under tenancy. Approximately 10% of the inbye land is used for the production of hay and silage, of which 80% is hay. Such land tends to be improved and has a higher rate of fertilizer application.

Over 90% of the holdings have sheep, with an average of 853 ewes – 565 on the moorland and 288 on the inbye. Ewes tend to be kept for three to six years and then sold to lowland farms for another few breeding seasons. The main source of income on such farms is from the selling of store lambs, usually at around six months. Seventy per cent of these farms also have beef cattle, averaging 32 suckler cows and 58 calves at various stages of fattening. Calves are mostly sold as stores at 12 to 18 months, with a few fattened for sale at around 24 months. The practice of grazing cattle on the hill has declined and is now virtually non-existent; this is regarded as one of the factors encouraging the spread of bracken in recent years. A small number of farms also have dairy herds, on average 41 cows. However, 40% of the dairy herd is kept on the small areas of land lying outside the ESA boundary.

On average each holding employs two family members and one hired worker with varying amounts of casual labour for shearing, gathering and other seasonal activities. Most of the participants were aged between 40 and 60, having been farming for 23 years on average. Approximately one quarter held agricultural qualifications of some sort. Around one third had additional sources of income, including haulage, contracting and various enterprises associated with tourism such as camp sites. However, in most cases the primary farming activities remain the most important financially.

The Non-Participants

Although the uptake of the North Peak ESA was high, even in the initial years, there still remained a core of land, around 7100 hectares (of which 6600 is moorland and 500 hectares inbye), which was eligible for the ESA but not entered. There were some problems in identifying all those who might own or farm such land, especially since on the moorland fringe there is a higher density of farms, often with dispersed holdings. A survey was carried out in 1990 on a sample of potential non-participants in order to determine firstly whether they were indeed eligible and, if so, to elicit information both on the characteristics of the holding and why the land had been withheld from the ESA scheme. It was found that there was a considerable difference between participants and non-participants in terms of the holding. The average holding of the non-participant was less than one-third of the size of that of participants, with 39 hectares of inbye and 191 hectares of moorland. There was, however, a much wider relative distribution of holding sizes, ranging from 4 to 1100 hectares. A further contrast is that 79% of the land on these holdings is owner-occupied with the remainder farmed on full tenancies. In addition, whereas on the participating farms most of the holding lay within the ESA boundary, for the non-participants only 40% of the inbye and 10% of the moorland on these farms was eligible.

Prior to being contacted for interview 82% had heard of the ESA, of which half had considered entering some land. However, it was considered that the restrictions associated with the ESA outweighed the level of payments available. For a farmer with 15 hectares of eligible inbye the total annual payments under Tier I would be only £150. For most this did not warrant the bureaucracy and curtailment of freedom involved. It was estimated that payments would have to be at least doubled to encourage this type of farmer to enter their land. Despite this, most of those interviewed claimed to have an interest in the environment. Many non-participants knew of others who had joined and recognized that it did suit their farms.

Evaluation of the North Peak ESA

An important feature of new schemes such as the ESAs is an evaluation of their success. This can be measured in a number of ways: the take-up of land and land-managers into the scheme; the extent to which it has achieved its objectives in terms of protecting the landscape, wildlife and historic interests and the ways in which farming practices have been changed. How these changes in farming practices and their impact upon production levels have affected participants' incomes can then be assessed. Finally, it is worth considering the degree to which such schemes can be considered as cost-effective in terms both of the extent to which any savings in budgetary support costs might be brought about, but also in comparison to alternative measures which could be taken to achieve the same objectives.

As described above take-up in the North Peak was high from the initial stages and MAFF's standard target of 75% of eligible land being entered has been met. Scheme uptake, however, is not necessarily a good indicator of success (although, of course, a low take-up – as was the case in the Test Valley – would tend to preclude a verdict of success from being given). What needs to be considered in addition is the extent to which the ESA has an impact in both environmental and socioeconomic terms upon the land on which payments are made. As with all of the ESAs, environmental monitoring was carried out by ADAS staff and includes an assessment of the impact on landscape, the flora and fauna and on sites of historic interest.

The Environmental Impact

The environmental monitoring (MAFF, 1993e) has on the whole revealed very little change within the North Peak during the first few years. Between the baseline survey in 1988 and the follow-up in 1991 only 2% of the ESA experienced any change in land cover. This can be attributed mostly to bracken spraying over 532 hectares leading to a substitution by other vegetation types, and some loss of meadow and pasture to cultivated land due to the ploughing and reseeding of grass. It is interesting to note that this activity is not permitted within the ESA guidelines but that special permission had been obtained in these cases. Although it is clearly desirable that the operation of the ESA be flexible, such events show that violations of even the most basic guidelines can be allowed. The impact on the vegetative condition of the moors is not clear at this stage. This is not entirely surprising since it would be expected that moorland regeneration, particularly of the most eroded areas, will be an extremely long-term process. Interestingly, however, the report of biological monitoring finds an unclear relationship between stocking levels and grazing levels, i.e. the reduction in the number of animals on the moor will not automatically improve the quality of the moorland vegetation.

In terms of one of the key landscape features, the drystone walls, some impact can be reported. A small increase in the length of continuous walls has occurred on agreement land, whilst at the same time, the proportion of discontinuous walls on non-agreement land has risen. There has been little change in the condition of traditional farm buildings, not surprisingly since there is no direct financial provision made for their upkeep and improvement.

Impact on Moorland Management

The impact on management practices has been mixed. The optimal cycle for heather burning varies from 12 to 15 years on the low-lying moors to 20 to 25 years on the higher, wetter ones. Comparing the extent of heather burning in the period 1989 to 1991 with that in 1988/89, there has been an increase in both the area and number of burns of 45 and 55% respectively. This is due in part to favourable conditions for burning during the first few years of the ESA; however, for means of comparison, on non-agreement land the number of burns increased by 35% but the area covered rose by only 3%. Despite this increase actual burning is still less than both the area committed and the optimal requirement to comply with ideal cycles. For the bracken spraying too, actual areas sprayed were less than those specified. This was exacerbated in later years due to the introduction of a draft code of practice on bracken spraying which arose out of concern by organizations such as the Peak Park Authority and English Nature that blanket aerial spraying would risk destroying colonies of rare ferns which were to be found in the moorland cloughs. In total 38% of the bracken on agreement land and 7% on non-agreement land was treated. Clearly most of this work done was a direct result of the ESA, and interestingly it was not a feature of the original guidelines but arose during the specification of management agreements. Most spraying was done using helicopters at an average cost of £108 per hectare.

One of the most significant parts of the ESA may be the fencing out of regeneration plots, in total 43, covering 145 hectares. It is too early to assess how well this regeneration process has gone. Clearly the most encouraging results are found where the conditions were least severe and where an obvious change has occurred almost immediately by removing bracken.

Impact on Farming Practices

The overall strategy of participants seems to have been to enter land into the tier which most closely corresponds to existing management practices so that the most intensively used meadows and pastures were only entered into Tier I. This has had the overall result of inducing only fairly small changes in both farming practices and output levels.

Fertilizer and lime

Although on Tier I land fertilizer applications are allowed up to the level of their pre-scheme usage, there has been a reduction on inbye rates from an average of 73 kg to 63 kg of nitrogen per hectare between 1987 and 1989. On Tier II inbye no fertilizer was permitted; however, prior to this land joining the ESA, fertilizer was applied on only 11% of such land at an average of 33 kg N per hectare. The overall average reduction was thus 1.3 kg N per hectare.

Lime is not permitted on any of the agreement land. Prior to the introduction of the scheme it was applied roughly every 6½ years on Tier I and every 9 years on Tier II. In the absence of the ESA, therefore, it would have been expected that 15% of Tier I and 11% of Tier II land would have been limed each year. Hence some savings will have been made from reductions in the use of fertilizer and lime.

Herbicides and other sprays

On most of the ESA land herbicides are not permitted as a general rule but spot treatment of selected weeds is allowed and in some cases encouraged. There are likely to be some savings in chemical costs through more selective use of herbicides but considerably more labour input is required in order to treat weeds by hand. Most of those interviewed considered that, taking both of these factors into account, they were probably no better or worse off than with their previous methods of treatment.

Labour requirements

In the North Peak there has been a significant impact on labour use on farms and shooting estates through the moorland management agreements. Three-quarters of the agreements have specified an annual shepherding requirement, on average an additional 182 man days per moor or one day for every 11 hectares.[2] In order to meet this requirement some farmers have absorbed this additional work into existing available, and hence presumably slack, labour on the farm. Others have taken on employees specifically to fulfil the shepherding requirement, often school leavers in the family for whom the ESA has provided an opportune, albeit temporary, job. Extra employment for shepherding has been created on roughly 22% of the holdings with Tier II agreements surveyed, amounting to a total of nine full-time jobs over the whole of the ESA.

---

[2]These moors have traditionally not been widely shepherded, with more emphasis on the use of hefted flocks, i.e. those where the breeding ewes have a detailed knowledge of the home range including the location of feeding points and shelter.

Shooting estates have also taken on additional full-time staff because of the availability of funds. Employment of keepers increased by 23%, the equivalent of four full-time posts, and a number of trainees have also been taken on for the duration of the ESA. Combining the shepherding and gamekeeping jobs, a total of 22 full-time posts, equivalent to 21% of the 1987 farm labour force, can be attributed to the scheme. It is evident that this constitutes a significant local impact.

The other main component of the moorland agreements, heather burning, is a labour-intensive process. Heather is burned by teams of four or five people (usually local farmers, farm workers and others who can be available at very short notice), covering approximately 5 hectares per day. The amount of heather that can be burnt in a season depends upon the weather conditions. The general practice in the area is to burn as much in any season as is possible given the suitability of conditions and the local labour constraints, hence it is unlikely that this component will lead to a net increase in employment.

Capital

The ESA had no discernible impact on sales or purchases of machinery on farms, although a number of the sporting estates have purchased all-terrain vehicles. The requirement to remove a quarter of the overwintering flock from the moor may have an impact on the need for buildings since not all of the sheep taken off the moor have been sent away. One instance was found of an overwintering shed being constructed due at least in part to the ESA guidelines and availability of payments. This, however, represents a large-scale investment that most of the participants were unwilling to undertake, particularly when the initial ESA scheme was operating under a five-year time horizon.

Impact on output levels

In general, changes in output levels in the North Peak have been small with the main effect on stock numbers resulting from stocking rate and over-wintering restrictions on the moorland and their impact on the inbye land. Additionally, a small change in the level of hay and silage production has resulted from restrictions on cutting dates. In order to isolate the net effects of the ESA scheme from the observed gross effects it is necessary to make some assumptions about what was likely to have happened to livestock numbers in the absence of the ESA scheme.

Ewe numbers
The Tier II moorland guidelines set a maximum stocking rate of one ewe (plus lamb and follower) per hectare. In addition, on all ESA moorland a quarter of

Table 5.2. North Peak ESA moorland stocking rates.

Year	Tier	Weighted average stocking rate (ewes/ha)
1987	I	2.34
	II	0.71
1989	I	1.74
	II	0.63

the normal flock must be wintered off the moor from January to March inclusive, hence reducing the seasonal stocking rate at a time when the moorland vegetation is most sensitive. Table 5.2 shows that stocking rates were higher on Tier I in 1987 and remained higher in 1989. Given the magnitude of the difference between the tiers it is not clear that the additional £10 per hectare paid for Tier II would compensate for the necessary stock reduction; the fact that a block of moorland remained in Tier I confirms this. It can be seen that even prior to the introduction of the ESA the average stocking rates on Tier II land were less than those required by the scheme guidelines. This is due in some part to the effect of the institutional landowners and the licence system. For instance, once the National Trust acquired moorland in the North Peak the number of gaits was reduced to a more environmentally appropriate level and hence again some redundancy of the guidelines can be noted. In fact stocking rates had to be reduced on only 6% of the ESA moorland within the sample.

The movement of sheep off the moorland led to a reallocation of livestock enterprises on the inbye, in some cases with cattle displaced in order to maintain the same number of ewes over the whole farm. It was estimated that there would be a reduction of approximately 1000 ewes in the ESA as a whole as a result of stocking rate restrictions. The overwintering guideline did not reduce the flock size but did lead to increased costs in the sending of hoggs away from the farm. The practice of removing sheep is not new. Prior to the introduction of the ESA most farms wintered ewe hoggs off the moor, either on their own inbye or on winter keep on lowland farms. In addition, farmers are now removing over 30% of their ewes from the moor. These will generally be moved onto the inbye and a corresponding number of the inbye flock wintered away. The period of away wintering has actually increased from an average of three months prior to the scheme to 5.3 months subsequently. Given average costs of winter keep of 38 pence per week, plus carriage of £1 per head each way, the average cost per animal of away wintering is around £10.66 per season.

In order to ascertain what may have happened to the sheep flock had the scheme not been introduced a review of local and national trends was carried out using Agricultural Census data. The general pattern revealed was that of an accelerating increase in both sheep and cattle numbers up to 1989, but with a subsequent reduction in the rate of increase from 1990 onwards, possibly in response to policy changes. Taking into account the patterns revealed in the census and the local conditions of the North Peak it was estimated that sheep numbers would have continued to increase by 3% per annum up to the end of the ESA period in 1992, equivalent to a projected increase of approximately 1100 ewes by 1992. Taken together with the observed changes this 'policy-off' effect implies that the net impact of the ESA has been to reduce the size of the ewe flock in the North Peak by approximately 2200 ewes by the time that the original scheme had expired.

Cattle numbers
As already noted, there has been some substitution of sheep for cattle on inbye land as an indirect result of reducing Tier II moorland stocking levels. The resulting reduction at the scheme level is approximately 135 breeding animals by the time the ESA was fully implemented. As would be expected there was no impact on the dairy herd. The net impact on the cattle herd can be estimated in the same way as that used above for the sheep flock. Taking into account changes in beef numbers in similar parishes it was estimated that cattle numbers would have continued to rise by 2% per annum had the ESA not been introduced in the North Peak. Combining this with the small reduction in cattle numbers that did result from participation leads to a net or overall reduction of around 165 animals.

Grassland conservation
Most of the hay and silage in the North Peak is made on Tier I grassland since this land has to be improved to the extent that it is possible to operate a tractor on it. Generally only the least productive land was entered into Tier II since the £10 payment differential was judged inadequate to compensate for the changes in management required under the higher tier.

Impact of the North Peak ESA on Participant Incomes

From the basis of the changes in input use and output levels as a result of the ESA it is possible to arrive at estimates of the impact of the scheme on those participating on both a per hectare and a per farm basis. Additional costs associated with complying with the scheme guidelines can be considered, along with the associated payments, to present a breakdown of the impacts according to the type of land, tier and participant.

When considering the income effects several key components must be taken into account. These are outlined in Table 5.3. The total value of

Table 5.3. The overall income effect of the North Peak ESA.

Effect (£)	1988	1989	1990	1991	1992	Total 1988–92
Payments (a)	628,932	687,934	688,790	699,510	699,510	3,404,676
Reduction in livestock gross margins (b)	–	125,350	113,371	114,679	117,140	470,540
Savings in fertilizer and lime (c)	42,287	45,069	45,369	45,616	45,616	223,957
Compliance costs (d)	357,650	391,536	391,703	397,926	397,926	1,936,741
Net effect (a+b)−(b+d)	313,569	216,117	229,085	232,521	230,060	1,221,352

payments given to participants rose from £628,932 in the first year up to £699,510 in 1992 – a total of £3.4 million over the length of the scheme. The net reductions in livestock were valued using gross margins from the North West Farm Business Survey results for hill farms. In the absence of any clear indication of what gross margin figures for 1991 and 1992 might be it was assumed that those for 1990 would continue to hold for the remaining life of the scheme. As shown in row (b) of Table 5.3 there is no reduction in livestock gross margins for 1988 since the ESA was introduced midway through the production cycle. The total value of livestock gross margins lost was estimated at almost half a million pounds. Some of this was offset by savings in inputs. The value of the reduced application of fertilizer and the cessation of lime are shown in row (c) in Table 5.3. Finally, to arrive at the net income effect, the costs of scheme compliance are included in row (d). These amount to almost 2 million pounds over the five-year period. The overall income effect in each year varies from over £300,000 in the first year when the full scale of livestock reductions had not taken place down to a little over £200,000 in the remaining years. Hence the overall enhancement to participators' incomes was estimated to have been £1.2 million by 1992. This is equivalent to 36% of the value of the scheme payments.

The overall impact on the incomes of participators can be disaggregated to show the relative contributions of the inbye and moorland components by tier. In addition, as shown in Table 5.4, the net income effect can be compared with the share of the total payments and the proportion of all land entered into the scheme accounted for by each component. The Tier II moorland is clearly the dominant component in terms of land entered, payments made and contribution to income. The income changes on the inbye land are high

Table 5.4. Income effect by tier.

Land type	Income effect (£m)	Proportion of total increase in net income (%)	Proportion of total payments (%)	Proportion of all land entered (%)
Tier I inbye	0.158	13.0	3.2	6.0
Tier I moorland	0.050	4.1	3.0	5.6
Tier II inbye	0.206	16.9	5.9	5.6
Tier II moorland	0.807	66.0	87.9	82.8
Total	1.221	100.0	100.0	100.0

in proportion to the share of land entered and total payments.

The detailed income effects can be further illuminated by considering the impact on a representative hectare in each tier of the ESA. These effects are summarized in Table 5.5. For both types of inbye land the increase in incomes was estimated to be greater than the value of payments given. On the moorland the net income effect is almost the same for both tiers although Tier II involves a higher level of both payments and compliance costs.

The final breakdown of income effects of particular interest in the North Peak is the disaggregation by category of participant. An earlier section detailed how the payments and responsibilities of the ESA agreement were divided between the various parties. Table 5.6 shows the aggregate effect in each of the five years on the three individuals in a 'typical' Tier II agreement

Table 5.5. Per hectare income effects in the North Peak, 1988–1992.

Income component (£/ha)	Tier I inbye	Tier II inbye	Tier I moorland	Tier II moorland
Payments (a)	50.00	100.00	50.00	100.00
Compliance costs (b)	19.50	19.50	18.10	60.75
Reduction in livestock gross margins (c)	28.21	12.77	7.05	12.02
Savings in fertilizer and lime (d)	69.38	35.15		
Net effect (a−b−c+d)	71.67	102.88	24.85	27.23

Table 5.6. Division of costs and payments on Tier II moorland in the North Peak ESA (average value per year).

Income effect	Grazier	Landowner	Shooting tenant	Overall impact
Payments: % of total	50	35	15	100
£/ha (a)	10	7	3	20
Average cost of compliance: £/ha (b)	5.53	4.53	2.09	12.15
Reduction in gross margin: £/ha (c)	2.42	–	–	2.42
Net income effect: £/ha (a−b−c)	2.05	2.47	0.91	5.43

on a per hectare basis. It can be seen that on the assumptions used here all parties enjoy an increase in their net income. No allowance is made for changes in rental values on this land. Average stocking rates on Tier II moorland have been reduced by 0.08 ewes per hectare and since rental payments depend on the number of stock grazed, the overall rental payment made by the grazier might be expected to fall. However, in the cases where stocking rates have been reduced, the licence charge per ewe has been adjusted upwards so that the landowner's total rental remains unchanged. Hence, there is in general no transfer of rents between parties as a result of the ESA scheme.

Potential transfers between tenants and landlords are formally recognized also in agreements concerning inbye land, some 58% of which is tenanted. A proportion of scheme payments, ranging from 15 to 50%, is made directly to landlords through agreements covering half of this tenanted land. In most cases this is regarded as in lieu of a rent increase. Beyond these formal transfers no evidence was available at the time of survey that any increases in rents can be attributed to the scheme.

Impact of the North Peak ESA on Budgetary Costs

In the socioeconomic monitoring exercise one of the areas of interest was the extent to which schemes such as the ESA could be considered as 'self-financing', i.e. the extent to which the cost of payments given could be accounted for through savings in budgetary support costs; in the North Peak this comprises savings in HLCA payments and beef intervention costs. Estimates of the support costs associated with different categories of sheep and

Table 5.7. The budgetary impact of the North Peak ESA.

Budgetary component	Total 1988–92 (£m)
(a) Scheme payments	3.405
(b) FEOGA reimbursements to UK exchequer	0.851
(c) Net cost of scheme payments	2.554
(d) Exchequer savings from livestock production	0.156
(e) Net cost *excluding* reimbursements (a−d)	3.249
(f) New cost *including* reimbursements (c−d)	2.398

cattle were provided by MAFF and these were used to determine the total exchequer saving. Table 5.7 compares the costs of payments and the exchequer savings. As a result of EC Regulation 1760/87 up to one quarter of the cost of schemes like the ESAs can be refunded from FEOGA. Because the payments per hectare in the North Peak were relatively low, the full 25% refund was available; this is shown in row (b) of Table 5.7. The net overall budgetary effect of the North Peak is shown both with and without FEOGA reimbursements to be roughly £2.4 and £3.25 million respectively. The budgetary savings resulting from reduced livestock numbers are seen to be insignificant in terms of the overall level of costs and payments, even taking into account the FEOGA refunds.

Impacts of the Scheme: A Caveat

The foregoing discussion has focused on changes which have been observed to have occurred at the farm or estate level in order to determine the impact of the ESA. However, any adjustments which have been highlighted are clearly only the initial stage of a longer term dynamic process which will continue to influence output, input use and incomes as farmers learn more about how compliance with the scheme affects their farming systems. Only when the full impact of the scheme has been manifested and farmers have completed their adjustment process will the long-run equilibrium be reached. However, as is usually the case when evaluating the long-run or equilibrium effects of changes in agricultural policy, the mechanism will have been adjusted or substituted with a new instrument before the full effects have become apparent.

Of interest in this regard with ESAs such as the North Peak is the extent to which the reduction in the use of variable inputs like fertilizers, lime and herbicides will lead to a reduction in its long-term productivity such that forage production or carrying capacity are significantly reduced. Only three years into the ESA some farmers were already noticing a weed build-up. Because permitted methods of treatment were considered too labour intensive some encroachment has been allowed to occur. Many farmers considered that the inability to apply lime would have implications for the productivity of their grassland; however, this may be due in part to their lack of information as to the likely impact. Conversely, the effects of improved moorland management should lead to an enhancement in the quality and extent of moorland vegetation and in the long term on the condition of the hill ewes. The regeneration of bare and eroded areas may even allow for an increase in the carrying capacity of the moors.

Attitudes to the ESA Scheme

In the follow-up survey carried out in late 1990 participants were questioned about their views of the North Peak ESA, having had two full years in the scheme. With regard to the impact on their incomes the overall feeling was that there had been no change. However, many admitted that it was hard to be precise since during the first few years of the ESA the Variable Premium was removed and lamb prices had also fallen. At the time of the re-survey there was a fairly considerable degree of uncertainty as to whether the ESA would be renewed at the end of the five-year period, although there was a fairly strong feeling (75%) that it should be (see Table 5.8). On the whole the ESA was still viewed favourably. Three-quarters stated that they would join another scheme with the same payments and guidelines, although there was a considerable body of feeling that the provisions for the inbye land were not as favourable as those for the moorland, especially for those farms without large moorland areas.

Numerous suggestions were made as to how the ESA could be improved. Direct payments were advocated by many, especially for drystone wall maintenance and repair. In addition, it was felt that rather than making payments to cover the whole of the Tier II moorland, more should be paid for each hectare actually regenerated. Different policies were advocated for individual moors according to the existing condition and management of the moor since it was recognized that each moor had a different carrying capacity and required distinct types of management.

The respondents' views of the extent to which the ESA has had an impact on farming practices, the landscape and ecology and the rural economy are also summarized in Table 5.8. Many expected any change in the landscape of

Table 5.8. Attitudes of participating farmers to the North Peak ESA.

Question asked	Yes	No	Don't know
Has the ESA had an effect on farming practices?	50	19	31
Has the ESA had an effect on the landscape and ecology?	63	19	19
Has the ESA had an impact on the rural economy?	63	13	25
Should this ESA scheme be renewed?	75	6	19
If this ESA scheme was renewed (with the same conditions) would you join again?	73	0	27

the North Peak to be fairly long term and certainly improvements in the quality of the moorland vegetation were expected to require longer than the initial five-year period.

The Revised North Peak ESA Scheme

The new North Peak ESA introduced in early 1993 (MAFF, 1993e) takes into account some of the shortcomings recognized in the operation of the first scheme. The scheme has been restructured with, on the whole, enhanced payments in return for more specific management prescriptions. In addition, the designated area has been extended by over 5000 hectares to include some of the surrounding degraded moorland. In common with the other ESAs but of particular relevance to the North Peak is the addition of an optional conservation plan. This means that farmers can receive grant aid of up to 80% for conservation works which they undertake, including rebuilding and maintenance of drystone walls and traditional buildings, control of bracken and scrub and supplementary treatment of eroded moorland. This has the effect of making the payments more transparent, allowing the farmer to decide more precisely what is to be done. The conservation plan will be likely to increase the amount of such work that is carried out in the North Peak although the value of payments will undoubtedly be greater. A simplified structure of the new North Peak ESA is shown in Box 5.2. Many of the guidelines are similar, for instance between Tier II inbye and Tier IA in the revised scheme, although with the condition that all unimproved enclosed land (i.e. all land that does not normally receive inorganic fertilizer) must be entered into Tier IA. For the second tier there are two options: extensification

Box 5.2. The revised North Peak ESA scheme.

Tier I (All farmland and moorland)

To maintain the environmental value of the wildlife habitats and landscape of the North Peak ESA and to protect its features of historic and archaeological interest.

Tier IA (£10/hectare): Suitable for improved meadows and pastures.
Tier IB (£30/hectare): Unimproved grassland and rough grazing.
Tier IC (£25/hectare): Moorland.

Tier II (Moorland enhancement)

To enhance the landscape and ecological value of moorland areas by improving the quality and diversity of their moorland vegetation cover. This may include the regeneration of areas of suppressed and eroded moorland.
All degraded moorland (i.e. with more than 25% bare ground or less than 25% dwarf shrubs) must be entered.

Tier IIA (£40/hectare): Moorland extensification — (stocking rate of not more than 0.1 livestock units (LU)/ha; reduced winter stocking rates).
Tier IIB (£80/hectare): Moorland enclosure — (exclude grazing livestock by temporary fencing, with programme of controlled grazing)

Conservation plan

50% grants for: restoration of ponds and wet areas; creation of species-rich meadow; control of bracken and scrub; planting, laying, gapping and renovation of hedges.
80% grants for: supplementary treatment of suppressed and eroded moorland; renovation of traditional farm buildings; rebuilding additional drystone walls; works to protect historic and archaeological features.

and enclosure. Again the payments are targeted much more closely to the land where work will be undertaken with flexibility as to how much land will be enclosed at any given time.

In an area such as the North Peak where much of the environmental enhancement is essentially long term in nature, the introduction of ten-year schemes is an improvement. It also gives some signal to farmers and other land managers of MAFF's commitment to supporting the production of environmental goods by farmers, although there is still of course an opt-out clause on both sides after five years. Many of the farmers in the North Peak are faced with increasing uncertainty with regard to future levels of agricultural support and this is likely to push them towards schemes such as the ESA which provide a guaranteed and often fairly substantial payment. However, there is some caution with regard to recent and possibly further changes in the way in which CAP support is to be given. With eligibility for livestock premia based on historical claims then any reduction in overall stocking levels on the farm may prejudice future rights to support premia. It is too early yet to say whether uptake into the new scheme is as high as that in the old, although most indications suggest this is likely.

Evaluation of the North Peak ESA: Summary and Conclusions

There has been criticism from the RSPB amongst others (RSPB, 1991) that the North Peak ESA is too compartmentalized and that, because there are not only separate components covering the inbye and moorland but that some of the participants' inbye lies outside the designated area, environmental slippage can occur. Certainly the incentives for entering inbye into the ESA were considerably weaker than those for the moorland and, because of the complex institutional structure, some farmers were able to withhold eligible inbye that they owned whilst still being party to an ESA agreement on the moorland. Clearly this circumvents the requirement that a participant should enter all eligible land under their control and may lead to some intensification of operations on this excluded land in order to compensate for the restrictions imposed on the land that is entered. During the course of the socioeconomic monitoring no evidence was found of any such 'halo' effect although such pressures are likely to build up with time.

The environmental monitoring has shown that the overall impact of the ESA has been to maintain the conservation value of this area with distinct enhancement of some features such as the repair of drystone walls and the eradication of bracken. More importantly, perhaps, the original ESA has initiated a long-term process of moorland regeneration which the revised scheme should be able to effectively consolidate. The effect of the May 1992 CAP reforms may have the result of reducing the incentives to intensify production. This is likely to be true of stocking rates but is less clear with regard to forage production on the inbye. However, one threat that is likely to become increasingly important in areas such as the North Peak is that of dereliction, with the moorland fringes subject to low levels of usage and encroachment of bracken and scrub.

To summarize the socioeconomic impact from the above discussion it seems clear that there has been a significant and positive effect on the incomes of those participating and also upon the employment on land enrolled. These will combine to result in additional 'knock-on' or indirect effects on the local economy, estimated at approximately £0.4 million in extra income generated and a number of additional jobs. The effect on agricultural outputs has been fairly limited and thus in consequence very few savings have been made in terms of budgetary support costs on production forfeited. There does seem to be an extremely positive attitude towards the ESA by its participants, especially the landowners and sporting estates. In addition, one of the benefits has been improved communication between the various parties with agreement on a joint strategy; this has been facilitated by the availability of funds.

On the part of the farmers, most recognize that in the future, any agricultural support that they are likely to continue to receive will come increasingly from measures such as the ESAs rather than directly from the support of production, although the overwhelming philosophy amongst farmers was that food production should remain their primary activity.

6

ITEMIZED PAYMENT SYSTEMS WITHIN A SCHEME
The Case of Breadalbane

Sarah J. Skerratt

Introduction

The socioeconomic evaluation of the Breadalbane Environmentally Sensitive Area (ESA) was carried out by a research team (T.J. Perkins, N.B. Lilwall and S.J. Skerratt) at the Scottish Agricultural College (SAC), from 1987 to 1990. This chapter outlines the characteristics of the area which resulted in its designation in 1987, and the features of the ESA Scheme which are particular to Scottish ESAs. The aims, objectives and methodology of the research project are presented, followed by results concerning: the impact of the Scheme on the local farm economy, and on farmers' attitudes to conservation; and evaluation of the uptake of the Scheme, focusing in particular on farmers' attitudes towards the ESA. In addition, there are a number of methodological comments on this specific evaluation, which have implications for similar evaluations of this type. These are briefly presented, and recommendations are made.

Breadalbane ESA

Description

Location

Breadalbane ESA lies within the Southern Highlands, and is located mainly in Tayside Region (Perth and Kinross District). It is the largest ESA in Scotland, covering an area of approximately 120,000 hectares, excluding the major lochs of Rannoch and Tay. It stretches from Glen Lochay in the west, to Strathardle in the east. The majority of the ESA is designated as a Less Favoured Area (LFA).

The nearest large town outwith the ESA is Perth, with a population of 41,654. Within Breadalbane, the towns and villages primarily service the agricultural industry, although some have a distinct tourist role, such as Pitlochry, at the northern fringe of the ESA, and Aberfeldy, the largest settlement located wholly within the ESA, with a resident population of 1469. The main transport links comprise the A9 road (Perth to Inverness), and the mainline railway (Perth to Inverness).

Agriculture

Approximately 85,000–90,000 hectares of Breadalbane ESA are farmed, the remainder comprising either large-scale forestry or shooting estates. There are approximately 160 farm businesses within Breadalbane ESA, each comprising one or more farm *holdings*. In addition to these, there are 72 'insignificant' holdings, which employ less than 1100 man hours per annum; many are holiday or second homes, or retiral homes where the land is let as summer grazings. The tenureship of the ESA's land area divides almost equally between owner-occupied (50.1%) and tenanted (49.9%). Within the ESA, there are a small number of estates covering an extensive area, particularly in the western section of the ESA. These estates are either farmed 'in hand' or with one or more tenant farmers.

Breadalbane is dominated by extensive hill sheep farming (Scottish Blackface), combined – on lower altitudes – with the rearing of store cattle. In addition, there are a small number of arable farms on the alluvial floodplain of the River Tay near Aberfeldy and Fortingall.

Geography

The topography of the ESA is diverse, and ranges from mountainous peaks through to gorges and lochs. The National Trust for Scotland Reserve of Ben Lawers (3984 ft), and also Schiehallion (3554 ft), are areas internationally recognized for their rare arctic and alpine vegetation. In addition, there are the scenic lochs of Tay and Rannoch, with their surrounding agricultural land interspersed with wooded slopes of a species-rich mixture, including a remnant of the ancient Caledonian Pine Forest, the Black Wood of Rannoch. The ESA also contains the beautiful, thickly wooded gorge of Glen Lyon, which, at over 20 miles in length, is reputed to be the longest glen in Scotland. The Forest of Clunie (1500–2000 ft), a plateau of rough grazing and heather moor, is one of the ESA's most significant environmental features, particularly as a habitat for the upland breeding wader population; it lies adjacent to a Scottish Wildlife Trust reserve, the Loch of the Lowes, renowned for its ospreys.

Designations

Two National Scenic Areas (NSAs) lie wholly or partly within the ESA boundaries: Loch Rannoch and Glen Lyon; and River Tay (Dunkeld). A third NSA, Loch Tummel, lies adjacent to the ESA's northern boundary.[1] In addition, there are 29 SSSIs (20,957 hectares) which cover approximately 17.5% of the ESA's land area. Milton Wood and Ben Lawers comprise the two National Nature Reserves. There are also a number of Scottish Wildlife Trust reserves, and local authority landscape designations.

Archaeology

The ESA is rich in archaeological remains, particularly stone circles, neolithic and bronze age burial mounds, round house settlements, and crannogs in Loch Tay.

Ecology and nature conservation

Of particular significance within Breadalbane ESA is the inbye land of the glens and the unimproved herb-rich pastures, which are able to support up to 350 plant species on one site. In the glens, such land also supports scrub birch, hawthorn, blackthorn and rowan, thus providing valuable habitats for small birds. A second feature of this ESA is the areas of semi-natural birch woodland, with juniper, Scots pine, alder, ash, hazel and oak.

Designation and Policy Mechanism

Background

Breadalbane ESA was designated on 1 May 1987 under the Agriculture Act 1986. Such areas were to be of recognized importance from an ecological and landscape point of view. In addition, farmers would have to stipulate that there would be 'no further intensification of agricultural production and that the stock density and the level of agricultural production will be compatible with the specific environmental needs of the area concerned' (EC, 1985a).

Following publication of Regulation 797/85, a joint working party was set up in Scotland to examine the five areas that had been shortlisted for possible ESA designation. The working party comprised officials from the Scottish Office Agriculture and Fisheries Department (SOAFD), the Scottish Development Department (Rural Environment and Nature Conservation Divisions, and the Historic Buildings and Monuments Directorate), the Countryside Commission for Scotland and the Nature Conservancy Council.

---

[1]Included in the ESA, post-April 1992.

Box 6.1. Attributes of, and threats to, the Breadalbane area (from Skerratt *et al.*, 1992).

Inherent conservation and landscape attributes

- High scenic quality and outstanding beauty.
- Unimproved, inbye pastures of the valleys and glens.
- Arctic/alpine vegetation.
- Wetlands and areas of open water, including major lochs.
- Semi-natural woodlands of broadleaves and Scots pine.
- Archaeological sites: stone circles, burial mounds, homesteads and crannogs.

Perceived threats to the existing area

- Possible intensification of hill sheep farming, leading to detrimental effects within sensitive habitats.
- Low farm profitability resulting in increasing tendency towards:
  – selling land for afforestation;
  – reducing expenditure on traditional farming operations and conservation features.

The five shortlisted areas were Breadalbane, Loch Lomond, Orkney, the Machair lands of the Uists and Benbecula, and Whitlaw/Eildon. Following the working party recommendations, Breadalbane and Loch Lomond were designated as ESAs in 1987.

Specific designation criteria

Breadalbane ESA was shortlisted as an ESA both because of its inherent conservation and landscape attributes (see above), and perceived threats to the status quo (see Box 6.1).

Aims and objectives

The Scheme's overall aim is 'to encourage positive conservation measures and traditional farming practice, while protecting sensitive habitats from agricultural intensification' (SOAFD, 1989). It therefore encourages conservation-friendly farming within specific geographical areas deemed to be of high conservation value. Within such areas, financial incentives are given to farmers and crofters to encourage them to protect and enhance environmental features on their land. In addition, they are discouraged from agricultural intensification and from farming practices which may cause environmental damage; traditional farming operations are promoted.

The objectives of the Breadalbane ESA are as follows:

(a) to protect the open hill rough grazing from land reclamations,

overgrazing and the inappropriate use of herbicides and pesticides;
  (b) to provide similar protection for the unimproved, enclosed land in the valleys;
  (c) to rectify the neglect of traditional farm dykes and hedges;
  (d) to encourage natural regeneration of farm woodland;
  (e) to ensure that new developments such as vehicular tracks and farm buildings do not damage the landscape.

(SOAFD, 1989)

These aims and objectives are addressed through a series of Management Guidelines.

Management Guidelines

The Breadalbane ESA Scheme is entirely voluntary. However, each farmer wishing to join the scheme for a period of five to ten years is required to produce a simple, balanced Farm Conservation Plan based on, and incorporating, the 16 Management Guidelines. These are summarized in Box 6.2.

Payments

The payments discussed below represent those in operation at the time of the ESA evaluation. The revised payment levels, implemented in 1992, are reported in Appendix 6.1. The ESA Scheme provides payments to the farmer for undertaking conservation work agreed in the Farm Conservation Plan and maintenance according to the 16 Management Guidelines. The farmer can

Box 6.2. Summary of Breadalbane ESA Management Guidelines (from Skerratt *et al.*, 1992).

- Avoidance of overgrazing or poaching.
- No new land reclamation work on the open rough grazings and agreement to follow good muirburn practice.
- Limits on the application of herbicides and pesticides on rough grazings.
- Limits on the application of lime and fertilizer and herbicides to unimproved, enclosed pastures.
- Agreement to obtain written approval before constructing vehicular tracks, removing edges or dykes, or carrying out planting outside of the forestry grant schemes.
- Agreement to obtain written advice on the construction of farm buildings and to discuss capital grants schemes before undertaking any work.
- No pollution on the farm and compliance with tree felling control procedures.
- Maintenance of stockproof dykes and hedges and agreement not to damage features of archaeological interest.
- Preparation and agreement of a farm conservation plan.

Box 6.3. Conservation work funded under the ESA (from Skerratt *et al.*, 1992).

- Repair and maintenance of existing dykes (walls).
- Hedge restoration.
- Tree planting – underplanting of existing areas.
- Fencing of woodland, wetland and permanent pasture.
- Eradication of bracken.
- Heather regeneration.
- Archaeological site protection.

claim up to £4500 per annum for five years. This payment is made up of two parts: the flat-rate payment (up to £1500 per annum) and the item payments (up to £3000 per annum).

The *flat-rate payments* are based on the amount and type of land within the farm unit. A total of £1500 per annum may be claimed. Farmers can claim £15 per annum for each hectare of enclosed land and £2.50 per annum for each hectare of rough grazings. The ESA Scheme defines enclosed land as 'land enclosed by fences, hedges, walls or dykes for the controlled grazing of livestock, cropping or the maintenance of farm woodland. This will normally mean land below the hill dyke or fence' (SOAFD, 1989).

The *item payments* comprise payments for the specific conservation work of the Farm Conservation Plan (see Box 6.3). These are calculated on the basis of standard costings for particular items of work at the rate of £X per linear or square metre for dyking and fencing, or £Y per hectare for other features, and so on. The amount paid per year is calculated on the basis of the amount of relevant work completed. A maximum figure of £3000 per annum per farm business can be claimed for these item payments, or £100 per annum per hectare, whichever is the lower figure. A flat-rate payment of £240 per annum is paid where the farm business covers an area of less than 16 'adjusted' hectares.[2]

The farmer receives the first annual flat-rate payment soon after the agreement is signed, and then at yearly intervals for the remaining period. The item payments can be claimed at any time provided the work has been completed. However, for any work completed during a calendar year, all claims must be submitted by the end of January of the following year.

It is possible for the farmer to join other schemes whilst the ESA scheme is running on the farm. It is not possible, however, to apply for other forms of grants or aid from Government funds for the work agreed in the conservation plan; it is therefore not possible to obtain double funding.

---

[2]An adjusted hectare refers here to the total number of hectares of enclosed land plus one-sixth of the total hectares of other agricultural land.

The Research Project

Objectives of the Research Project

The three main objectives of the evaluation are as follows: firstly, to record the current farming and socioeconomic conditions in the designated ESA of Breadalbane, and the control area (not designated as an ESA) of Glenshee and Glenisla, the latter area being immediately to the east of the ESA and selected on the basis of its comparability of farming type, landscape and topography; secondly, to assess the impact of the ESA on farmers, the rural economy and the rural landscape and to evaluate the likely uptake of the ESA in the Breadalbane area; and thirdly, to evaluate the likely impact on farming systems, the rural economy and the rural landscape, of selected policy options. For brevity of discussion, this chapter will concentrate on the second of these objectives.

Methodology: Data Types

For impact assessment, data were required on: the farm business, the local economy, the environment, and attitudes and behaviour. The ESA uptake evaluation aimed to represent more clearly the decision-making behaviour of the farmers within the designated area, with respect to: participation in the ESA Scheme; and how conservation objectives could relate to the everyday farming and management of the farm business. The types of data required were subdivided into three categories: (i) the individual farmer; (ii) the farm characteristics; and (iii) the policy initiative – the ESA and its implementation.

Data were collected through two surveys in both the ESA and control area. The first survey was carried out from July to December 1988; it involved face-to-face interviews with farmers, using a structured questionnaire. The survey sample comprised a 100% census survey within the ESA, and a random sample of 33% of the control area farmers, which was stratified on the basis of farm size and tenure type, in order that the ESA and control samples were approximately equivalent in these two respects (the criteria of size and tenure being predetermined by the availability of control area data at this stage of the research). A randomizer programme was used for sample selection. The overall response to this survey was 78% of farmers in the ESA area, and 73% of the control area sample.

The issues covered in this questionnaire can be subdivided under three headings, physical, attitudinal and response to the ESA Scheme. Physical comprised data on: farm size, land use, farm buildings, labour, farm woodlands, on-farm non-agricultural activities, inputs to the farming system. Attitudinal questions addressed: farm conservation, farm objectives. Responses to the ESA Scheme included: attitude towards the Scheme, factors considered when deciding whether or not to join; perceived advantages, disadvantages and suggested improvements; expected impact of the Scheme on the farm business; and details of the Farm Conservation Plan.

The second survey was carried out towards the end of the three-year study, from January to March 1990, using a telephone questionnaire (with assistance from the Research Unit in Health and Behavioural Change, Edinburgh University). As far as possible, the issues raised were broadly similar to those of the first survey to allow for comparison of data; in addition, the survey sample (census in the ESA, 33% sample in the control area) was identical. The overall response to this survey was virtually the same, although some farmers preferred to answer questions face-to-face rather than over the telephone, or vice versa; thus the farmers did not necessarily take part in both surveys.

Within the questionnaire, similar issues were covered as in the first set of interviews. The more complex financial questions were omitted, however, due to the telephone medium reducing the possibility of discussing farm accounts (both in terms of the time taken, and the inconvenience for the farmer of reading out accounts over the telephone).

Results

Impact

Data from the first and second surveys (see above) led to results concerning: the impact of the Scheme on the local farm economy, and on farmers' attitudes to conservation; and evaluation of the uptake of the Scheme, focusing in particular on farmers' attitudes towards the ESA. The main results of the study fall within four categories: farm business, local economy, landscape and attitudes.

Farm business: land use and stocking

More than half the farmers interviewed indicated that they had made some adjustment to their cropping patterns and stocking level over the previous two years (i.e. 1986–1988). The most common shift appeared to be away from arable (particularly barley) towards increased cattle and sheep numbers. No adjustments, however, were brought about as a direct result of the ESA Scheme.

It is worth noting at this point that, although the SOAFD publications, such as *A First Report* (SOAFD, 1989) stated that: 'the scheme is designed to resist pressures towards damaging intensification' and 'protect open hill rough grazing from land reclamation, overgrazing ...' the actual stocking density limit of 0.5 livestock units (LU) per hectare (on open rough grazings) was higher than most Breadalbane farmers' stocking density (Skerratt *et al.*, 1992). Thus, in the researcher's view, an opportunity for confronting the issue of overstocking was not fully addressed.

Farm business: labour

Although there was no specific employment objective in the Scheme, the ESA's effect has been slight, since the majority of ESA-funded conservation work has been undertaken by contractors (see below) rather than by existing on-farm labour. In 2% of cases, however, the farm workforce has directly been affected by the opportunity which the ESA represented for the employment of younger people under the (then) Youth Training Scheme. More detail concerning this issue of employment is given below.

Farm business: destination of ESA monies

A farmer participating in the ESA Scheme is able to claim up to £4500 per annum for each of the five years, up to £1500 of this being the flat-rate payment, and up to £3000 being the 'itemized' payments (see Appendix 6.1).

Firstly, flat-rate payments: more than 80% of the participating farmers stated that such monies were being – and would continue to be – used for on-farm expenditure; that is, the money was being ploughed back into the farm business. This payment, however, was increasingly being used to top-up itemized payments which were falling short of the full cost. Eighty-three per cent said that there was no chance of any off-farm investment of these monies; and more than a quarter of the respondents were using this flat-rate payment to help reduce debt.

Secondly, itemized payments: these were for specific conservation activities, such as dyking, fencing and tree planting. A small number of farmers carried out the work themselves, and were thus able to keep the monies in lieu of their time. However, in the majority of cases, much of the conservation work was carried out by contractors. The itemized payments were therefore used directly for the purpose of maintaining or improving the existing farm conservation features.

Farm business: farming system

Very few respondents reported any change in the running of the farm business and their farm management, as a direct result of the ESA Scheme. The Management Guidelines appeared to be 'well-tailored' to the Breadalbane farming systems. The one area of infringement and difficulty, at least initially, was linked with the fencing of woodland areas for regeneration (or where specific underplanting occurred) and a small number of wetland areas. These required a resultant change in grazing location from areas which had previously been used for shelter. In addition, in the earlier stages of the Scheme's implementation, there was confusion over the precise time periods for which areas should have been fenced off, although it seems that this issue has since largely been resolved, due to SOAFD consultation with Scottish Natural Heritage (SNH) and the FWAG.

Local economy: labour supply and demand

In addition to the above comments, it is necessary to look at the percentage of farmer involvement in each of the ESA-funded activities (see Table 6.1). It can be seen that 100% of participating farmers, for example, carried out some dyking as part of their conservation plan; 89% of these participating farmers fenced off woodland, and so on. In order to carry out these activities, farmers seemed to follow one of two options: use of available farm labour, with additional training as required; or use of contract labour. This choice depended on the nature of the activity (whether dyking or tree planting, for example), the availability of on-farm and/or contract labour, associated costs, time input for the work, training requirements, and the perceived required standards for the completed work.

It was found that contract labour was used, to varying degrees, for five out of six of the conservation activities, the highest contribution being for dyking and fencing (see Table 6.2). Since dyking was carried out on 100% of

Table 6.1. Farmer involvement in each of the ESA-funded conservation activities. (From Skerratt *et al.*, 1993.)

Activity	% ESA participant farmers involved each activity
Dyking	100
Fencing off woodland	89
Tree planting	86
Fencing off wetland	58
Fencing off unimproved pasture	44
Bracken control	42
Archaeological site protection	35
Hedge restoration	16
Heather regeneration	7

Table 6.2. Labour inputs for each ESA-funded activity. (From Skerratt *et al.*, 1993.)

	Labour inputs		
Activity	Own labour (%)	Contract labour (%)	Both (%)
Dyking	9	85	6
Hedge restoration	75	25	0
Tree planting	73	20	7
Fencing	26	55	19
Bracken control	77	23	0
Heather regeneration	100	0	0

Table 6.3. Projected expenditure* on labour and materials to 1996. (From Skerratt *et al.*, 1993.)

Type of work	Total expend. (£k)	Farm labour (£k)	Contract labour (£k)	Materials (£k)
Dyking:				
Item payments	603	73	530	0
Extra cost	106	0	106	0
Fencing	444	78	144	222
Hedge replanting	21	5	2	14
Tree planting	21	5	2	14
Bracken eradication	25	10	3	12
Total	1220	171	787	262

*At 1990 prices.

participating farms, and was also the activity that perhaps required the highest degree of training, 33 full-time jobs were required in the area as a direct result of the ESA agreements. A number of the dykers came from outwith the area, some of whom were previously established. In 1989, these dykers stated that they were booked up for at least the next five years on ESA-funded work. Table 6.3 illustrates the degree of government expenditure according to the type of ESA work; the significance of the contract labour share is evident.

The ESA has thus, in this instance, had an impact on the local economy in terms of employment. It should be noted, however, that more than 60% of the dykers lived outwith the ESA and came into the area specifically for the work on a day-to-day basis; there was thus a leakage of ESA funds from the ESA itself (this issue is addressed below).

Landscape

The SAC evaluation concentrated on the level and extent of conservation work being carried out with ESA funding, using the control area for comparison. This focus was determined by the concurrent research being carried out by the Macaulay Land Use Research Institute and The Countryside Commission for Scotland into the ecological, conservation and landscape impacts of the Scheme in Breadalbane.

As can be seen in Table 6.4, the ESA has facilitated significant conservation work which, with reference to the control area, would not have been carried out to the same extent without such funding. Within the ESA, advice was available, others in the area were carrying out the work, and, of course, financial assistance was present; all of which are strong incentives for

Table 6.4. ESA and control area conservation activity – ESA-type work. (From Skerratt *et al.*, 1993.)

Type of conservation work	ESA %	Control area %
Dyking	61	6
Hedge restoration	10	0
Tree planting	79	46
Fencing:		
Woodland	35	0
Wetland	34	4
Permanent pasture	27	0
Bracken eradication	25	0
Heather regeneration	5	4
Archaeological site protection	20	0

carrying out the work. The control group therefore demonstrates relatively clearly the opportunity and incentive afforded by the ESA Scheme.

Attitudes

The evaluation focused on the ESA's impact on attitudes to conservation, and on-farm conservation. The observations must be qualified, since the responses occurred just two or three years after the Scheme's introduction (1987) and, in many cases almost immediately after the farmer had joined the Scheme. There is a necessity for a greater time-period to have elapsed in order to facilitate a more accurate assessment of the ESA's attitudinal impact (see below).

However, within the two surveys, three aspects of this issue were examined: firstly, whether the ESA had led to a change in farmers' *interest* in conservation; secondly, whether their *understanding* of conservation had changed; and finally, whether the ESA had changed their *awareness* of conservation practices on the farm. As is evident from Table 6.5, the ESA-induced changes are relatively low, with almost half the farmers reporting no change in interest in conservation as a result of the ESA Scheme. The majority of those giving this response stated that they were good stewards of the land prior to the introduction of the ESA, and the Scheme had thus not altered their attitude. The greatest percentage of respondents reporting an increase was for 'awareness of conservation practices on the farm', i.e. a greater awareness of both the functional and aesthetic aspects of farm conservation.

Table 6.5. ESA-induced attitudinal change. (From Skerratt *et al.*, 1993.)

ESA-induced change	Response (%)		
	Increase	No change	Don't know
Interest in conservation	40	45	4
Understanding of conservation	45	42	2
Awareness of conservation practices on farm	47	36	2

Table 6.6. Actual and projected* uptake to 1992. (From Skerratt *et al.*, 1993.)

Year (to 31 May)	Applications		Approvals	
	No.	ha	No.	ha
1988	76	34,690	41	14,927
1989	84	36,961	75	31,257
1990	97	51,270	82	38,158
1991[†]	106	55,968	97	51,216
1992[†]	118	62,304	112	59,136

*Projections based on 75% uptake from eligible units.
[†]Projected.

Uptake

Uptake pattern

Table 6.6 shows the actual and projected uptake of Breadalbane ESA to 1992. It demonstrates the rapid initial uptake, with the number of applications levelling off as time progresses. The uptake for Breadalbane ESA was particularly high compared with other ESAs in Scotland.

Factors affecting uptake

Those factors which appear to have affected Breadalbane farmers' ESA adoption/non-adoption decisions are now discussed. These can be subdivided into three sections: the individual farmer and farm characteristics, and the policy initiative – the ESA and its implementation. The major results are outlined below.

Individual farmers
At the individual farmer level, the age of the decision-maker seemed to be important. As can be seen from Table 6.7, as the age of the farmer increased, the willingness of the farmer to participate in the ESA Scheme appeared to decrease, with 67% of farmers in the 25–40 category taking part in the Scheme, as opposed to 27% of farmers aged 'over 65 years'. The research highlighted the fact that the younger farmers were more willing to 'give the scheme a try', whereas the older farmers preferred to continue farming the land in the way they had always done.

Another issue, which is a further comment on age, is that of retirement status; those nearer to their planned retirement were less likely to join, with

Table 6.7. Scheme participants: distribution within age category. (From Skerratt *et al.*, 1993.)

Age (years)	% Farms
16–24	NA
25–40	67
41–64	50
65+	27

an associated reluctance to see their day-to-day management of the farm altered in any way, and a concern over the five-year commitment required by the ESA.

Farm characteristics

The main factor which appeared to influence ESA adoption was farm size. The lowest uptake of the Scheme occurred in both the '0–50 hectare' range, and with the farms and estates at the top end of the size range. The highest ESA adoption was on farms of 50–100 hectares. The reasons associated with this were that on the smaller farms, the flat-rate payment (calculated on a per hectare basis) was significantly less than the maximum of £1500 per farm business per annum; in addition, the potential for positive conservation measures on these smaller farms was felt to be more limited, with an associated concern over the probable difficulty therefore in producing a 'balanced' farm conservation plan.[3] The incentives at this end of the farm-size scale were therefore felt to be lower. In contrast, the larger farms found difficulty, and therefore a disincentive, with the upper limit of £1500 for observation of the management guidelines on a sizeable hectarage of farm land. In addition, the response on these larger properties was that there was the potential for carrying out more positive conservation measures than were provided for under the maximum funding of £3000 per annum for each of the five years of the conservation plan. This was significant in the Breadalbane area, since there are a number of large estates covering many thousands of hectares. The 'ideal' farm size for taking full advantage of the ESA funding thus appeared to be 50–100 hectares.

Farm status – i.e. whether the farm is tenanted, owner-occupied or mixed – was anticipated by the researchers as being significant to the ESA adoption/ non-adoption decision. However, adoption of the Scheme was found to be almost identical within these categories, with 57% of tenants, 55% of owner-

---

[3]This was a very definite requirement stipulated by SOAFD in their ESA Explanatory Leaflets.

occupiers, and 52% of those of mixed tenureship, being involved in the Scheme. A significant factor here, however, is that it appeared that a number of the tenants who farmed within the larger estates were strongly encouraged to join the ESA Scheme by their landlords and/or factors, some estates topping up any shortfalls in the ESA funding which the tenant farmer would have otherwise incurred. In addition, two tenants within the area were not allowed to join the ESA Scheme, due to landlord preference.

Policy initiative
This category comprises, firstly, data on farmer response to the information and advice associated with the ESA's introduction and implementation, and, secondly, the specific advantages, disadvantages and suggestions for improvement which were cited by farmers when interviewed. It must be stressed that these are farmers' comments and feedback.

Extension: information and advice.   Table 6.8 illustrates the primary – i.e. the first and main – source of ESA-type information used by farmers within Breadalbane. The combined SAC input reached 43% of farmers, with SOAFD input accounting for 36%. Farmers were then asked to comment on the adequacy of the information they received at three specific stages of the ESA's implementation: when considering whether or not to join the Scheme; when drawing up the Farm Conservation Plan; and when actually carrying out the ESA-funded conservation work. As can be seen from Table 6.9, over 80% of farmers saw the ESA-related information and advice as adequate or completely adequate for the first two stages, and 70% for the third stage.

Table 6.8. Primary sources of information concerning the Breadalbane ESA Scheme. (From Skerratt *et al.*, 1993.)

Primary sources of information	% of respondents
SAC (Perth)	17
SAC advisers (Perth)	24
SAC (Edinburgh)	2
SOAFD (Perth)	27
SOAFD advisers (Perth)	2
SOAFD booklets	7
NFU	2
Neighbours	2

Table 6.9. Adequacy of information and advice concerning Breadalbane ESA. (From Skerratt *et al.*, 1993.)

Stage	Completely adequate	Adequate	Inadequate	Completely inadequate
When considering whether or not to join the Scheme	40	44	7	2
When drawing up the farm conservation plan	46	39	2	2
When carrying out the work	29	44	10	2

Inadequacy of the extension input was greatest when farmers were carrying out the work; however, this was stated in only 12% of cases.

The results indicate that the level of, and satisfaction with, the information and advice received by farmers was an important positive factor in their ESA adoption/non-adoption decisions, and for many farmers certainly encouraged their adoption of the ESA Scheme.

Farmers' comments concerning the ESA Scheme. The major advantages and disadvantages of the Breadalbane ESA and suggestions for its improvement, as stated by the farmers, are outlined below. Within the questionnaire, these particular questions were designed to be open-ended; thus after giving their responses, farmers were then asked to state the *main* advantage, disadvantage, and suggestion.

Advantages (see Table 6.10): Primarily, these concern the opportunity for repair and/or maintenance of dykes, and the associated jobs that the ESA

Table 6.10. Advantages of the ESA Scheme. (From Skerratt *et al.*, 1993.)

Main stated advantage	% of respondents
Dykes and work for dykers	20
Environmental activities that could not have been done otherwise	16
Farm and countryside more attractive	14
Stock control features	13
Financial input to the farm	13

Table 6.11. Disadvantages of the ESA Scheme. (From Skerratt *et al.*, 1993.)

Main stated disadvantage	% of respondents
Interference with farm system/management	28
Range of conservation items too narrow	22
Bureaucratic input	9
Uncertainty over the five years and future	9
Itemized payments not high enough	8

Scheme required. Secondly, the Scheme allowed for environmental activities to be carried out on the farm, activities which were seen as 'unaffordable' without ESA funding.

Disadvantages (see Table 6.11): 28% of respondents felt that the main disadvantage of the ESA Scheme was the interference with their farm system; as has been mentioned, this was primarily associated with pre-ESA grazing location, and particularly with the exclusion of stock from certain areas of the farm for long periods. One-quarter of farmers felt that the range of ESA-funded conservation items was too narrow (as the main disadvantage), particularly as the establishment of new features was not allowed under the Scheme; these may include planting of trees where there are currently no trees, and the creation of ponds. It was felt that there was scope for a more comprehensive farm conservation scheme.

Suggestions for improvement (see Table 6.12): Firstly, as mentioned above, a major suggestion was to broaden the Scheme remit in order to include new features. In addition, farmers suggested the possibility of non-agricultural land within the area – such as that owned by hotels – becoming eligible for ESA funding, thus increasing the scope for environmental improvements within the ESA as a whole.

Secondly, a point which was raised as the main issue by only 6% of respondents, but by a much larger percentage of respondents as part of their overall suggestions, is that of keeping the itemized payments for the conservation work in line with inflation. Concern had arisen that agreements were signed, say, in 1988, for a five-year period, but at 1988 prices. The costs of dyking, particularly, increase during the lifetime of a Farm Conservation Plan. It was therefore felt that index-linking of the itemized payments should be seriously considered if future ESAs were to be designated in Scotland.

Table 6.12. Suggestions for improvement in the ESA Scheme. (From Skerratt *et al.*, 1993.)

Suggestions	% Response
Broaden Scheme remit	12
Increased funding or index-linked payments	6
Scheme should be for more than five years	4
Opportunities to modify plan	3

Evaluation of Breadalbane ESA

Socioeconomic Impact

The ESA's overall socioeconomic impact has been limited. The farm businesses within the area appear to have been little affected in terms of changes in land-use patterns and livestock, except for some shifts in grazing and sheltering locations where areas have been fenced off.

The ESA-funded conservation activities have largely been carried out by contract labour, and thus farm-level labour situations have remained unchanged. The ESA monies, however, have been invested in the fabric of the farm, and this may have implications both in terms of their financial value and aid to farming activities such as stock control. However, the proportions of ESA grants invested in the participating farms could have been increased with less use of contract labour and more encouragement of the training and associated use of on-farm labour (see below). The local economy has seen little change due to the ESA; the major effect was connected with the labour required to carry out the ESA-funded conservation work; however, as mentioned elsewhere in this chapter, this impact was significantly reduced due to labour commuting from outwith the designated area, often on a daily basis.

The majority of ESA participants felt that the Scheme led to a positive landscape impact, primarily in terms of the repair and maintenance of dykes, particularly since farmers had been increasingly replacing dykes with fences due to the former's prohibitive cost and required time input. In addition, the encouragement of woodland regeneration in certain areas of farms which were formerly grazed was felt to have a positive long-term impact (for a detailed botanical assessment, see Nolan and Still, 1993).

The issue of the extent to which farmers' attitudes to the environment were changed by the ESA was difficult to assess because many farmers felt that they had already been farming in a way that was beneficial to the environment, thus creating and maintaining the sorts of features for which the ESA had been designated. This was particularly felt to be the case in this predominantly LFA, extensive hill farming area. For some farmers the ESA was merely facilitating a *continuation* of these practices which had recently become impossible to carry out due to the financial 'squeeze' on farming. However, what can be pinpointed is the way in which the ESA appeared to increase farmers' awareness of the scope for integrating conservation activities, as represented by the ESA, with everyday farming practices. Also of importance here was the opportunity for planning and negotiation between farmer and adviser (during the ESA adoption procedure) which led to a realization for a number of farmers that there was room for the discussion of often differing land-use objectives. The ESA appeared to be a positive experience for the majority of farmers who joined, in that the Scheme was voluntary, and was publicized as 'experimental' (thus suggesting possibilities for its improvement). In addition, the application procedure and form-filling were not particularly onerous (as compared with other schemes), and the payments were received fairly speedily and covered a significant percentage of the costs involved. However, as is noted above, farmers did comment on the necessity for index-linking the itemized payments due to the five- (and now up to ten-) year duration of an agreement.

Uptake

The adoption rate of Breadalbane ESA ranks the highest of all the Scottish ESAs. The factors affecting uptake appeared to be the farmer's age, education and nearness to retirement. The factor of tenure (at this stage of the research), does not seem to play a significant part in the adoption process, except in the context of the influence of landlords on the large tenanted estates within the area. However, the amount of potential ESA-funded work and the significance of the financial incentives (the flat-rate element of which is calculated on a per hectare basis) is related to farm size. Uptake could have been increased with a recognition of the restrictions that small and large farm size can bring (see Results), and the opportunity for flexibility in order to encourage the participation of such farm units.

In addition, the ESA-funded conservation works had benefits for livestock farmers; for example, the dykes provide good stock control and shelter, and areas where trees have been underplanted will also provide shelter within the next few years. The small number of lowland arable farmers in the area did feel that the Scheme had little to offer them in this way; for example, they would have preferred the opportunity for planting trees in *new* areas which could have subsequently provided shelter. Within the Scheme, therefore, there needs to be the opportunity for catering to this diversity of farm type, size and tenure (see below).

Certain details of the Scheme itself increased its uptake; these included: the relatively easy application procedure; the easy form-filling and crucial assistance (from SAC) with the Farm Conservation Plan; and the timely payment of the Flat Rate Grant. In addition, the flat-rate payment was felt by many farmers to be a sufficient incentive for involvement in the Scheme. However, uptake could have been increased had an in-built price review system been incorporated into the ESA, since farmers are committing themselves, up to five years forward, on the basis of cash payments at today's price levels.

Comments on Methodology

Introduction

The above results and evaluation need to be viewed within the context of the methodological approaches used, since these influenced the selection of data, its analysis and subsequent conclusions. Although the following comments are specific to this research project, their wider evaluation implications are also noted, with brief recommendations therefore being made concerning methodological improvements for future ESA-type evaluations.

Comments

These can be subdivided into two broad areas: the objectives of the evaluation; and the overriding emphasis on timeliness of the evaluation feedback.

Firstly, the lack of clarity of the evaluation's aims needs to be highlighted, since this had implications for the types of data collected, including the extent to which attention to a broader range of factors (see below) was seen as appropriate. As the research period progressed, increasing emphasis was placed upon evaluating the extent to which Breadalbane ESA was meeting its objectives, rather than combining this with an in-depth assessment of the ESA's objectives themselves (as had been initially envisaged). This development, related to the UK-wide evaluation of the ESAs, reduced the possibility, within the given time-scale and funding, of: assessing Breadalbane ESA as a policy mechanism; discussing issues related to the implementation of the ESA policy; or assessing its uptake in any great depth. This 'evolution' of the aims led to confusion over what should be accomplished within the evaluation; it also resulted in the progressive narrowing down of the research avenues being pursued, and increased rigidity concerning the issues being discussed, with a consequent loss of in-depth, analytical material which may have been more informative to policy development in the longer term.

Secondly, it is recognized that the timely Report on the Scheme's progress, impact and uptake was useful, and also necessary to the ESA policy review of 1992. Sole reliance on a snapshot mode of assessment can, however, lead to a trade-off between the reliability of, and confidence in, the data being produced, and the completion of the evaluation within the agreed time-scale. The implications of this can be illustrated through the following examples: research emphases, data collection methodology, the brevity of attitudinal assessment, and the use of standardized categories. These are now discussed in turn.

Research emphases

The focus upon evaluation completion within the given time-frame resulted in an overriding emphasis upon answers rather than questions, upon certainties rather than uncertainties – an approach which tended to preclude flexibility and questioning. The associated reliance upon 'tried and tested' methods and data is addressed by Rich (1981). He highlights policy-makers' preference for safe, familiar sources and types of information, and argues that this is due to the need for policy decisions to be 'subject to the least possible risk' (p. 11; see also Wilensky, 1967). Consequently, there is often a bias towards information types that are assumed, perhaps implicitly, to be likely to verify initial assumptions, rather than giving the opportunity for following up inconclusive (as yet), but perhaps significant, information.

The implication for the Breadalbane research project was to reduce the requirement and opportunity for a detailed assessment of broader issues related to impact and uptake, with an associated aim of generalizability, and a subsequent loss of location- and time-specific detail (including the landlord–tenant hierarchy, the Scottish and LFA identities of the area, contemporaneous agri-conservation policy developments and associated farming uncertainties). The analysis of ESA adoption/non-adoption was reduced to a discussion of a one-off decision (yes/no) on the part of the farmer, with little account being taken of the number of ESA-related decisions which play a part in the final outcome (for comparable examples see Gladwin, 1989, and Gladwin and Murtaugh, 1980). Also, the range of factors affecting such decisions was given little scope for analysis; these include farm household objectives and perceptions (including perceptions of themselves as farmers; see Seabrook and Higgins, 1988); awareness of, and susceptibility to, influences from neighbours and colleagues; the 'public' nature of farming; motivations at different stages of a farming career; symbolism of the land; and intergenerational conflict and/or continuity. Factors such as these may well play a significant role in the Scheme's impact and uptake; however, the sole reliance upon a minimum data set accessed within a limited time-period, significantly reduced opportunities for their incorporation and assessment.

Data collection methodology

Due to the need for a relatively rapid evaluation of the ESA, one of the emphases was upon methodological approaches that would provide the required data in the minimum time, with the result that questionnaires became the sole methodological tool.

Within the project, two formal sets of interviews, one face-to-face and the other by telephone, were carried out using structured questionnaires. This conventional method was seen as appropriate to the anticipated survey data and quantitative analyses. Kuhn (1970, p. 59) comments that 'consciously or not, the decision to employ a particular piece of apparatus and to use it in a particular way carries an assumption that only certain sorts of circumstances will arise'. Thus, although such approaches facilitated the collection of those quantifiable factors associated with the farming system and the ESA-funded conservation activities, they also precluded the inclusion of data less suited to quantification. These include farmers' perceptions of the ESA, such as 'traditional' or 'progressive' (and what these terms imply); how the ESA relates to their view of why and how they farm; why they appear to take risks in some situations and not in others, and whether the ESA is perceived as a risk. Leach (1967, p. 77) states that 'there is a wide range of sociological phenomena which are intrinsically inaccessible to statistical investigation of any kind'. This calls for a recognition of the limited nature of the questionnaire methodology as the sole approach for addressing certain critical issues within such an evaluation.

In addition, the Project's singular reliance on questionnaires and interviewing of individuals resulted in a lack of information concerning the relationships between farmers, and within farming households; this is a particularly significant omission when addressing the uptake of this voluntary Scheme. Leach comments that this 'statistical orientation presupposes that the field of observation consists of "units of population", "individuals"' rather than 'the data being made up of "systems of relationship"' (1967, p. 77). The focus on the individual also implicitly reinforces the view of the farmer as an autonomous, decision-making unit, whereas the reality of the decision-making nexus is far more complex and dynamic (see, for example, Berlan Darque's (1988) discussion of the 'power and negotiation' involved in the decision-making of farming couples).

Attitudinal assessment

The assessment and evaluation of ESA-induced change concentrated particularly on farm conservation activities and farmers' attitudes towards conservation. Although elements of the former were visible, for example, the number of dykes rebuilt, trees planted, areas fenced off, and so on, attitudinal change was far more difficult to isolate (in terms of being attributable solely to the ESA) and assess. This was due in part to the questionnaire methodology (see above), which treated the two types of data in the same manner.

However, the 18-month period during which the two sets of interviews were carried out (summer 1988 and early 1990), was too short a time for accurately assessing any attitudinal changes which may have occurred, particularly since the uptake process is staggered, with some farmers joining just before the end of the evaluation period.

Standardized categories

Examples of categories used within the ESA evaluation include: whether the farmer is a 'tenant' or 'owner-occupier', a 'landlord', an 'older farmer' or 'younger farmer', 'with successor' or 'without successor'. Such classification is considered necessary for both the understanding, and prediction, of policy-related behaviour such as uptake. However, it also conceals information which may be of significance, due to the inherent diversity within each of these categorizations. For example, when applying tenureship categories, no consideration is given to the reasoning behind the tenureship arrangement and associated farming and non-farming objectives; the biographies of those within the categories; and the significance that both the individual farmers, and the farm households, place on these criteria when making their own ESA-related decisions (see Gasson and Hill's (1984) work, *Farm Tenure and Performance*, particularly pp. 37–38, 101–109). These assumptions of uniformity (Leach, 1967, p. 80), which emphasize generalizability (and predictability for other similar policy scenarios), reduce the opportunity for both applying and questioning these groupings of farmers. Thus standard relationships continue to be addressed through conventional channels and perspectives, when an inclusion of a broader range of data would begin to facilitate a fuller understanding of the *extent* to which these categories determine ESA responses.

Recommendations

The recommendations outlined below are necessarily brief; they are intended as pointers within the very specific context of ESA-type policy evaluation methodology.

The precise aims of the evaluation – both the funder's and the researchers' – must be clarified and communicated throughout the project, in order that the research requirements can be fully met. This would enable the core set of issues to be recognized and addressed, and may also facilitate a degree of flexibility which would permit research beyond such focal areas. The latter may comprise a combination of both formal and informal approaches, whereby the researcher moves from 'being wide open to whatever (they) can learn', towards increasing focus, with final systematic questioning, the results of which 'will often pose further questions' (Agar, 1980, p. 136).

The time-scale of such evaluations would therefore need to be extended, such that both 'certainties' and 'uncertainties' can be probed. These on-going evaluations would incorporate the regular submission of evaluation reports on the scheme's impact, uptake and progress, in order that the policy-makers' information needs can be met alongside continuing, necessary in-depth research. If such a situation is not possible, due to funding constraints, a lesser alternative would be a period of research at a specified time following the scheme's implementation and first evaluation.

In addition, data collection methodologies should comprise a range of approaches which are sensitive, and appropriate, to the data under consideration, in order that certain data types are not precluded from the outset. For example, the use of questionnaires for the collection of farm production, financial, and farm conservation activity information; semi-structured/ unstructured interviews when looking at attitudes, perceptions, and how these are constructed and perpetuated; and a period of staying in the area to enable a focus on inter-personal relationships (see above) and an understanding of their significance in the 'public' activity of farming and the adoption/non-adoption of a voluntary ESA-type scheme. In addition, the complementarity of these data sets needs to be examined, with the aim of increasing the overall accuracy and coherence of the evaluation.

Finally, the diversity within the standardized categories should be openly stated in order to qualify the generalized, and often predictive, comments made within policy evaluations such as Breadalbane ESA. The interviewees' perceptions of these categorizations, and their significance in their ESA-type decisions, should not be inferred, but rather become a subject of enquiry itself. The categories may maintain their significance within evaluations, or they may be revised.

Conclusions

This chapter has discussed the socioeconomic impact and uptake of Breadalbane ESA over the period 1987–1990. The following comments aim to briefly summarize the key points concerning the Scheme.

Negative Aspects of Breadalbane ESA

Firstly, Breadalbane ESA has not sufficiently confronted the overgrazing issue, which was cited as important in the early stages of the ESA's designation and implementation. Specific areas, such as herb-rich meadows and wetlands, have been catered for under the ESA provisions, due to funding which has allowed them to be fenced off. However, the open hill rough grazings had been specifically identified as requiring protection from overgrazing; but the stocking density level set within the Management Guidelines has not led to any changes in the farmers' average annual stocking density.

Secondly, feedback from farmers indicated that payments became 'insufficient' after the first two to two-and-a-half years of the Scheme's operation; the greatest increase in costs was for the dyking work, due to both inflation and the increasing prices charged by dykers. As a result, farmers were increasingly having to use a proportion of their flat-rate payment to meet the rising costs.

Thirdly, the exclusion of non-agricultural land is seen as a disadvantage, since such land is significant to the ESA as a whole, in both hectarage and landscape terms, and its exclusion results in a piecemeal approach. This is therefore seen as a missed opportunity, although it is recognized that the ESA is an agricultural measure, and changes of this sort would require an amendment to the Statutes.

Finally, the majority of the dyking and fencing work was carried out by contract labour. Although it is recognized that new jobs have been created as a result, a 'leakage' of resources has been identified, in that ESA monies leak firstly from the farm business to the contractor; and secondly, from the Breadalbane area, since more than 60% of the contractors are from outwith the area.

Positive Aspects of Breadalbane ESA

Firstly, the ESA is positive in terms of its overall uptake – almost 70% of eligible farms (up to March 1992). Secondly, the Scheme has brought about a considerable amount of enhancement work: stone dykes have been renovated and rebuilt; semi-natural woodlands have been fenced off to allow for regeneration; areas of herb-rich pasture, and some wetland, have been fenced off so that grazing may be controlled and poaching reduced. Thirdly, most of the income from the flat-rate payment has been ploughed back into the farm business, with over 50% of the farmers receiving the maximum payment of £1500 per annum. Fourthly, the Breadalbane ESA Scheme has shown the potential for integrating conservation with day-to-day farming. The aesthetic and functional aspects of conservation are being demonstrated, such as the maintenance and repair of dykes – which are both a landscape and stock control feature. Fifthly, the ESA has had a positive visual impact, at least in the short-term, primarily with respect to dyking and tree planting. And finally, the ESA's knock-on requirement for 33 full-time jobs, 15 of which have been filled by those resident within the ESA, is an obvious advantage and has contributed towards the maintenance of the traditional craft of drystone dyking.

ESA Recommendations

The two essential elements in the Breadalbane Scheme should be retained; the combination of a substantial flat-rate payment and a balanced Farm

Conservation Plan ensures both high uptake for the Scheme, and a broad coverage of conservation features.

Schemes such as Breadalbane ESA should allow for the funding of new features, such as ponds and new woodland, as these would add to the attractiveness of the Scheme from the farmers' point of view. Although these features can and do attract funding from other sources, there is considerable appeal in developing a single, comprehensive conservation plan and working through it over a five to ten-year period.

As farmers gain in conservation experience, it is quite likely that they will see scope for improvement in their Farm Conservation Plans. Consideration should therefore be given to allowing modifications to the original Plans, for example in the second or third years (a fee could be charged to cover the cost of this second approval). Such a system would allow for more feedback from the farmer on some of the Scheme's details, and may subsequently have the effect of increasing uptake, and giving farmers a more positive attitude to farm conservation.

Although it is recognized that the creation of jobs was not one of the ESA's objectives, the ESA's financial resources could well have been contained within Breadalbane to a greater extent if, for example, there had been increased awareness of training opportunities in the area and associated liaison with bodies such as the Agricultural Training Board, at earlier stages of the ESA's implementation.

There needs to be a working awareness within the Scheme's design, of the (adoption) implications of certain features within this ESA. Firstly, the complexities of tenureship arrangements must be recognized in order that the appropriate individuals can be approached, and account taken of the constraints and opportunities of tenants and landlords, factors and managers. Although the Local Area Advisory staff are aware of the various estates and their farming arrangements, there are no details within the ESA mechanism which cater for them.

As mentioned above, the Scheme also needs to address the diversity of farm size and type. For example, a finer tuning of the flat-rate incentive payment for farms of less than 50 hectares, no charge for their Farm Conservation Plan, and the possibility of signing up for a shorter time-period (in recognition of the comparatively limited amount of work available for ESA funding), may encourage farms of this size to join the Scheme. A higher ceiling for itemized payments, even for say three out of the first five years, may encourage more of the larger farms to join.

It was stated that, overall, the ESA's socioeconomic impact has been limited. The above comments and recommendations, if met, would encourage higher adoption levels for the Scheme, and allow for a greater positive financial input to the farms and the area. In addition, farmers' awareness of their increased role in determining aspects of the Breadalbane ESA policy may well encourage greater participation in ESA-type schemes, and have longer term positive implications for involvement in farm conservation activities *per se*.

Evaluation Methodology

The influences of the project's methodology on the socioeconomic evaluation of the Breadalbane ESA have been outlined. Such methodological approaches were, of necessity, linked with policy reformulation, in that they affected the results which informed both the detailed changes, and shifts, in this agri-conservation policy. The methodological attributes of similar evaluations need to be continually assessed, in order that their effects may be explicitly recognized and noted, with a view to working towards a consistent, coherent, methodological framework within which thorough and meaningful individual evaluations may be realized.

Acknowledgements

Acknowledgements are due to T.J. Perkins, N.B. Lilwall, J. Traill Thomson and I. White. The socioeconomic evaluation of Breadalbane ESA (1987–1990) was funded by the Ministry of Agriculture Fisheries and Food. Research into the uptake of the ESA (1990–1992) was funded jointly by the Scottish Office Agriculture and Fisheries Department and the Scottish Agricultural College. Research into a methodological critique of ESA-type evaluations (1992–1994) is funded jointly by the Newby Trust Ltd and the Devonport Charitable Trust.

Appendix 6.1. April 1992 Changes to Breadalbane ESA.

Payment Levels Increased
Flat rate: from a maximum of £1500 per annum to a maximum of £2000 per annum.
Itemized: these have been increased in recognition of the increased actual cost of the works, from £3500 to £4000 per annum (maximum).

Ponds and Styles
These are now funded, and represent an expansion of Tier IIb.

Biennial Review of Payments
The payments are reviewed every two years, with possible revision of the amounts paid. However, the levels may increase or decrease, that is, they are not automatically index-linked.

Enlarged Geographical Area
The original ESA has been enlarged to the north, to include the Loch Tummel area, and to the east to cover the eastern and northern extent of Strathardle.

Time-Scale Increased
It is now possible to join Breadalbane ESA Scheme for a period of ten years, with an opt-out clause after five years. The original arrangement was for five years only.

Changes in Application to Join the Scheme
In the original Breadalbane ESA, each applicant was required to draw up a Farm Conservation Plan, and an outline of expected conservation activities over the five-year period. The revisions means that the applicant now has to draw up two Farm Plans, one descriptive and the other showing the proposed conservation activities for the first five years; and a separate 'Schedule of payments' expected from SOAFD.

For details, see SOAFD (1992).

7

ESAs in the Context of a 'Culturally Sensitive Area'
The Case of the Cambrian Mountains

Garth Hughes

Introduction

The Cambrian Mountains ESA (Mynyddoedd Y Canolbarth) is a scenically attractive, but relatively poor, livestock farming area, of hills and uplands in the central part of Wales, with overall dimensions of about 20 miles east to west and 40 miles north to south, rising to 2467 feet at Pen Pumlumon. The upper Wye and Severn river valleys dissect the area from the east, the Rheidol and Ystwyth rivers from the west, and the Teifi and Cothi from the south.

The Cambrian Mountains was the first ESA in Wales and was designated because its valuable landscape and wildlife habitats were considered to be threatened by agricultural intensification and further afforestation. Geographically, it was the largest of the first generation of 19 ESAs introduced to the UK between 1986 and 1988, and was designated in two stages. The first designation order was made by the Secretary of State for Wales (1986) (Statutory Instrument No. 2257) and designated the northern and southern parts of the Cambrian Mountains as an ESA (the 'Original Area'). This came into force on St David's Day, 1 March 1987. A second order followed in 1987 (SI No. 2026; Secretary of State for Wales, 1987a), which designated the central part of the Cambrians as an ESA (the 'Extended Area'), and this became operational on 1 January 1988. A second ESA also became operational in Wales on this date in the Lleyn Peninsula (Penrhyn Llyn) (SI No. 2027; Secretary of State for Wales, 1987b). These five-year schemes are now coming to an end, but are being renewed, and new ESAs are also being introduced in other parts of Wales as elsewhere in the UK.

Land Use and Agriculture

Almost 80% of the Cambrian Mountains is in agricultural use, the rest being afforested with coniferous plantations, although there are some small patches of natural deciduous woodland. About two-thirds of the agricultural area is semi-natural rough grazings and one-third is improved land.

Poor climate, thin soils and steep slopes have traditionally limited agriculture in the area to the production of store sheep and cattle for fattening on lowland farms, although many farmers within the area now finish their own animals. The whole of the Cambrian Mountains ESA has been classified as being within the 'Severely Disadvantaged' part of the EC's Less Favoured Areas (LFAs). This policy provides financial support for farming in difficult farming areas, where it is considered that the survival of agriculture is important, in order to support the local economy and for the conservation of the countryside.

There are over 900 farm holdings with some land within the boundary of the Cambrians ESA, with an average size of about 126 hectares or 16 BSUs – a financial measure of farm size based on the number of standard gross margins imputed on the basis of a farm's stocking and cropping. Their size distribution is, however, severely skewed: 63% of farms are below the average size of 16 BSUs; 30% are between 16 and 40 BSUs; and 7% are of 40 BSUs and over.

In recent years, there have been something like a million sheep and 30,000 cattle recorded on these holdings at the June Agricultural Census. During the 1980s, as in the rest of Wales, there was a significant expansion in sheep numbers, largely stimulated by the introduction of an EC common policy for sheepmeat. However, in contrast, the number of cattle remained fairly stable throughout the decade.

The dominant form of agricultural land tenure within the ESA is owner-occupancy, although, as in the rest of the UK, the land tenure picture is complicated by the existence of farms of mixed tenure, that is partly owned and partly rented. Thus, 66% of farms in the Cambrian Mountains are owner-occupied; 14% are tenanted; 15% are mostly owner-occupied; and on 6% of the farms most of the land is rented.

Conservation Policy

The primary objective of designation has been the conservation of the substantial area of semi-natural rough grazing that still remains within the region, but which has been diminishing as a result of the intensification of agriculture and afforestation. The protection of semi-natural rough grazing is environmentally important because it is an integral part of the scenic attractiveness of the region, and also because of its botanical and wildlife

Box 7.1. Cambrian Mountains ESA: definitions and generalized prescriptions*.

Semi-natural rough grazing (SNRG)	Hay meadows	Broadleaved woodland
'Land where the vegetation consists predominantly of Ben (*Agrostis*), Fescue (*Festuca*), Bracken (*Pteridium aquilinum*), Purple moor grass (*Molinia caerulea*), Mat grass (*Nardus stricta*), Heather (*Calluna vulgaris* or *Erica*), Bilberry (*Vaccinium*), Cotton grass (*Eriophorum*), or Deer grass (*Tricophorum*).'	'A meadow cut in the traditional manner, the vegetation of which includes a mixture of native grasses, sedges and wild flowers.'	'Land used for broadleaved woodland where that use is ancillary to the farming of land for agricultural purposes.'
£30 per hectare	£30 per hectare	£45 per hectare
No ploughing, levelling, reseeding or cultivating	As SNRG	Retain broadleaved woodland
Graze so as not to cause overgrazing	Do not cut before 15 July and exclude stock for at least seven weeks before cutting	Exclude stock
No lime, slag or inorganic fertilizer	Maximum rate of inorganic fertilizer: one 50-kg bag/acre/year of 20:10:10	Obtain written advice on management of woodland (from ADAS, Coed Cymru, etc.)
Do not install or modify any drainage systems	As SNRG	
Do not use pesticides	As SNRG	
Herbicides may only be used to control bracken and seven other specified weeds (specified method of application)	As SNRG	
Burning of heather, grass and scrub must be in accordance with an agreed programme		
Do not construct new hedges, walls or fences (without PO's agreement) nor remove existing ones	As SNRG	
Obtain written advice on siting, design and materials for buildings, roads or other engineering operations not requiring planning permission.	As SNRG	
Conserve and maintain lakes, ponds and streams		

Reprinted by courtesy of the Welsh Office Agriculture Department.
*First generation scheme, based on Statutory Instrument 1986, No. 2257 (Secretary of State for Wales, 1986).

value. The semi-natural rough grazing generally occupies the higher and steeper land within the region, sometimes in large and extensive areas, although at lower altitudes it often forms a mosaic pattern of small areas interspersed with improved land. The contrast between the semi-natural rough grazing and the improved pastures on the flatter slopes and in the valley bottoms is often a striking and attractive one.

The vegetation of the semi-natural rough grazing is typical of thin, acid, upland soils and provides a habitat for a distinctive, interesting and rare range of birds and animals. Perhaps most well known in this respect is the last remaining significant red kite population of the UK which, although small, ranges extensively over the region. The protection of broadleaved woodlands, which now occupy only 4% of the area, is important not only in this context, but also because they represent an extremely attractive element in the landscape: contrasting the bleak but attractive vistas of the semi-natural rough grazing, and the uninteresting, monotonous blocks of coniferous plantations that have, increasingly, become a feature of the region's landscape over the last 50 or so years.

Other conservation objectives of the Cambrian Mountains scheme are the rare species-rich hay meadows, the protection of lakes, ponds and streams, and archaeological sites.

Protection has been provided through the standard ESA model: voluntary five-year farm management agreements which prescribe farming practices. In return, farmers receive annual payments per hectare, fixed by the Agricultural Departments for each conservation objective within each ESA. In the first-generation scheme, the basic payment in the Cambrian Mountains had been £30 per hectare per annum, increased to £45 per hectare per annum in the case of broadleaved woodlands.

Management prescriptions in the Cambrian Mountains have been totally proscriptive rather than creative. In other words, very much the 'Thou shalt not ...' variety, i.e. stocking limitations and controls on the use of fertilizers and chemicals (see Box 7.1). This is in contrast to some of the ESAs in the rest of the UK, and particularly in Scotland, where more emphasis has been given to payments for undertaking conservation work. The Cambrian Mountains ESA is also distinctive in that management agreements are taken out on eligible land rather than the whole farm. This contrasts with the Lleyn Peninsula and some of the other ESAs in 'upland UK' where management agreements are for the whole farm.

Land Enrolment

The Cambrian Mountains ESA has only been moderately successful in enrolling eligible land in comparison with many of the other ESA schemes, where enrolments of 75% and over of eligible land have occurred.

The main recruitment problem in the Cambrians has been in enrolling common lands and broadleaved woodlands. It has been difficult to obtain agreements on semi-natural rough grazing when a number of farmers exercise common grazing rights. Consequently, the area of commons enrolled within the scheme has been disappointing. Thus, the proportion of total semi-natural rough grazing within the Cambrian Mountains ESA included within the scheme is only 57% (43,875 hectares, December 1992), if common lands are included when estimating the scheme's coverage, but almost 75% if they are excluded.

The uptake of broadleaved woodlands has also been very disappointing because of the importance of this type of woodland to the landscape and wildlife of the area (just 17% of eligible woodlands or 555 hectares); although for hay meadows it has been very good (72% or 543 hectares). Clearly, the scheme has underestimated the importance of these woodlands to farmers as a shelter for livestock and grazing, and the expense of providing stockproof fencing for woodlands included in the scheme. There are also 32 hectares of archaeological sites, and 22 hectares of lakes, ponds and streams for which management agreements have been signed. (All areas relate to December 1992 and including some land in expired agreements.)

The number of farmers participating in the schemes in July 1992 was 363 (38%) out of about 950 who have some land within the ESA boundary, of whom about 600 are eligible for the scheme (60% participation). However, a fairly generous interpretation of eligibility has been adopted and this figure should therefore be treated as a maximum. It is likely that some of the estimated 600 so-called eligible farms will have, either, only small areas of semi-natural rough grazing, or small areas interspersed with improved land, which makes membership of the scheme both difficult and unrewarding.

The average area of land under management agreement per participant was about 120 hectares, which was 61% of the average size of participants' farms. As might be expected in a scheme whose principal focus is the inclusion of semi-natural rough grazing, the largest farms account for most of the land under management agreement. Thus, farms of 16 to 40 BSUs provide half the land under management agreement and farms of 40 BSUs and over account for a further one-third. Farms of 16 BSUs or less provide only about 17% of the land under management agreement and are under-represented in the scheme.

Socioeconomic Evaluation

An evaluation of the socioeconomic effects of ESA designation is of particular interest:

- Where agricultural policy still contains a strong element of income support, as it does in the LFAs: the Cambrians is wholly within the severely disadvantaged part of the LFAs.

- Where agriculture is important to the local economy. It is estimated that at least 20% of employment in mid-Wales, in terms of full-time job equivalents, is accounted for either directly or indirectly by agriculture (Bateman *et al.*, 1991).
- Where there are policies already in place to support rural incomes and employment. The Cambrian Mountains are almost entirely within the area of the Development Board for Rural Wales, and the area is in one of the four objective 5b regions in the UK which qualify for special EC financial support.
- In Culturally Sensitive Areas: in Wales there is a further reason for attaching importance to an investigation of these socioeconomic effects, namely language and culture. There has been much discussion, mostly inconclusive, as to whether there is such a thing as rural culture, and, if there is, whether it can and should be preserved. These things are hard to quantify. But in Wales the Welsh language constitutes a cultural value that clearly does exist, that can (with problems) be measured, and that is recognized as being worth preserving. In the Cambrian Mountains, the language has been in decline. Nevertheless, a significant proportion of the population are still Welsh speaking, particularly in agriculture, and it is government policy to support the survival of the language.

Most of the socioeconomic evaluations of the first generation of ESAs have examined the effects of ESAs on such elements as farming incomes, employment and the rest of the economy. Also investigated have been the budgetary implications of the ESA schemes, farmers' reasons for joining or not participating in the schemes, as well as farmers' views on their operations and administration. All these issues have been examined in the case of the Cambrians (Hughes and Jones,1991; Hughes and Sherwood, 1993) but in this chapter the emphasis will be on discussing the effects on farm income, employment and the local economy.

To undertake a socioeconomic assessment of ESA designation it is necessary to determine what might have happened without ESA designation (a policy on/off comparison). The methods used to make these assessments in the Welsh studies were farm surveys of participants and non-participants, and a study of farming trends. Broadly similar objectives and approaches were adopted in other studies, although in some cases control samples of farmers from outside the ESAs were used. However, a satisfactory control sample was not readily available in the case of the Cambrians.

A sample of 139 farmers with management agreements in the Cambrian Mountains were visited in 1990 and 1991. This sample, stratified by farm size, represented nearly one-half of the total participants in the scheme at the time the sample was taken. Some farmers were also re-surveyed at a later date, by post and by telephone; and a sample of farmers within the Cambrian Mountains who had not taken out management agreements were also visited.

In general, the farmers involved in these surveys were extremely cooperative and non-response was not a problem.

The Effects on Farming

An assessment of the effect of management prescriptions on farming activities was used as a basis for evaluating some of the socioeconomic effects of ESA designation in the Cambrians, in particular on farm incomes and employment. The farm surveys provided much of the information required for this analysis.

As might have been expected, the effects varied between farms but, in general, the majority of farmers have not had to significantly change their farming activities as a result of joining the scheme. In some cases this was because farmers were already farming within the prescribed limits, but also farmers were often able to compensate for restrictions placed on their farming of management-agreement land by intensifying on the rest of their farms. This was especially the case when reduced stocking densities were necessary to comply with management prescriptions.

Stocking Densities

The establishment of maximum livestock stocking densities for the semi-natural rough grazing, 'compatible with the maintenance of the existing vegetation types', has been a key feature of the Cambrian Mountains scheme. This required the prescription of individual farm stocking rates because of the variation in vegetation types that exists between farms in the Cambrians, whereas in some other ESAs, for example in the Lleyn, uniform stocking rate prescriptions have been considered appropriate.

Our investigation suggested that just over 40% of farmers in the Cambrian Mountains with semi-natural rough grazing management agreements, representing two-thirds of semi-natural rough grazing under agreement, expected to reduce stocking densities on their semi-natural rough grazing as a result of joining the scheme. However, most of these expected to be able to compensate by intensifying grazing and/or renting additional land. Thus, only 17% of farmers with semi-natural rough grazing agreements had to reduce their overall farm stocking as a result of joining the scheme.

It was apparent that the smaller farms have had to make less adjustment to the scheme than the larger ones. This suggests that the smaller farms have only been willing to undertake management agreements if their management prescriptions mean no reduction in their stock numbers. This may be because there is less scope on small farms to compensate for reduced stock numbers on management-agreement land by increasing grazing elsewhere, and may help to explain why smaller farms are under-represented in the scheme.

There was also some evidence that the impact of the scheme has grown over time, not simply through greater participation, but also because later entrants appear to have had to make larger adjustments in their stocking than those who joined in the first two years of the scheme.

There are also restrictions on the grazing of broadleaved woodlands and hay meadows included in a management agreement in the Cambrian Mountains ESA, but these appear to have had a negligible impact.

Fertilizer Use

The conservation of semi-natural rough grazing and traditional hay meadows requires controls on the use of lime, slag and inorganic fertilizer since the plant species that make up these vegetation types are extremely vulnerable to the use of even small quantities of these substances. Consequently, their use on semi-natural rough grazing has been proscribed and restricted in the case of hay meadows. Thus, hay meadow management prescriptions prohibit the use of lime and require that 'the farmer shall not increase existing application rates of inorganic fertilizer and shall not in any year apply more than 25 kg of nitrogen, 12.5 kg of phosphate and 12.5 kg of potash per hectare to such meadows'.

However, in many cases, farmers did not have to make significant changes in their use of these items, either because fertilizers were not generally used, or because applications were within the prescribed rates. Thus, only 15% of farmers interviewed were in the custom of applying fertilizer or lime to their semi-natural rough grazing before they joined the scheme, and only 30% of farmers that had hay meadows under agreement had to make reductions in their fertilizer use. Nevertheless, the environmental significance of these controls should not be underestimated because of the low tolerance levels of the vegetation types to the use of chemicals. This has been recently demonstrated in a study undertaken by the Institute of Grassland and Environmental Research. 'Our aim was to discover whether there is a safe low-level fertilizer than can enhance agricultural production without harming wild flowers. But work at the 20-hectare test site on Tadham Moor near Glastonbury revealed that there is no such level. Even small amounts of fertilizer, such as 25 kg of nitrogen per hectare, result in the loss of species' (Kirkham et al., 1992).

Herbicides and Pesticides

The use of pesticides is prohibited on land included in a management agreement and only selective herbicides can be used. Very few of the farmers interviewed in the Cambrian Mountains said that they spent any money on these substances before they joined the scheme, and that when they did, the amounts were quite small. Thus, the effect of this prescription is essentially one of future prevention rather than changing current practices.

Farming Income

To estimate the farming income effects of the ESA it was necessary to reduce the gross value of ESA payments to farmers for any loss of income from farming as a result of joining the scheme, in order to determine the net income effect. To make these adjustments the impact of the scheme on farming activities was assessed, using the evidence of the farm surveys and an examination of livestock farming trends prior to designation (a policy on/off comparison).

The estimated gross annual value of ESA payments on eligible land in the Cambrians in January 1992 was £1.22 million (eligible land enrolled multiplied by payment per hectare). The net value of this to farmers was an estimated £700,000 or 60% of the gross annual value of ESA payments (i.e. about £18 per hectare compared with a gross payment of £30 per hectare, or approximately £2200 per participant). This could be described as a fairly strong positive net income effect. Such effects have also been characteristic of some of the other ESAs, for example Breadalbane (Lilwall *et al.*, 1991); Lleyn Peninsula (Hughes and Sherwood, 1993); North Peak (MAFF, 1993e); Shropshire Borders (MAFF, 1993d); and West Penwith (MAFF, 1992e).

How important are these income effects? This can be considered from the point of view of the farming community and the local economy. Our estimates suggest that the average net annual value of ESA payments per participant of £2200 was equivalent to about 15% of the annual net farm income that could be obtained from hill farming in the Cambrians in recent years (1987 to 1991). However, such is the annual variation in hill farming incomes, that the annual value of ESA payments could be as high as 30%, or as low as 10% of net farming income.

However, not all farmers within the Cambrians ESA are able, or willing, to participate in the scheme. Therefore, an estimate has been made of the impact of ESA payments on total farming income in the Cambrian Mountains ESA, by multiplying net farm income per BSU on hill farms in the Farm Business Survey of Wales, by the total number of BSUs attributable to farms with some land in the designated area of the ESA, and then taking the estimated net value of ESA payments as a percentage of this total. This estimate was made for a number of recent years to allow for the large annual variations that exist in farming incomes in the area. These estimates suggest that ESA payments contribute between 5 and 14% of aggregate net farming income, depending upon year.

The significance of these farm income effects, however, lies not just in their absolute and relative size with respect to farming incomes, but in the security of income that they provide, particularly in hill farming areas where fluctuations in annual income can be very large.

It should also be noted that the distribution of payments is skewed in favour of the larger farms. The medium size and large farms represent about 55% of participants in the scheme, but receive over 80% of the value of ESA payments. This is not simply a reflection of the fact that payments are on a per hectare basis, but also the fact that small farms are under-represented in this scheme.

Farm Employment

Farm employment effects will depend upon the effects that ESA schemes have on farming activities and the extent to which the schemes involve conservation work. Since the effects of the Cambrians ESA on farming activities were often relatively small, and because the scheme was essentially proscriptive, it is unsurprising that the farm surveys showed that ESA designation has not changed the quantity of labour employed on farms participating in the scheme, and that farmers did not expect there to be any change during the life of the scheme. A similar result was also obtained in our study of the Lleyn Peninsula ESA where management agreements were also proscriptive. In contrast, in ESAs where there are payments for conservation work there have been significant increases in employment, for example Breadalbane (see Chapter 6) and the North Peak (see Chapter 5).

In the long run, it is possible that ESA designation may add to the Cambrian Mountains' tourist potential and that farm tourism may benefit correspondingly. However, at the present time, this is impossible to assess.

Impact on the Rest of the Economy

This will depend upon a number of factors:

1. Agriculture's size relative to the rest of the economy. As already mentioned, this can be large in areas like mid-Wales.

2. The impact of the ESA's prescriptions on the output and input of traditional agriculture. These are usually negative, their magnitude depending upon participation in the scheme and its restrictiveness. In practice, in the Welsh ESAs, as in some of the other first generation of ESAs in the hills and uplands, the changes required have not been large.

3. The conservation work stimulated by the scheme. This is generally positive but absent from the Welsh schemes.

4. The net effect of the scheme on the incomes of farm families. This has been strongly positive in the Cambrian Mountains, as it has been in many of the other ESAs.

5. The value of the multipliers. These can be significant for traditional agriculture; see, for example, Midmore's work (1991) on input–output analysis and the derivation of income and employment multipliers for the various sectors of agriculture in Wales. However, their values may differ for conservation schemes and, of course, will depend upon how the local economy is defined. Therefore, caution should be exercised in using multipliers derived for traditional agriculture to estimate the local economy impacts of ESA schemes.

In the Cambrians, there have been some effects through (2) above, but the main effects have been through (4). In the Lleyn, virtually all the multiplier effects have been through (4). Neither of the Welsh schemes has had any effects through (3) because of the way the schemes have been designed.

In the Cambrians, the net income effect could be increased by about 20% and in the Lleyn by about 30% if the multiplier effects are taken into account, but these would be diffused throughout Wales and only a proportion would actually be felt within the local economies of the ESAs.

Thus, conservation policies can have both positive and negative effects depending upon their form. Although in the Welsh ESAs, the wider effects have on balance been positive, it is apparent that the design of the schemes themselves is important in determining the local effects on income and employment. This raises the question of whether conservation policies in areas like the Welsh ESAs should be designed to take greater account of income and employment effects, or whether conservation policy should be kept separate from policies to support the local economy. In this respect, an ESA scheme which gave greater emphasis to conservation work by farmers than the existing schemes would be beneficial, because it would generate employment and provide smaller farmers with an opportunity to obtain more support than schemes in which payments are geared to land area.

Welsh Language and Culture

Agriculture is an important source of employment for the Welsh-speaking population of Wales. This was confirmed by an analysis of the 1981 Census of Population (Jones, 1989). This showed statistically significant differences between the employment structure of the Welsh-speaking and non-Welsh-speaking populations and that the correlation was particularly strong in the case of agriculture.

This situation partly reflects the fact that the Welsh language has been in decline and that the agricultural workforce is older than the rest of the workforce. However, to quote Jones:

> the physical stability and inheritance pattern of the agricultural industry may also be an important contributory factor in the language's continued predominance within this sector.

During this century, as children have inherited farms from their parents, so they have become tied to particular areas. Farmers seldom sell their inherited farms to purchase farms elsewhere, unless by so doing a considerable monetary gain is possible, which is very seldom likely. A sentimental attachment to the inherited land and an inherent knowledge of this land's production capabilities combined to discourage inter-farm mobility. Unforced movement out of the industry is also rare. Farming skills are transferable only to a few industries and, in addition, many farmers have limited formal educational qualifications, having left school at the earliest possible opportunity in order to work on the farm. (Moreover, school examinations often coincide with hay or silage-making and it takes a very dedicated student to be able to forego such distractions.)

Workers in other industries encounter far fewer obstacles to mobility. Few people inherit family businesses which constrain them to a particular profession or area and few people are constrained by their career to remain in a particular area. Indeed, it is often the case that career opportunities may be enhanced by moving away from rural Wales.

The greater degree of mobility in other industries has resulted in the greater dilution of the Welsh language within them. Moreover, entry into farming requires considerable capital outlay and, therefore, other industries in rural Wales are far more likely to absorb inward migrants than agriculture, thus accentuating dilution of the language within their ranks. Recent trends, however, may contradict this. People selling houses in the south-east of England may have sufficient capital funding to purchase sizeable farms in rural Wales.

In both the Welsh ESAs, the Welsh language is widely spoken, especially in the Lleyn and the western and southern parts of the Cambrian Mountains, but not so much in its eastern area. Thus, for example, in the county district of Dwyfor, which covers the Lleyn Peninsula, 72% of the population were recorded as Welsh speaking at the 1991 Census of Population, which was substantially lower than the 82% recorded at the 1981 census. In Ceredigion, which includes much of the western part of the Cambrian Mountains, the percentage of Welsh speakers in 1991 was 56% (62% in 1981), but in Montgomery and Radnor, which include the eastern parts of the Cambrians ESA, it was respectively only 21 and 5% in 1991 (24 and 5% in 1981). Of the 139 farmers interviewed in the Cambrian Mountains, who had signed management agreements, 58% were Welsh speaking. In the Lleyn ESA, 90% of the 80 participants in the scheme interviewed were Welsh speaking.

For many years there was little public or official concern over the decline of the Welsh language; indeed, at times its use was actively discouraged. However, since the 1950s the climate of opinion has changed from one largely of indifference, and even antipathy, to one of concern and active support; and it is now official government policy in the UK to promote the survival of the Welsh language. Consequently, the Welsh ESAs are in what might be described as 'Culturally Sensitive Areas'. This makes ESA policy additionally interesting in the Welsh context, insofar as ESA payments, by helping farming to survive at a time when support for the traditional agriculture is being reduced, may, indirectly, have cultural benefits by helping to maintain the agricultural population.

Estimates of the farming income effects of the Cambrian Mountains ESA showed that, for those participating in the scheme, ESA payments could make a useful contribution (as much as 30% in a bad farming year). In the Lleyn Peninsula, they could also make a useful contribution in relative terms, although less so in absolute terms because of the small size of farm in this area. However, whether the participating farms are the most vulnerable, and whether the level of ESA payments made will be critical to their survival, is difficult to determine without further investigation. Nevertheless, in a period of declining farm incomes, ESA payments of this size can clearly help, and it has been noticeable that with the increasing uncertainty generated by CAP reform about the future of traditional agriculture, the Welsh ESA schemes have become more attractive to farmers. If incomes from traditional agriculture continue to decline and ESA policy expands, the cultural value of the policy will be enhanced.

The nature of the ESA schemes is important in this respect. Schemes which are geared to providing payments for farmers to undertake conservation work will be of more value in generating employment, and thus in helping to maintain a Welsh-speaking population, than those so far employed, in which the emphasis is on controlling farmers' activities rather than encouraging conservation work. A scheme which gives more emphasis to farm conservation work would also allow greater participation by small farmers, whereas the current schemes favour the larger farms in the distribution of payments, since they are geared to land area. It is interesting to note that small farms have been under-represented in both the Welsh schemes.

Summary and Conclusions

The Cambrian Mountains scheme has been fairly successful in enrolling semi-natural rough grazing when only one grazier has been concerned, and recruitment has compared favourably in this respect with other ESAs. However, the recruitment of common lands, which occupy significant areas of semi-natural rough grazing, has not been very successful because of the problems of obtaining agreements when a number of graziers are involved. This has detracted from the overall success of the scheme. The uptake of broadleaved woodlands has also proved disappointing and it is now clear that the scheme underestimated the costs to farmers of signing agreements on these woodlands.

As might have been expected, the farming effects of management prescriptions varied between farms but, in general, the majority of farmers have not had to significantly change their farming activities as a result of joining the scheme. This result is not particularly surprising, firstly, because the emphasis of the scheme has largely been on maintaining the status quo and many farmers were already farming within the prescribed limits. Secondly, in the Cambrians, management agreements were invariably part-farm, rather than whole-farm agreements, because the scheme only allowed agreements to be signed on land of a particular vegetation type. Thus, farmers were often able to compensate for restrictions placed on their farming of management agreement land by intensifying on the rest of their farms. This was especially so when reduced stocking densities were necessary to comply with management prescriptions. Thirdly, in hill areas, farmers do not use very much fertilizer and other chemicals on their rough grazings and so the changes required by the schemes in the use of these inputs were predictably small. Nevertheless, even small changes in the use of chemicals can be significant environmentally because of the low tolerance of the vegetation types and because of their cumulative effects.

In the Cambrians, the ESA scheme has had fairly strong positive income effects on participants, both in absolute and relative terms (60% of the annual gross value of ESA payments, or on average £2200 per farmer). This was equivalent to between 10 and 30% of average net farm income on participating farms. Strong income effects have been characteristic of many of the first-generation ESAs, and this is inevitable when management agreements are rewarded by a uniform payment per hectare, and the income foregone per hectare varies between participants in the scheme. If farmers are primarily motivated to join ESA schemes for financial reasons – and the evidence from the Welsh studies suggests that this is the case – then, for farmers at the margin of entry, the rate of ESA payments can be considered as being equal to the income foregone as a result of participation in the scheme. In these circumstances, intra-marginal farmers will receive payments in excess of the income they forego by joining the scheme.

However, not all farmers in the Cambrians have the opportunity to join (unlike some schemes, for example, the Lleyn Peninsula). This is because qualification depended upon a farm possessing particular vegetation types, and many farmers within this ESA either did not have eligible land or the amounts were small. Consequently, only some 60% of farmers with some land within the ESA boundary were eligible to join, of which 60% have done so. Inevitably, in a scheme in which payments are geared to land area, it has been the largest farmers who have benefited the most. It also means that, in absolute terms, the financial incentive for small farmers to join the scheme is very much weaker, and this may explain their under-representation in the scheme.

The potential income benefits that ESAs can provide are likely to become more important in the future. Reform of the Common Agricultural Policy (CAP) will mean a decline in price support for traditional agriculture. At the moment, the EC appears to have accepted that this will need to be compensated for. In the longer term, however, the position is uncertain, and farm families will probably need to diversify their sources of income. Whilst farmers in Wales may be disadvantaged in many aspects of traditional agriculture, it is the case that they do have a comparative advantage in the production of environmental conservation: they own and farm some of our most environmentally valuable parts of the countryside.

ESAs represent one potential source of diversification and the opportunity to benefit from this and other environmental policies is growing. On 22 June 1992 the Secretary of State for Wales announced 'his intention that new ESAs be designated in Anglesey and Radnor by the end of 1992, and in Preseli and the Clwydian Range by June 1993.' Thus, another 18% of the agricultural area of Wales will be within an ESA, to add to the 10% currently within the Cambrian Mountains and the Lleyn Peninsula ESAs. The designation of the Brecon Beacons National Park and the northern part of the Snowdonia National Park would also add a further 10% to the ESA total. Thus, the designation of four, and possibly six, new ESAs in Wales, plus the renewal of the existing schemes, means that in the foreseeable future almost 40% of the agricultural area of Wales will be within an ESA, and nearly one-third of farmers will have the opportunity to join a scheme.

Nevertheless, although growing, the money available through ESA schemes is still small compared with other expenditures under the CAP. The Cambrian Mountains and the Lleyn ESAs have provided about £8 million gross for farmers during the life of the first-generation schemes, i.e. just under £1 million per annum. This compares with annual sheep subsidies to farmers in these ESAs of about £15 million per annum (1991 rates). If all six proposed ESA schemes in Wales were to be implemented, then, gross ESA payments could total about £155 million (for a ten-year scheme and a 70% take up). This would be equivalent to about £10 million per annum over a 15-year period (assuming 70% of farmers joined in the first five years of the scheme). In comparison, total sheep subsidies in Wales, at 1991 rates, are of the order of £160 million per annum.

Although environmental conservation payments will be a new and welcome additional source of income for many more farmers in Wales, they probably will not be sufficient, or grow quickly enough, to compensate for the decline in support for traditional agriculture. Farm families will need to be alert to opportunities for additional income sources. Pluriactivity amongst farm families will need to grow, and policies designed which will help farm households to remain viable by diversifying their sources of income, not only on the farm, but by the provision of full- and part-time work within travel-to-work distance of their farms (D. Bateman *et al.*, 1993).

Conservation in agriculture is not just a matter of substituting one form of income for another. Conservation policies can have effects on the rural economy that are different from traditional agriculture. The effects will depend upon how policies are designed, and policy-makers will need to consider to what extent the local effects need to be taken into account. The case for considering the socioeconomic consequences of environmental conservation policies may be greater in areas like mid-Wales or the Lleyn Peninsula than in more prosperous farming regions, because of the particular problems and policies of these areas. In Wales, there is the additional policy dimension of language and culture.

One of the main conclusions from the Welsh ESA study, and it is also to some extent true of the other ESAs, is that in the Welsh ESAs there should be more emphasis on conservation work undertaken by farmers. There are three reasons why this is important.

1. Public perception and acceptability: there is a danger that these schemes lack credibility and will discredit conservation policy, in the same way that agricultural policy has suffered as a result of agricultural surpluses. There are two reasons for saying this. Firstly, paying farmers to reduce their intensity of production on conservation grounds does not accord with the polluter pays principle, which probably commands a wide measure of public support. Secondly, paying farmers who are largely unaffected by the scheme lacks credibility because it appears to be paying something for nothing. A number of farmers commented on this in our farm surveys both in the Cambrian Mountains and in the Lleyn Peninsula.

Public acceptability would be more likely in schemes in which payments were being made for conservation work. Such schemes would be more defensible when further funding is being sought, particularly when the existing schemes have largely been a net addition to government expenditure: (i) because the EC contribution is only about 7% when allowance is made for the UK contribution to the European Agricultural Guidance and Guarantee Fund (EAGGF = FEOGA) and the abatement of EC contributions to UK expenditure as a result of the Fontainebleau Agreement; and (ii) because of the small savings in production subsidies as a result of the schemes. Any idea that the ESAs would be largely self-financing has not proved to be the case.

2. Environmental conservation: ESAs which give greater emphasis to farm conservation work (including public access, although there may be a conflict here) would increase the conservation value of these schemes by adding to the capital stock of environmental goods, rather than maintain it at the level (non-optimal) at the time policy was introduced.

3. Socioeconomic benefits: more emphasis on conservation work by farmers would also generate employment and provide smaller farmers with an opportunity to obtain more support than under schemes in which payments are geared to land area. This would be important in areas like mid-Wales where policies of support for the local economy exist.

Are ESAs the right approach to policy? In schemes where a significant number of farmers do not participate there may be a problem. The non-participants may be the very ones that are wanted inside the scheme because they represent the greatest threat of intensification. Conversely, those already in the scheme may have represented a smaller threat. In this sense, an ESA scheme may be inefficient. Consequently, it could be argued that it is a costly approach to conservation policy. Should we therefore consider a greater use of other policies, for example cross-compliance (for example, in the LFAs on stocking rates), or even conservation auction markets? Furthermore, con-servation policies by their very nature need to be long term; but what happens in ten years' time – do we go on paying farmers for ever? If we are intent on a long-term policy then, perhaps, we should think of more radical and permanent solutions to conservation, like land purchase (or the purchase of specified development rights). Management agreements provide only tempo-rary relief to the 'problem' – at the end of the agreement the problem and the expense still remain.

There is also the question of whether a rationalization of conservation policy is now desirable in view of the proliferation of conservation schemes that has taken place in recent years. For example, within Wales, the Welsh Office Agriculture Department (WOAD), in addition to administering the ESAs, the Farm and Conservation Grant Scheme and the Farm Woodland Premium Scheme, is developing a Moorland Extensification Scheme, an Organic Farming Scheme, and a 20-Year Set-Aside Scheme (to be known as the Habitat Improvement Scheme). The Countryside Council for Wales also has conservation management schemes for agriculture which include: Tir Cymen (a farmland stewardship scheme operated by the Countryside Council for Wales); Sites of Special Scientific Interest; National Nature Reserves; a Hedgerow Renovation Scheme; and various grants for the conservation of the landscape and the countryside. Money is also available for conservation from the National Parks Authorities, the Forestry Commission and Local Author-ities. Finally, EC regulations on the Less Favoured Areas – 75% of the area of Wales – allow the variation of LFA payments to farmers for reasons of environmental conservation. Rationalization would not only avoid confusing farmers but may be administratively more efficient and provide for better environmental conservation management of the countryside. Wales, where many governmental responsibilities have been devolved to the Welsh Office and other bodies, could be a suitable region for experimenting with a more integrated approach to policy.

Finally, it should be pointed out that new changes in the Cambrian Mountains ESA scheme (Original Area) were announced by The Secretary of

State for Wales on 9 April 1992 and came into effect on 30 June. There were five main changes: (i) ten-year management agreements, with a break clause at five years; (ii) increased payments for broadleaved woodlands and hay meadows; (iii) additional Tier II top-up payments for heather and broadleaved woodlands, which require farmers to adopt additional prescriptions; (iv) farmers can adopt a 'conservation plan' under which they can receive up to 80% of the cost of undertaking various conservation work (for example, hedge and tree planting, creation of heather, florally rich hay meadows, ponds, etc.); and (v) lower stocking densities on semi-natural rough grazing (Secretary of State for Wales, 1992). The Cambrian Mountains (Extension Area) and the Lleyn Peninsula ESAs are also under review.

8

A BASELINE ASSESSMENT FOR A NEW ESA
The Case of the Mourne Mountains and Slieve Croob

Joan Moss

Introduction

The Mourne Mountains and Slieve Croob Environmentally Sensitive Area (ESA) Scheme (Mournes ESA), the first of its kind in Northern Ireland, came into operation on 1 May 1988, and the first management contracts were agreed in late 1988/89. The area encompasses the enclosed agricultural land in the foothills and lower slopes of the mountains – approximately 4% of the total land and freshwater area of Northern Ireland (see Fig. 8.1). The area enjoys a reputation for having one of the most beautiful and unique landscapes in Northern Ireland. It is this feature and its high wildlife value, which led to its designation.

A socioeconomic evaluation was commissioned by the Department of Agriculture for Northern Ireland (DANI) to investigate the impact of the Scheme in economic and financial terms at both farm and provincial levels. The evaluation was designed as a two-stage procedure to firstly establish the baseline data at the outset of the scheme and a follow-up study when the five-year management contracts were completed.

General Objectives of the Baseline Study

These were (i) to establish the social and economic data necessary for end-of-scheme evaluation; (ii) to identify social characteristics associated with participation in management agreements; and (iii) to investigate landholders' perceptions of and attitudes to the ESA Scheme and broader conservation issues at the commencement of the Scheme.

In this chapter the main findings of the Baseline Study (Moss and Chilton, 1992) are presented. There is a discussion of how the Scheme, with its

154 *J. Moss*

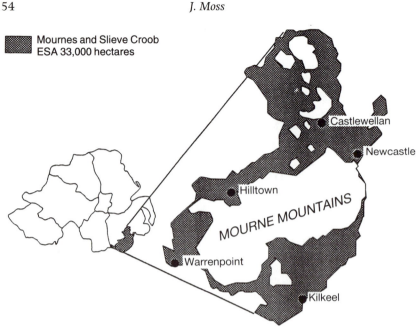

Fig. 8.1. Mourne Mountains and Slieve Croob ESA, Northern Ireland.

emphasis on landscape enhancement, relates to the environmental consequences of the farming activity in the area. The distinguishing characteristics of participants are identified and there is a discussion of how information
on participants/non-participants can assist in recruitment strategies for new
ESA schemes and the modification of existing schemes. The chapter concludes
with an analysis of the participant and non-participant landholders' awareness of the impact of their farming activity on the environment and their
attitudes to a range of environmental issues.

Geological Processes

Geological processes spanning millions of years have led to the development
of the Mourne countryside and were directly influential in determining land-
use potential and natural vegetative cover (DOENI, 1986). The actual massif
has a base of ancient slate and shale formed in the Silurian period (440
million years ago), but the granite core was not formed until the Tertiary era
(50 million years ago). A slow sinking of the surrounding shale led to the
development of the mountainous core.

Since their formation, periodic climate changes culminating in the last Ice
Age have also had a profound effect on topography. A diverse range of

landscapes now exist in the area from upland U-shaped valleys and corries with accompanying screes, to a shallow coastal plain and drumlins at the lower levels. There is a variety of distinct soil types ranging from the poor, infertile soil of the uplands (formed from the hard, acidic granite), through the deep acid soils of the coastal plains to the more fertile soils in the northern foothills.

Landscape

This combination of factors has therefore endowed the area with a rich diversity of landscape with greatly differing characteristics. For instance, the fertile agricultural land of the northern foothills of the Mournes soon gives way (in both westerly and northerly directions) to the rough mountainous areas of Hilltown and Slieve Croob. South of Hilltown, however, the topography softens and is characterized by drumlins and river valleys. Land in this area, generally speaking, is more agriculturally productive than the rougher uplands. The south-eastern coastal plain is quite densely populated and is noted for its many small farms and a 'traditional' farmscape of drystone walls, small fields and vernacular buildings.

Ecological Resources and Wildlife

The total area, including the mountainous core, has a wide diversity of natural environments and habitats. Within the main massif there are many corries and deep, glaciated valleys with poor peaty soils underlain by acidic granites and areas with widespread growth of heather and summit grass-lands. Numerous insects depend on the upland flora and a variety of small mammals (e.g. small populations of Irish hare, stoat, badger, etc.) and a range of birds (e.g. ravens, red grouse) can be found. Other habitats include valuable freshwater environments (streams, small lakes), coastal zones and a small amount of semi-natural woodland.

The ESA Scheme is concerned amongst other things with the issue of wildlife resources on agricultural holdings and the potential, if any, for nature conservation on them; consequently the complexities and requirements of resource management of habitats not on these holdings will not be discussed in any further detail. It is worth noting at this juncture, however, that agricultural practices occur outside the designated area (by some of the landholders participating in the Scheme as well as others) because of the option to utilize common grazing rights in the mountainous cores. This area has a high ecological and conservation value as cited previously, but is currently unprotected by ESA designation although it is, to a certain extent, affected by agricultural practices.

Agriculture in the area has been based on mixed systems of pastoral husbandry and rotational cropping which has led to a distinctively farmed landscape of stone wall and hedgerow field boundaries surrounding improved pasture, interspersed with unimproved areas (scattered woodland/scrub, bogs, unimproved pasture, etc.). The use of seaweed, and later of lime, allowed the area of intensive agriculture to be extended from the coastline into the lowlands and foothills. The Mournes countryside is therefore partially a human creation, but man has also had an impact on the natural ecosystems – either through destruction or simply by benign neglect. Tall, wide hedgerows, undrained wet hollows, unsprayed verges and old, unploughed meadows are particularly valuable ecological sites. Farmland is, by its nature, an unstable habitat and is less able to sustain a large number of plant or animal communities, so these semi-natural pockets assume a high degree of importance, providing a more stable environment to support wildlife (DOENI, 1986). Sympathetic management both to protect and improve these areas is therefore desirable in order to maintain or enhance the ecological diversity.

Farm Structure

The Northern Ireland Agricultural Census for 1988, the year the ESA Scheme was instigated, depicted the designated area as a region of 1833 family-owned holdings averaging 18 hectares in area and usually farmed by a single individual, whether full-time or part-time. Beef cattle and sheep farms dominated and accounted for 45% of holdings. Eight per cent of holdings were classified as dairy farms and 6% were crop and livestock farms. There was insufficient farming activity to generate a farm business size of at least 1 British Size Unit (BSU) on 13% of holdings and a further 25% of holdings had no recorded farming activity. In total less than 4% of holdings were 16 BSU or greater and 23% fell between 4 and 16 BSU.

Land Use and Livestock

In terms of land use/cover, grassland accounted for over 90% of the total utilized area of approximately 33,000 hectares. Spring barley, the main arable crop, covered half the arable area but amounted to only 3% of the total utilized area. Woodland cover was minimal. As already mentioned, beef cattle and sheep were the major livestock – cattle and calf numbers having increased slightly (by 5%) over the 1980s. Sheep and lamb numbers, however, have increased dramatically by approximately 56% over the same period, broadly reflecting the trend in sheep numbers throughout Northern Ireland. The increase in the sheep population had implications for land use and environmental management.

The ESA Scheme

Justification for ESA Designation

The quality of the landscape depends on the retention and maintenance of the traditional stone walls, hedges and other landscape features. Also it is very largely dependent on a reduction in the trend towards more intensive farming practices on the better quality land in the area, coupled with a reversion to the traditional and less intensive pattern of mixed farming.

Therefore, designation and appropriate incentive payments should assist and encourage landholders by way of maintenance programmes and approved production practices to preserve and enhance the many varied, and environmentally desirable, aspects of the area.

(DANI, 1987)

Figure 8.2 indicates how current agricultural practices impinge on the environmental components (e.g. landscape, wildlife and archaeology) of the Mournes and Slieve Croob area.

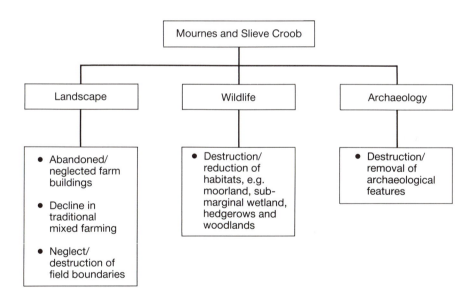

Fig. 8.2. The effect of agricultural practices on the area.

Management Objectives

These were: (i) to encourage farmers to protect and enhance any valuable landscape and wildlife features on their holdings; and (ii) to encourage the retention/adoption of extensive farming practices (DANI, 1987). Box 8.1 summarizes the Management Guidelines for the Scheme.

Components of the Scheme

An incentive of £30 per hectare per annum for the duration of the five-year management plan/contract was paid to help achieve these objectives. The ceiling of £1000 per farm fixed at the outset of the Scheme has since been lifted and no longer applies. The Scheme is voluntary and may be terminated at any time, subject to certain provisos (e.g. repayment of certain monies if necessary). The plan comprises various tasks such as wall maintenance, hedge/tree planting, painting/maintaining vernacular buildings and adherence to a General Schedule referring to a number of defined agricultural practices (see Appendix 8.1). The remedial effects of the Scheme are illustrated in Fig. 8.3.

Uptake – at August 1990

Eligible land comprising 13,925 hectares from the 1988, 1989 and 1990 contracts was under agreement (i.e. approximately 42% of eligible land) at the

Box 8.1. Management Guidelines – Mourne Mountains and Slieve Croob ESA.

- Maintain existing walls, farm buildings, gates, dykes, ponds, streams, rivers and associated vegetation, hedges and existing field patterns using traditional methods and materials.

- Maintain existing areas of heather and undertake regeneration measures.

- Obtain departmental approval before starting any reclamation work.

- Avoid the use of pesticides or herbicides on hedge bottoms; restrict the use of herbicides in pastures to weed wiper or spot treatments of named species.

- Obtain written advice on the management of woodland and existing hedgerow trees; obtain written advice on any tree planting proposals.

- Avoid release of pollutants.

- Avoid damaging any historic or landscape feature.

- Obtain written advice prior to the commencement of any construction, renewal or engineering work on buildings or roads.

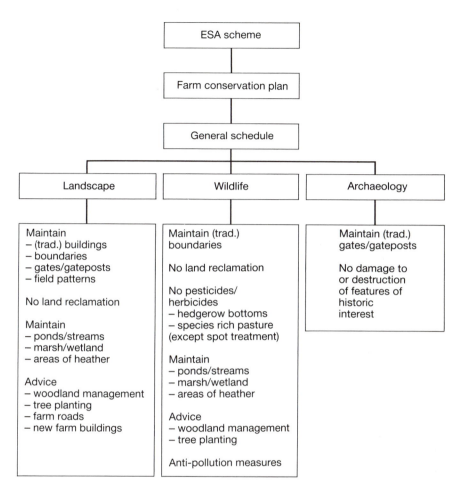

Fig. 8.3. Effects of the Scheme on the environmental components of the area.

time of the baseline study. Table 8.1 gives aggregate details of the 615 management agreements (i.e. 33% of landholders) standing on 31 August 1990. Recruitment continued within the Scheme. Over the five-year period the Scheme would have facilitated the maintenance of approximately 260,000 metres of walls and 80,000 metres of hedging each year along with the construction of a further 20,000 metres of new walling and the planting of 37,000 metres of new hedging. In addition, about 20,000 metres of other boundaries (e.g. ditches and banks) were under contract to be maintained annually. Approximately 18,000 new trees would be planted and 16 hectares of woodland would have active maintenance carried out on an annual basis.

Table 8.1. Percentage of landholders utilizing main agricultural management techniques and modern facilities (1980–90).

Management activity/facility	Participants (%)	Non-participants (%)
Reclamation (1980–90)	39	19
Reclaimable land on farm (1990)	40	50
Reclaim*		
Intend to	37	28
Do not intend to	63	72
All†	11	6
Reseeding (1980–90)	95	79
Crops 1980	51	55
Crops 1990	48	29
Hay (1990)	59	50
Silage (1990)	68	44
Both (1990)	36	19
Neither (1990)	9	24
Use of:		
Pesticides – 1980	47	39
– 1990	40	27
Herbicides – 1980	51	43
– 1990	55	44
Fertilizers – 1980	98	95
– 1990	98	95
Slurry/manure disposal (1990)		
Slurry only	32	24
Manure only	28	23
Both	22	14
Neither	18	39
Storage facilities for slurry on farm (1990)	58	39
Erected new buildings (1985–90)	42	18
Renovated buildings (1985–90)	29	24

Source: Survey of Landholders – Mourne Mountains and Slieve Croob ESA.

*Proportion of those with reclaimable land.
†Proportion of those who have reclaimed land in the past, have reclaimable land on their holding and intend reclaiming it in the future.

Other environmental improvements included the maintenance of 110 buildings on average each year together with the painting of 2300 sheds, outhouses, etc. Seventy-eight new gates would be erected and 780 gates painted. This was the situation in August 1990. The Scheme was still open so it was not possible to quantify the total expected environmental enhancement from the Scheme, given the continued uptake of new management contracts.

Baseline Study Methodology

The study was designed to establish the baseline information for measuring the impact of the ESA Scheme over its five-year duration and also to compare the attitudes/opinions of participating and non-participating farmers and their farm businesses. The components of the socioeconomic assessment are presented in Fig. 8.4. One hundred landholders participating in the Scheme (participants) were randomly selected from the list of ESA management agreements in early 1990. A further sample of 100 landholders not participating in the Scheme (non-participants) was also randomly selected from the Agricultural Census records for the designated area. The two samples of landholders were interviewed between March and October 1990.

The survey was structured to generate information on topics such as farm resources, agricultural systems and husbandry techniques, the farm family profile, off-farm income, on-farm employment and the degree of reliance on agricultural subsidies. Attitudes to and perceptions of the effect of the Scheme on the holding or (in the case of non-participants) the degree of awareness of the Scheme's existence and its effect were recorded. A general picture of farmers' attitudes to business, agricultural and environmental issues was also obtained. A number of statistical tests were then applied to the survey data. The first stage of the analyses led to the determination of descriptive statistics for the two samples. In the second stage chi-square tests and t-tests were used to identify any statistically significant differences between the two samples.

In the third stage of analysis a Euclidean dissimilarity coefficient matrix (measuring the level of similarity between different variables or cases: dissimilarity measures between entities decrease with greater similarity) was constructed for the pooled data for the two samples to enable application of hierarchical cluster analysis. The cluster analysis was applied to a number of key variables to allow examination of more than one variable at a time (i.e. rather than looking for statistically significant differences between isolated variables) to determine if these variables were in any way linked together, thus enabling an overall picture of the landholders, particularly those participating in the Scheme, to be obtained.

In order to take account of as many influences as possible affecting the landholders' likelihood of participating in the ESA Scheme, and to further aid in identifying any distinguishing characteristics, a number of other factors were examined. These included answers to open-ended questions pertaining

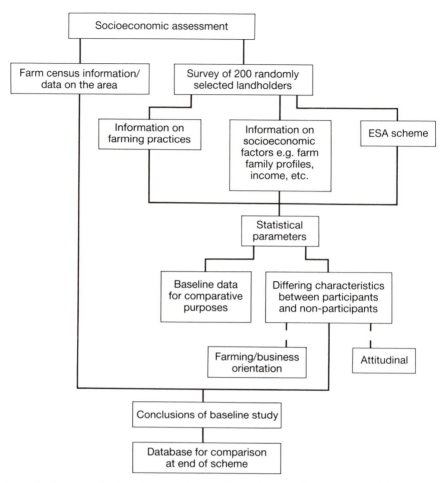

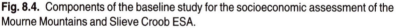

Fig. 8.4. Components of the baseline study for the socioeconomic assessment of the Mourne Mountains and Slieve Croob ESA.

to views/opinions and knowledge of issues and anecdotal evidence from the informal conversations accompanying each interview.

Baseline Survey Results

Farming Practices

Table 8.1 indicates the main land management techniques utilized in the ten years prior to the survey by the participants and non-participants. Thirty-nine

Table 8.2. Percentage of landholders engaged in ecological resource/landscape management activities (1980–90).

Management activity	Participants (%)	Non-participants (%)
Post and wire fencing		
Repair existing	87	82
Plan continue/start repair	87	82
Put up new fencing in past five years	79	58
Plan new fencing	56	37
Drystone walls		
New wall built	41	13
Plan build new walls	26	11
Removed	27	18
Currently maintained	77	64
None on farm to maintain	11	25
Stone clearance from fields	9	37
Hedges		
New hedges planted	13	2
Intention to plant	34	17
Currently maintained	70	75
None on farm to maintain	26	17
Tree planting		
Past	24	23
of which:		
– conifers	10	18
– broadleaves	8	1
– mixed	6	4
Intend to plant	57	30
Woodland management	23	33
Ponds		
On farm	7	7
Intend maintaining	5	7
Created	0	0
Intend create	4	4
Wetland		
On farm	29	35
Plan to maintain	23	24
Heather		
On farm	17	12
Management: – grazed	15	12
– other	2	0

Source: Survey of Landholders – Mourne Mountains and Slieve Croob ESA.

per cent of the participants had carried out land reclamation in the period 1980–90 and 11% of these expressed the intention to carry out further reclamation, given that they still had reclaimable land on their holding. The majority (95%) had reseeded at least some of their land, most of which was previously grazed (an average of 14 hectares per holding). About half the landholders had had crops on their land at some time, but these amounted to very small areas (average 3 hectares). Less than 10% of the participants made neither hay nor silage; of the remaining landholders, a larger proportion made silage (68%) as opposed to hay (59%), and 36% made both.

Pesticides and herbicides were used to some degree by about half the participants. Only 2% had not applied fertilizer to their land. No details were available on the amounts and types used as most of the landholders did not follow any strict land management programme; rather they applied as growing conditions dictated. Almost 60% had storage facilities for slurry and approximately 40% had erected a new building(s) on their holding. The corresponding figures for the non-participants are also presented in Table 8.1 and the significance of any differences is discussed later.

Table 8.2 gives an indication of the types of management input that had an effect on the ecological resources or landscape value of holdings in the ten-year period prior to the survey and similar work planned for the following five years. Almost 80% of the participants had put up new post and wire fencing over the ten years and 56% of the landholders planned to erect new fencing of this type. The rate of maintenance of traditional type boundaries was high (77% maintained their drystone walls and 70% maintained their hedges) and about 40% had built new walls in the past (average of 332 m per holding). Only a small proportion (13%) of participants had planted hedges (average of 230 m per holding) but 34% expressed the intention to do so in the future. These figures indicated a general trend away from constructing boundaries out of traditional materials, although the rate of maintenance of existing (traditional) boundaries appeared quite high. Approximately one quarter of the participants had planted trees (mostly conifers) but over half intended to plant in the next five years. The proportion of their holdings with ponds was very low (7%) and no participant had created a pond over the period, although 4% expressed an intention to do so. Fifteen per cent of the sample used grazing as the principal technique for heather management (17% of the sample had heather on their holding). The corresponding figures for the non-participants are given for comparison and, as stated earlier, significant differences are discussed later in the chapter.

Comparison of Participants and Non-Participants

The survey data were analysed to identify the distinguishing characteristics of participants and non-participants in the Scheme. The resulting information

Table 8.3. General characteristics of participating and non-participating landholders.

Landholder status	Average age (years)	Average size of holding (ha)	Farming status (%)			
			Full-time	Part-time	Retired	Other
Participants	52	23	58	31	9	2
Non-participants	60	17	36	38	19	7
Level of significance	***	**			***	

Source: Survey of Landholders – Mourne Mountains and Slieve Croob ESA.

** = 0.025 level of significance; *** = 0.01 level of significance.

would assist policy-makers and advisory staff in the field to formulate appropriate tactics for the effective targeting of landholders most likely to join the Scheme (or similar schemes) in the future. There was strong evidence to suggest that there existed a number of key differences which characterized the two groups of landholders. Using the methodology described earlier in the chapter, significant differences at the 0.05 significance level or higher existed for over 20% of the 300 variables recorded in the survey of landholders.

The participants were younger (the average ages for participants and non-participants were 52 and 60 respectively), owned larger holdings and

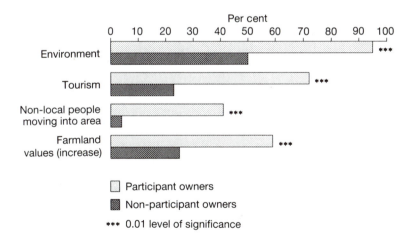

Fig. 8.5. Impact of the ESA Scheme as perceived by landholders.

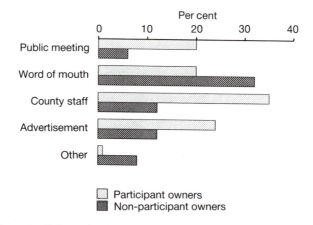

Fig. 8.6. Channels of information through which landowners first heard about Scheme.

operated larger farm businesses. The average holding size for the sample of participants was 23 hectares, being higher than the average of 18 hectares for all holdings in the area, while non-participants had a mean holding size of 17 hectares. Over half the participants farmed full-time (as opposed to approximately one-third of non-participants) with the perceived hours per week of on-farm work for participants averaging about 61 hours compared to 48 hours for non-participants (see Table 8.3).

Participants had a generally more positive attitude towards the impact of the ESA Scheme on the immediate area (see Fig. 8.5). The channels of information whereby the two groups first heard about the Scheme also differed, most notably in the fact that participants were more likely to have heard about it through DANI County Advisory Staff and public meetings (see Fig. 8.6).

Agricultural/Farm Management

Considering the joint issues of farming techniques employed and the degree of 'progressiveness' of the landholder, the participants had, on the whole, a more active approach to land management and a more commercial approach to their farm businesses (see Fig. 8.7). Non-participants were more likely to let their land in conacre (a traditional system of short-term letting) and less likely to have participated in one or more agricultural grant schemes in the past ten years, to grow crops or to utilize advice from official sources (on average, the participants had four contacts [in addition to ESA contacts] with Department of Agriculture officials – whereas the corresponding number of contacts for non-participants was two). Participants displayed a stronger tendency to engage in 'modern' farming techniques such as silage making

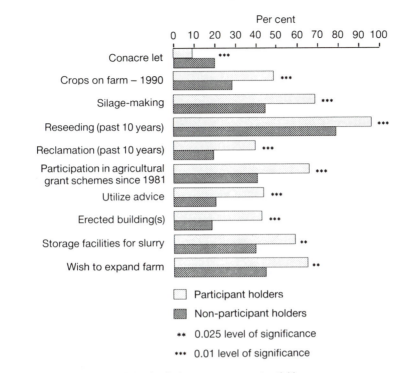

Fig. 8.7. Landholders' participation in farm management activities.

and regular reseeding of pasture. They were also more likely to have reclaimed land in the past ten years, to have erected more buildings, to have owned more modern machinery and to have had storage facilities for slurry on the farm. A higher percentage of participants also expressed a wish to expand their farm if the opportunity arose.

Environmental Management

It was also evident that the participants had shown more of a propensity to undertake environmentally orientated work on their farm in the past. A larger number of participants had already carried out some form of active boundary maintenance or had created new boundary features (see Fig. 8.8). Fewer non-participants anticipated planting trees in the future but the two groups showed little divergence concerning the actual rate of tree planting prior to the survey.

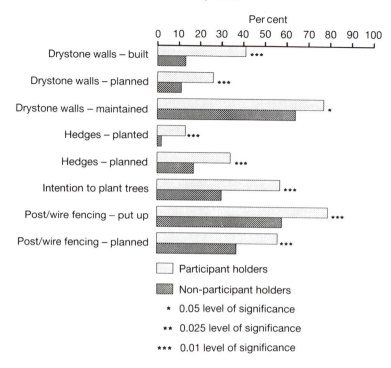

Fig. 8.8. Environmental management on holdings.

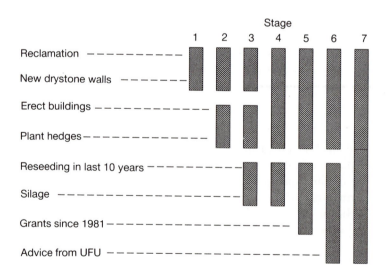

Fig. 8.9. Clustering of key variables.

Clustering of Key Variables

The basic aim of cluster analysis is to find the 'natural groupings', if any, of a set of individuals or variables. More formally, cluster analysis aims to allocate a set of individuals or variables to a set of mutually exclusive, exhaustive groups such that those within a group are similar to one another while those in different groups are dissimilar (Chatfield and Collins, 1980). The process of hierarchical clustering (Gnanadesikan, 1977) is one in which every cluster obtained at any stage is a merger of clusters at previous stages. Broadly speaking, a cluster analysis has been successful if it brings to light previously unnoticed groupings in a set of data or helps to formalize its hierarchical structure. The objective in clustering variables is to see if it is possible to discover subsets of variables which are so highly correlated amongst themselves that any one of them, or some average of them, can be used to represent the subset without serious loss of information. By using cluster analysis it was possible to take measurements on the variables important (determined by the prior analysis as highly significantly different between participants and non-participants) to the landholders to identify any relationships between those variables.

The cluster analysis lent support to a hypothesis of association between the variables highlighted in Figs 8.7 and 8.8. At each stage of the clustering procedure (see Fig. 8.9) the linkage among certain variables was revealed. The first four stages identified a clustering of some land management techniques, with (past) 'reclamation' and (past building of) 'new drystone wall' having the strongest association, i.e. first in the hierarchy. The second cluster (i.e. second strongest level of association) was formed from the variables relating to the erection of buildings in the past five years and the planting of hedges. A third cluster ('reseeding' and 'silage' making) was formed before the two previous clusters merged (Stage 4) implying that the link between reseeding and silage making was stronger than that of the relationship between the two previously formed clusters. The variables relating to the uptake of grants and the taking of advice from the Ulster Farmers' Union were more closely related to the cluster concerned with reseeding and silage making and hence joined with these in preference to the other cluster (Stages 5 and 6). The two separate clusters then joined together at Stage 7 before the introduction of new variables (Stages 8 onwards – not shown) which simply added on one at a time to the Stage 7 cluster with no new, separate relationships being identified, i.e. the important relationships were identified in the first stages of clustering.

These results pointed to a strong level of association between the more 'modern' land management techniques and the continuation of a number of 'traditional' management techniques, particularly with reference to traditional boundary maintenance – which is a significant contribution to the overall landscape value of the area. This could be taken to infer that, while landholders were keen to utilize 'modern' practices, this is not always necessarily detrimental to the landscape potential of the area. For instance, the strong level of association between past reclamation and the building of new walls would seem to bear this out. It was recognized, however, that some of the new walls were constructed because of the need to dispose of the stone rather than a conscious act to enhance the landscape. Similarly, the linkage between new buildings (i.e. enhancement of the farm business) and the planting of hedges – both probably to improve livestock management, given the enterprise mix within the area – was an example of the integration of land management practices and landscape (or ecological) enhancement. The inclusion of the other 'progressive' land management techniques (e.g. reseeding and silage making) and the variables relating to uptake of grants and advice, supported the hypothesis that it was the more 'progressive' landholders (in terms of farm management and propensity to take up schemes/grant aid) who availed themselves of the opportunity to participate in the ESA Scheme.

Attitudes to the Environment/ Awareness of Environmental Issues

The coupled issues of attitudes to and awareness of the environment and the impact of farming was investigated. As detailed later, the two landholder samples exhibited very few significant differences in their response to the attitude/opinion questions and consequently the views of the combined samples are presented. To gauge the level of awareness of the landholders of the influence of agriculture on the environment they were asked an open-ended question concerning impact. While over 40% of the combined sample of 200 thought agriculture had 'improved the land', 29% of the landholders expressed the view that the only noticeable effects were harmful (see Table 8.4). The most frequently cited major harmful effects were: a reduction in wildlife; pollution, especially slurry and spraying problems; and boundary removal. It would be misleading, however, to consider these general comments as being indicative of a high level of awareness since specific examples of detrimental effects were mentioned by less than 30% of landholders.

Conservation Awareness

The general level of conservation awareness would appear to be relatively low despite the conservation-orientated work already undertaken by some of the landholders. Conservation meant nothing to 13% of the landholders (see Table 8.5). Just over half of them were able to suggest at least one definition of conservation. The suggestions tended to be vague, e.g. maintain the

Table 8.4. Landholders' responses to the question 'In your opinion, in what ways (if any) has farming influenced the environment in the past 20 years?'.

Unprompted responses	Proportion of landholders (%)
Improved the land	41
Reduced wildlife	28
Pollution problems	27
Pesticide/herbicide problems	20
Slurry problems	14
Hedge/ditch removal detrimental	14

Source: Combined samples of participating and non-participating landholders.

Table 8.5. Landholders' main responses to the question 'Can you give a brief description of what the term conservation means to you?'.

Unprompted responses	Proportion of landholders (%)
Maintenance of countryside	24
Protect wildlife habitats	23
Help look of landscape	23
Tree planting	21
Hedge/boundary maintenance	17
Nothing	13
Maintenance of heritage	9

Source: Combined samples of participating and non-participating landholders.

countryside as it is, or tidy up the countryside, with few practical measures identified. Twenty-three per cent of landholders did, however, mention protection of wildlife habitats and 21% cited tree planting.

General Attitudes to Farming and Conservation

The landholders were invited to express their opinions in terms of 'very much agree', 'agree', 'neutral', 'disagree' or 'very much disagree' on a number of attitudinal statements relating to farming and conservation. Table 8.6 lists the statements, ranked in terms of the strength of agreement, beginning with the statement which inspired the highest level of agreement (i.e. highest positive score) down to the single statement which elicited an aggregate level of disagreement (negative score). There was little variation in opinion between the participants and non-participants except for two statements. A significantly higher proportion of the participants were of the opinion that conservation saved money whereas a significantly higher proportion of the non-participants agreed with the statement that there were no benefits for farmers from conservation. (It should be noted that the test for differences was applied to raw survey data, not the numerical scores which were used as a measure of the strength of aggregate opinion.)

As might be expected, the landholders held stronger (i.e. with more certainty) opinions on issues/questions relating to farming itself, with a high consensus of agreement on the statements such as 'There is more to farming than just producing food', 'A good farmer needs to be brought up on the land' and 'Non-farmers should not tell farmers what to do with their farms'. It is perhaps notable that this first statement (i.e. 'There is more to farming than just producing food') elicited the strongest level of agreement, implying that landholders recognized that they had a wider role to play than simply that of food production. The positive responses to statements such as 'A farmer is like a business person with the countryside as the office', 'Using official advice is important in farming' and 'Farmers in the future will need some formal training' implied quite a high degree of business orientation. However, on a cautionary note, it must be remembered that this was what the landholders thought rather than what, in some cases, they actually did. As the issues became more complex, e.g. 'There is no real future for traditional farming', 'There are no real benefits for farmers from conservation', 'Agriculture will become less important in rural areas in the future', the landholders became more divided in their opinions, indicated by the proximity of the average score to zero (where zero indicates that the whole sample on average was neutral/undecided or there was an equal distribution of landholders in each category).

As stated previously, these were the attitudes/opinions held by the landholders at the time of the survey. Any major changes in attitudes of the participants or non-participants by the time of the follow-up survey (i.e.

Table 8.6. Attitudinal statements ranked in terms of strength of agreement.

Attitudinal statement	Score*
There is more to farming than just producing food	+1.38
A good farmer needs to be brought up on the land	+1.17
A good farmer always tries to produce the maximum crops/stock from the land	+1.14
Non-farmers should not tell farmers what to do with their farms	+1.10
Farmers need to learn more about conservation	+1.07
Conservation costs money	+1.00
Using official advice is important in farming	+0.95
A farmer is like a business person with the countryside as the office	+0.93
Environmentally friendly farming will cost the public more than farming as we know it	+0.84
Farmers in the future will need at least some formal training	+0.76
Modern farming has damaged the environment more than some farmers think	+0.74
A farmer should look after the countryside for everyone else	+0.74
Farming will become less intensive in the future	+0.40
Conservation is all about keeping things as they are and not allowing more production	+0.36
There is no real future for traditional farming	+0.28
Conservation saves money	+0.05
There are no real benefits for farmers from conservation	+0.03
Agriculture will become less important in rural areas in future	+0.03
Conservation is an option only for the better-off farmers	−0.39

Source: Survey of Landholders – Mourne Mountains and Slieve Croob ESA.

*Scores were between +2 and −2 where +2 would indicate all the sample answered 'very much agree' and −2 would indicate all the sample answered 'very much disagree'. Zero was the neutral point on the scale.

identified by the emergence of statistically significant differences between the opinions of the two groups) may be associated with participation or non-participation in the Scheme. Any widespread changes in the aggregate sample may partly arise out of the area being designated, so heightening environmental awareness in the total population in the area or partly from changes in attitudes of society at large.

In addition, a number of common themes and views emerged from the informal conversations which accompanied each interview: for example, it was felt that the number of people able to make a living from farming in the area will further decline in the next few years. The ESA Scheme was not perceived by the landholders surveyed as helping to keep people on the land (although, of course, this perception may change once the Scheme has been in operation for a few years), but approximately 20% of the participants (without prompting) stated that it was a good, positive idea. Most of the remaining landholders saw it as a minor scheme not having too much impact on farms or incomes (which were the main foci of concern for landholders interviewed at a time of uncertainty and depressed farming income) – indeed, a recurring comment was that the rate of payment was not high enough to make much impression on the farm (or in their pockets). Although difficult to measure, the non-participants seemed in general to have a more pessimistic view of the future for agriculture and seemed to be expecting or hoping for some sort of rescue package, more so than the participants, who were slightly more optimistic in their outlook.

Participants' Attitudes to the ESA Scheme

Almost 40% of the participants had applied to join the Scheme immediately it was brought to their notice – for the remainder there was an average lag of 6 months before application. DANI County Staff and advertisements were the most frequently cited sources of information on the Scheme. The main reason given for entering the Scheme was the availability of cash for maintenance work. Concern for the environment was the second most popular reason. Additional income and the increased capital value of the land were also mentioned by a relatively small proportion of participants (see Table 8.7).

When asked why they thought the Scheme had been introduced, over half the participants said they assumed it was to improve the scenic value of the area, and a fifth of them specifically mentioned tourism. Only 14% thought the Scheme's main purpose was to channel money to farmers. The vast majority of the participants (over 90%) considered the General Schedule of conditions accompanying their management plans to be reasonable. They had not been in the Scheme long enough to pass judgement on its overall effectiveness. Of those who had received payments, only one-third felt their costs had been totally covered. Almost 40% of the participants claimed they would carry out tasks additional to those they would normally do, because of the Scheme. Only 8% were considering leaving the Scheme and the main reason given was inadequate finance for the prescribed work.

Table 8.7. Reasons for entering the Scheme.

Reasons	Participating landholders (%)
Cash assistance – maintenance work	81
Concern for environment	38
Additional income	14
Increase the capital value of land	12
Maintain income	5
Steady source of income	5
Create additional employment	3
More efficient utilization of existing workforce	2

Source: Survey of Landholders – Mourne Mountains and Slieve Croob ESA.

Concluding Comments

The small size of the holdings in the scheduled area and the reliance on beef and sheep products made it difficult to envisage a return to relative prosperity for farmers without the opportunity to avail of extra income (from either farm or non-farm sources). The ESA Scheme could be considered as a source of additional income and it seemed from initial analysis that proactive farmers were keen to take part (i.e. younger, farming full-time, engaged in more modern land management techniques, etc.), which indicated that the ESA funds were being channelled, at least in some part, to those reliant on agriculture for their main source of income.

The rich and diverse character of the landscape in the designed area has largely arisen out of the land management and husbandry techniques employed by those working the land. If society wishes the traditional farmscape to be preserved, this may be at a cost to the farmer if future economic pressures dictate changes in farming practices which further alter the landscape in some undesirable way. Then it can be argued that society has some duty to help mitigate the effects on the farmers' incomes of fulfilling these requirements. Likewise, landholders could be said to have a duty to society as custodians of the countryside for future generations. If they are receiving public monies it can be argued that the public has a legitimate interest in how the funds are utilized and the resultant impact on the environment.

In terms of the Mournes and Slieve Croob ESA, the objectives of designation were firstly to protect or enhance the landscape and wildlife potential of the area, and secondly to promote the adoption or retention of extensive farming practices. Clearly the likelihood of achieving the former could be said to be very high due to the conservation work-plan component of the Scheme, which will encourage positive practical actions. Some of the prescriptions (such as maintenance of ponds and wetlands) contained in the General Schedule will help prevent any further deterioration in landscape and ecological resources on the holdings.

When considering the chances of achieving the second objective, the assessment depended on the definition of extensive farming. If it meant the prevention of further intensification (since in the context of the Mournes ESA, stocking rates were considered by DANI to be optimal) then the Scheme may have gone some way towards aiding this process, i.e. prevention of reclamation, non-removal of field boundaries, etc., which would prevent further land becoming available for agricultural use. This argument, however, becomes somewhat obscured if the landholder has no restrictions imposed on the amount of stock on the land (i.e. the present situation in the Mournes ESA Scheme). Given the current 'optimal' stocking levels this is not a problem but difficulties could arise in the future if the landholders' response to economic forces external to the Scheme was to intensify their farming activity. If land is relatively scarce this may also cause landholders to intensify. The General Schedule provided very little in the way of conditions to actually promote extensive farming practices.

In operational terms, the Mournes and Slieve Croob Scheme appeared to have got off to a good start. In general, the participants were younger, more likely to be farming full-time and utilized the more progressive farming and land management techniques. They were also more likely to be known to official advisory staff and were generally more receptive to taking and acting upon their advice. Paradoxically, more of their number had also carried out conservation-type work on their farms prior to the Scheme, even if they were not fully aware of the environmental impact of their work.

It appeared, therefore, that the farmers or landholders most likely to undertake an environmentally orientated scheme were those that had been farming or managing their land in a less traditional manner in the immediate past. This was somewhat at variance with initial expectations, namely that such schemes would encourage retention of traditional farming practices. If the more modern approach to farming in the area, however, has not been environmentally detrimental then this is not an issue. Problems may arise in other areas where the modern approach is detrimental because then the cost of getting farmers to change to environmentally friendly practices would be higher. The older landholders in the Mournes ESA were more likely to farm in a traditional manner but less likely to participate in the Scheme. When one of the objectives of an ESA Scheme is to attract landholders farming in a traditional manner, additional efforts may be necessary to recruit the older landholders.

It was noteworthy how little notice was taken of the General Schedule by the majority of participants – most said they agreed with it mainly because there was nothing in it that particularly curtailed their operations. This may not have been a problem in the Mournes, since it implied that they were already managing their land in the desirable manner. The main issue, however, was that the concept of integrating actual farming practices with sympathetic environmental management (as opposed to carrying out some-what cosmetic activities, e.g. painting buildings) did not seem to have got through to the farmers. This could lead to difficulties in the future if the Scheme is perceived mainly in terms of 'prettying the landscape' for others (e.g. loss of credibility, loss of interest on the landholders' part, low levels of re-participation and non-curtailment of environmentally unfriendly agricul-tural practices). The potential for integrating conservation with agriculture, e.g. in terms of recycling of resources, prudent use of artificial inputs, etc., so making it more relevant to farmers, could be missed.

One problem which could arise in the future may centre around the issue of what happens once all the positive work is done, i.e. how to amend, if at all, rates of payment, contract details, etc. The situation may well occur whereby people use the Scheme to tidy-up the farm or holding, withdraw and then return to their former practices (which may in some cases be antagonis-tic towards ESA principles). The ESA Scheme will obviously need to evolve to ensure the gains achieved during the life of the Scheme are perpetuated for the long-term benefit of the area. Possibilities include one-off payments for certain environmental improvements or the introduction of tiers of support within the Scheme.

Acknowledgement

The author wishes to acknowledge the contribution of Miss Susan Chilton to the original study.

APPENDIX 8.1. General Schedule for Mournes ESA.

1. The farmer shall prepare and agree with the Department a farm conservation plan for his land which shall identify any conservation features relevant to the requirements in paragraphs 2 to 17.

2. The farmer shall maintain stockproof walls and hedges in a stockproof condition using traditional methods and materials.

3. The farmer shall maintain any weatherproof traditional farm building which he owns or the exterior of which he has a liability to repair in a weatherproof condition using traditional materials.

4. The farmer shall retain and maintain traditional gates and gate posts.

5. The farmer shall maintain existing field patterns and shall not remove any hedge, dyke or wall except with the written permission of the Department.

6. The farmer shall not carry out any land reclamation work unless written prior approval has been obtained from the Department.

7. The farmer shall not apply pesticides or herbicides to hedgerow bottoms except with the written permission of the Department.

8. The farmer shall not apply herbicides to species-rich pastures except to control bracken, spear thistle, creeping or field thistle, curled dock, broadleaved dock or ragwort. Herbicides used for these purposes shall be applied by weed wiper or spot treatment. In the case of bracken, control shall be by means of Asulam or other chemical approved by the Department.

9. The farmer shall maintain existing ponds, streams and rivers and shall retain associated fringe vegetation.

10. The farmer shall retain existing areas of marsh and wetlands.

11. The farmer shall retain existing areas of heather and undertake measures necessary to regenerate the heather.

12. The farmer shall obtain written advice from the Department on maintaining farm woodland and existing hedgerow trees.

13. The farmer shall obtain written advice from the Department on any tree planting proposals which are not to be carried out under its forestry grants scheme.

14. The farmer shall ensure that no pollution due to the escape of silage effluent, sheep dip or other pollutant occurs.

15. The farmer shall ensure that in farming the land he does not damage or destroy any feature of historic interest.

16. The farmer shall obtain written advice from the Department before commencing the construction or reconstruction of farm roads.

17. The farmer shall obtain written advice from the Department before commencing the construction of new buildings or the carrying out of major renewal work to existing buildings.

9

THE ULTIMATE TEST
Measuring the Benefits of ESAs

Ken Willis and Guy Garrod

Introduction

An analysis of the uptake rate of ESA agreements and public exchequer expenditure arising from ESA prescriptions permits a judgement to be made about the effectiveness of each ESA scheme in relation to inputs. However, the ultimate economic test of an efficient policy is whether the outputs, or the value of the benefits the policy produces, exceed the value of inputs. The purpose of this chapter is to consider how the outputs of ESAs can be valued, and whether this value exceeds the costs of ESA policy.

Public exchequer costs of agreements vary between each designated ESA area. Each ESA has its own distinctive landscape character which frequently contrasts with the surrounding countryside. Despite their innate diversities, the benefits that ESAs provide, dependent upon the maintenance of traditional farming techniques, can be categorized into:

1. an increase in ecological and wildlife diversity;
2. preservation of traditional landscapes;
3. maintenance of features specific to each ESA, such as field boundaries, drystone walls, ancient trackways, and so on.

Other benefits which ESAs provide tend to be indirect impacts of management prescriptions and are frequently specific to an ESA. A prime example of this is the improvement in water quality, given the reduction in fertilizer and chemical use in many ESAs, which has improved the appearance of water courses and their wildlife interest, as well as resulting in some reduction in health risks.

Any methodology used to evaluate the benefits of ESAs must be able to distinguish between the benefits and costs *with* and *without* ESAs; i.e. to assess the net contribution of ESAs. Thus the benefits of ESAs need to be assessed with respect to:

1. the implementation of ESA management prescriptions, compared to
2. a continuing emphasis on agricultural policy with no curtailment through ESA schemes.

These two policy situations are illustrated conceptually in Fig. 9.1. Both of these positions are to some extent hypothetical. Some of the effect of ESA prescriptions may only fully work through into landscape and environmental benefits at some point in the future: so future annual benefits may exceed current measured annual benefits. But perhaps more uncertain is what the *without* ESA agricultural position will be in the future. Agricultural policy is subject to change, and the likely implications of the MacSharry proposals and of the CAP policy and price changes on farming would need to be taken in to account.

Moreover, there are many other organizations and policies which protect wildlife, landscape and historical interests in the countryside (see also Chapter 10) including the following:

1. English Nature, which has management agreements with respect to Sites of Special Scientific Interest (SSSIs) and nature reserves in many ESAs.
2. The RSPB, which has designated a number of reserves within ESA boundaries.

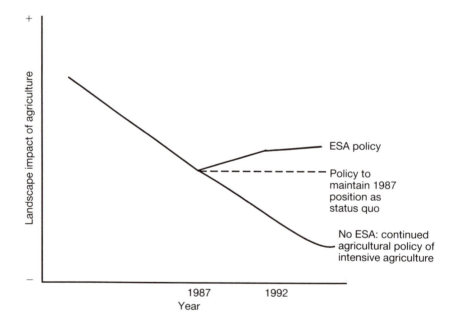

Fig. 9.1. The impact of ESA policy.

3. The Countryside Commission, which acts to protect the traditional landscape in ESAs.
4. National Park Authorities, which seek to maintain the cultural landscape in large areas of land often encompassing ESAs.
5. The National Trust, which holds some land in ESAs which it manages in a way designed to protect traditional farming, landscape and historical features.

A great deal of effort from agencies such as MAFF and English Nature is devoted to coordinating policies, programmes and practices towards conservation goals, and there is a large degree of commonality between environmental programmes with respect to ESA type objectives.

In evaluating the landscape, wildlife and historic feature preservation benefits of the *with* ESA position, the benefits attributable to these other policies should be excluded, if these policies would have continued to provide some 'ESA-type' landscape benefits in the absence of ESA policy. Clearly separability is a different problem, both in 'netting out' the contribution of these other policies to maintaining the traditional landscape and in determining to what extent the benefits of these other policies are dependent upon ESA policy and vice versa.

The physical outputs from ESA designations may affect the utility levels of individuals. Such utility changes could be positive or negative: some individuals may prefer ESA-type landscapes, while others may prefer the more intensive agricultural landscapes which would result if agricultural policies pursued elsewhere continued to be applied in ESAs. Any evaluation technique must be capable of estimating the net change in utility levels across individuals. The benefits, and costs, of ESA designation are also likely to impact differentially on various groups of the population. Obvious groups are:

1. Visitors to ESAs, who directly experience changes in the landscape, wildlife and archaeological-historical features in an area.
2. Residents in ESAs, who similarly directly experience changes, including perhaps changes in the value of their properties as a consequence of the ESA.
3. The rest of the general public living elsewhere in Britain who do not visit ESAs, or all ESAs, but nevertheless bear the cost of ESAs through taxation, and who also may receive non-use benefits from ESAs.

The benefits of ESAs to these three groups are of two types: (i) use values, and (ii) non-use values. Use values comprise changes in the utility level of visitors and residents directly affected by the ESA prescription. Visitors and residents will directly experience visual changes in the landscape and in the quantity of wildlife and historical-archaeological features that would otherwise be available. The impact of ESAs on use values might be exhibited in changes in property values, a change in the number of visitors to an ESA, change in the visit rate of existing visitors, and the amount of money they are prepared to pay to visit the ESA. Non-use values refer to the utility people derive from an amenity such as an ESA for various reasons other than visiting it. Existence values arise from the satisfaction individuals gain from knowing that the traditional landscape is protected and exists as a natural habitat for plants and wildlife. People gain utility from simply knowing that such species and habitats are protected. Non-users may also have an option value for ESAs: a measure of how much a non-user of a good is willing to pay to preserve the option to consume it in the future given his current uncertainty about his demand for the ESA landscapes.

A number of techniques could be employed to measure the benefits of ESA policies:

1. Opportunity cost (OC) approach: this enumerates public exchequer expenditure on ESA policy and then assesses whether politicians, decision-makers, experts and the general public regard this expenditure as justified, in terms of the utility derived from it exceeding benefits forgone elsewhere in the public sector.
2. Household production function (HPF): how much households actually spend on preserving (e.g. on membership of organizations) or consuming (e.g. visiting ESA landscapes), or spend on other consumption goods (e.g. books, broadcasts, etc.) associated with ESAs and their outputs.
3. Hedonic price model (HPM): assessing the impact of ESA policy through changes in people's willingness to pay (WTP) to acquire houses within ESAs.
4. Contingent valuation method (CVM): this values the benefits of environmental goods by asking people directly how much they are willing to pay to acquire them rather than go without ESA outputs.

The following section assesses which of these techniques are appropriate according to a range of criteria for enumerating and valuing the benefits of ESAs.

Techniques to Measure the Benefits of ESAs

Opportunity Cost or Effect on Production Approach

ESA agreements affect the production possibilities of farms, for example in terms of what can be produced, factors of production used, and consequently the quantity of outputs flowing, their value, and hence the profitability of farms. Thus the impact of an ESA is represented by the value of the change in the inputs and outputs that it causes. Payments to farmers under each ESA scheme are designed to compensate farmers for profits forgone. Public exchequer payments under ESA schemes therefore have opportunity costs: the benefits forgone elsewhere in public spending.

This approach is the most widely used of all the various valuation techniques in operationalizing government policy: it is the practical method adopted in 'buying out' production rights in the countryside. It forms the basis of the Land Compensation Acts, and for compensation under among others the Town and Country Planning Acts and management agreements under the Wildlife and Countryside Act (1981).

Defensive expenditure, or expenditure to prevent environmental degradation, may provide an estimate of society's willingness to pay (WTP) where individuals' expenditure averts the externality, to provide a private acceptable environmental good for those individuals. Thus defensive expenditure has been used to value air, noise and water pollution where individuals move dwelling and incur additional journey to work and other costs to avoid the externality, or fit double glazing to reduce noise levels inside the dwelling, or buy bottled supplies of clean drinking water. However, to the extent that individuals are still exposed in part to the externality, for example to noise in the garden, then WTP for private goods such as double glazing will understate the utility loss caused by the externality. Since ESAs are a public good not amenable to internalization, the value of ESAs cannot be determined in this way.

Where compensation payments for production profits forgone are made by decision-makers in government, the implicit assumption is that ESA benefits equal or exceed the opportunity cost or profits forgone. However, such a model assumes no relationship to the behavioural theory of individuals. ESA expenditure is politically determined. Economic theory is sceptical about the ability of voting rules to produce optimal outcomes. Majority voting rules result either in too little or too many resources being devoted to environmental goods, depending upon whether those with an environmental preference are in the majority or not (Willis, 1980). Other voting rules also result in distortions compared with market outcomes. Hence voting rules are an imperfect method of measuring individual utility and strength of preference on ESAs.

The advantage of the opportunity cost effect on production approach is that it distinguishes between the with/without ESA case: indeed, it is based on this distinction. The with/without case is valued in terms of 'market' prices of agricultural outputs. To the extent that 'market' prices are above the opportunity cost price on the world market, because of import quotas, tariffs and subsidies, then the effect on production approach will overestimate the opportunity resource cost of ESAs.

The effect on production approach only measures use value or the value of use forgone. It does not measure non-use values such as option and existence values which may be an important component of the value of an ESA. But opportunity cost values are readily aggregated across enterprises within an ESA, and also between ESAs, which is the other main advantage of this method.

Where the physical impact of ESA policy on production is well established and accurately measured and valued, then the effect on production technique is extremely robust. In this respect the effect on production approach is likely to be more robust than other techniques in valuing ESAs. It will of course be more limited in a predictive sense where the without ESA agricultural policy base situation is subject to on-going change, as under CAP reform and the MacSharry proposals.

Household Production Function

The environmental improvements generated by the ESA designation may provide considerable benefits for those households who utilize such areas for recreational purposes. Household production function models assess the value of an environmental change through the household's consumption of commodities that are either complements to or substitutes for the environmental change. Within the HPF framework, the travel-cost model (TCM) is widely used to measure the *in situ* value of recreation sites from the travel cost incurred to gain access to the site (see Bateman *et al.*, 1992). Travel cost is a complementary expenditure necessary to consume the environmental good. TCM studies have consistently shown that as the price (of access or cost of travel) increases, then *ceteris paribus*, the visit rate to the site falls.

The travel-cost method assesses the value visitors place on the current use of a site. It is an *ex post* evaluation of the gross recreational value of a site. In principle it could be used to value the benefits in terms of consumer surplus on individual recreational visits to ESAs: however, since ESA designation, either the consumer surplus per visit, or the number of visitors to the ESA may have changed, and both of these variables must be estimated to derive net ESA user benefits.

Thus, to estimate the net contribution of an ESA using the TCM approach some measure of *without* designation benefits is required. This could be derived either from a travel-cost study of visitors to an area before it was designated an ESA, or from a similar study based on visitors to non-uptake land within the ESA. However, travel-cost studies of areas within the current ESAs carried out prior to designation are simply not available, while identifying visitors to intensively farmed agricultural land within an ESA who visit for landscape, wildlife and historical features just like ESA visitors, but without the ESA enhancement, would be an extremely difficult task.

A more fundamental disadvantage of this approach is that the travel-cost method can only value use benefits: it cannot, by definition, value non-use benefits, such as existence values, option values of vicarious use values; nor can it estimate benefits which are expected to arise in the future as the impact of ESAs develops. Hence the value of such future benefits could not be established from a TCM.

In addition, TCM will undervalue residents' willingness to pay travel costs to visit an ESA; i.e. a TCM will undervalue the utility of people who have moved house to live in or near an ESA and hence avoid travel costs in visiting an ESA. However, these people's benefits can be assessed in theory through a hedonic price model of the local housing market.

Furthermore, TCMs assume that ESA recreation is separable from other kinds of recreational activities within an ESA; i.e. the demand for ESA-based recreational visits does not depend on the quantity consumed in any other recreational activity. Results will be biased if separability is not possible since some of the value of other recreational activities will be assigned to the ESA.

To summarize, the travel-cost method can more readily estimate the current aggregate visitor benefits from an ESA, rather than the net user benefits arising from designation. A variation of this approach, the hedonic travel-cost method, could, however, be used to distinguish between the respective contributions made to these benefits by the individual components which make up an ESA, such as landscape, wildlife and historical features. Such an approach would require a much larger sample than that required for a conventional TCM analysis.

The Hedonic Price Method

The amenity benefits of an improved landscape for those people choosing to live in an ESA may be measured by estimating the premium which an ESA location adds to the price of their accommodation using the hedonic price method. The HPM is based on the idea that in the absence of financial constraints, the amount which an individual is willing to pay for a particular good is dependent upon the individual characteristics of that good. Thus, the amount which an individual would be willing to pay for a new house would depend to a great extent upon its location, and the type of neighbourhood, as well as the number of rooms it has, its state of repair, whether it is detached, semi-detached or terraced, the central heating provided, the amount of garden area, the provision of garage space, and so on.

If this is so, then for otherwise identical goods, an improvement in the level of one characteristic of the good should raise its price by an amount equal to the value which the purchaser places on that improvement. For example, consider two identical houses facing opposite each other in the same street, sharing the same services and identical neighbours. The back windows of one house command a view of a brick wall, while from the back windows of the other house a pleasant green field can be seen. If both houses are auctioned simultaneously then any differences in price between them is attributable to the difference in view.

Hedonic pricing involves the derivation of a mathematical model which reveals the relationship between each good's characteristics and its sale price; i.e. it can take a set of normal sales transactions and use them to simulate a situation as in the housing example above and from that estimate the premium for an improvement in a particular good's characteristic. This approach allows a value to be estimated for the amount by which an extra unit of a particular characteristic will on average raise or depress the sale price of the good. If the characteristic involved is discrete, that is if it is either present or absent in the good and there is no in-between position, then the method will simply derive the premium which the presence or absence of that characteristic will generate.

Hedonic pricing has been used for over 20 years (e.g. Rosen, 1974), and the estimates it yields for environmental improvements are generally considered to be reliable. The estimates may, however, be particularly sensitive to missing data and to the mathematical specification of the model (Garrod and Allanson, 1991).

The hedonic price method can distinguish between properties within the ESA and those located outside of its boundaries, and can determine whether the within-ESA location currently adds a premium to house price. The premium which a household pays to live in the ESA landscape may reflect both members of the household's values as users of part of that landscape for recreation, and their values for simply knowing that the landscape exists and that they have the option to use it whenever they wish. The hedonic price method provides no way of disaggregating these benefits.

The situation with respect to an ESA will be further complicated by those houses just outside the ESA boundary, since the value of such houses could reflect part of the benefit of an ESA in terms of a view over part of the ESA landscape. In addition, the ESA scheme has been in operation for only a relatively short period, and should in the future result in further landscape, wildlife and cultural protection. The benefits of these anticipated improvements may not be obvious to house buyers and hence may not be incorporated into the current capital value of properties.

Moreover, the premium on the price of a house in an ESA (including the payment for the stream of expected future benefits) may still not reflect the benefits of the ESA scheme. For example, only a proportion of these benefits would be attributable to the ESA designation, while the rest would be attributable to the landscape which already existed at the time of designation. Those areas designated as ESAs were assigned that status because they were of sufficient importance from a landscape, wildlife or heritage point of view, to warrant preservation and possibly enhancement. If the features which led to designation in the first place are also likely to add a premium to local house prices, then a house within the ESA would generally command a higher price than an otherwise identical house a few miles outside the area. In the six years since designation it is unlikely that these areas would have changed sufficiently to have caused more than a marginal alteration to the existing house price premium. Thus, any benefits estimated for households within the ESA would have to be assumed to be generated by a combination of the environmental benefits offered by the area before designation and the enhanced environmental features generated afterwards. It is most unlikely that such combined benefits could be separated in the hedonic model.

In any case, the environmental improvements generated by the ESA scheme are the result of a combination of many individual improvements and changes such as greater diversity in wildlife, improved tree cover, cleaner waterways, more wildflowers and less noise from tractors and other agricultural machinery. The way these changes interact in a physical sense may be too complex to be modelled under a hedonic price framework, and the method would only be able to model the overall improvement by generalizing it to a single, common environmental improvement experienced by all houses within the ESA area. Even if this was satisfactory, the approach could be applied to an ESA if, and only if, a substantial amount of data were available on house sales within the area. Given the available data sources, such as building societies and estate agents, this may be hard to achieve for any given period, especially for the more sparsely populated ESAs such as the Somerset Levels and Moors or the Suffolk River Valleys.

The Contingent Valuation Method

The most versatile technique for valuing the benefits of ESAs is the contingent valuation method, which has been used for nearly 30 years in studies of recreation and the environment as a means of obtaining individuals' valuations for those goods, such as clean air, landscape and water quality, which do not usually have a price attached to them. CVM can, in theory, be applied to any good, though it is most usual to apply it to the case of unpriced goods such as aspects of the environment, non-priced open-access recreation and human health (Mitchell and Carson, 1989).

Contingent valuation depends on the definition of a hypothetical situation in which it seems natural for individuals to specify the payment which they would be willing to make or receive in response to the specified environmental change. The approach relies on responses to questions in which individuals from a target population are asked the maximum amount which they would be willing to pay, or the minimum amount of compensation they would be willing to accept, for some increase or decrease, in the current level of the specified environmental good. For example: What is the maximum you would be willing to pay in increased water rates in order to improve the water quality in this river to the extent that fish would be able to live in it again?

Although money does not usually change hands, this elicitation process involves the specification of a realistic payment vehicle such as an increase in tax, an entrance charge, a user permit, a donation to a charitable trust or, as in the above example, an increase in utility bills. These valuations are then aggregated in an appropriate fashion across individuals to determine the increase or decrease in benefits to the target population which would result from the environmental change.

In the case of environmental goods the target population, i.e. the range of individuals who can be asked to provide their valuations, is unrestricted. For instance, a particular site can be valued in terms of the amenity value it provides to local residents and the recreational value it has for visitors. In addition values can be elicited from people who never even use the site: this may be achieved by asking them how much they would be willing to pay to ensure the preservation of the site, in as much as its continued existence ensures that they derive utility from knowing it is preserved and that it is available for future generations to enjoy.[1] Identifying the size and structure of the target population is an important factor in the valuation process both for sampling purposes and later for the aggregation of benefits. Several sub-populations may be identified, the broadest of which are the user groups consisting of local residents and visitors, and the non-users which could in theory include the remainder of humanity, though in practice this is usually scaled down to the community of reference in the cost–benefit appraisal.

In the case of ESAs, CVM would be used to elicit a valuation from a respondent, which it is hoped would coincide with the unknown 'true' measurement of the benefit which they derive from the environmental improvement achieved by the designation. After a suitable preamble respondents would be presented with the valuation scenario complete with appropriate payment vehicle, and would then be asked to make their valuations. It would in theory be possible to disaggregate these valuations into their wildlife, landscape, heritage or other components, and similarly into use and non-use values.

Use values would reflect the proportion of the payment which respondents allocate in order to provide for current recreational access and amenity value, while non-use values include the following:

1. *Existence values:* the benefit which people derive from simply knowing that ESAs protect traditional landscapes, wildlife and archaeological features, even if they have no intention of visiting that cultural landscape area.
2. *Vicarious use values:* the extent to which people who do not visit an ESA, or any ESAs, nevertheless gain pleasure from pictures, books and broadcasts about features of these areas which are dependent upon the ESA designation (by comparison, while a TCM study could determine a household's expenditure on its vicarious consumption of ESAs in the same survey as that used to assess the cost of travel, it could not estimate the vicarious consumption of non-users).
3. *Option values:* the values that individuals would be willing to pay in order to ensure the future availability of the amenities produced by ESAs. Option values are the amounts which individuals are willing to pay to preserve the

---

[1]The comparable private market situation would be family heirlooms or art collections where individuals spend considerable sums to ensure their continuing existence.

ESA, given their uncertainty about their demand for future visits; and uncertainty about the supply of ESA-type benefits if payments to farmers are curtailed.

Any contingent valuation exercise studying the benefits of the ESA scheme must be subjected to intense scrutiny designed to detect any evidence of the presence of biases. These are sources of error and inaccuracy which, when present in a contingent valuation study, cause the results to deviate from the desired 'true' value. In simple terms, biases are the result of differences between the behaviour of respondents in the necessarily hypothetical situation of a contingent valuation study and what they would do if that situation really did exist – i.e. if they really did have the option of making a payment in order to ensure the preservation of the ESA designation. In an effort to obtain unbiased responses from what are often rather artificial exercises, the application to ESAs must include mechanisms designed to prevent biases from occurring, and tests to detect them when they do.

All in all, contingent valuation provides a uniquely flexible methodology for the measurement of environmental policy benefits and damage costs, and has been used for this purpose with increasing frequency over recent years. The technique is intuitively simple, although it can raise considerable practical difficulties in application. It is founded on a basic direct questioning approach where respondents are asked how much they would be willing to pay for some environmental improvement, or how much compensation they would be willing to accept for some reduction in environmental quality.

Using this basic technique it is theoretically possible to apply contingent valuation in almost all situations, which is a major advantage of this methodology over other approaches, such as the travel-cost method or hedonic pricing, which are only applicable in a limited number of circumstances. Furthermore, the method could be used to estimate both the use and the non-use benefits which the ESA scheme generates with respect to considerations such as landscape, wildlife, amenity and areas of historical interest. In addition, it could be applied with equal facility to individual ESAs or to ESAs in general (see Willis *et al.*, 1993).

Contingent valuation cannot be applied without great care being taken. The estimates generated by the method will be highly dependent on both sampling technique and the design of the questionnaire: the latter is perhaps the most crucial single aspect of any CVM application, and must address matters such as the choice of payment vehicle and the payment-elicitation method, as well as taking into account the need to minimize the various biases which may arise.

Benefits of an ESA:
The Case of the South Downs ESA

This case study illustrates, first, how the contingent value method can be used to estimate benefits, and second, how the benefits of an ESA may be compared with the financial and public exchequer cost of an ESA incurred by government.

The ESA scheme was designed to safeguard areas of the countryside where landscape, wildlife or historic interest is of national importance, recognizing the major influence which agriculture can have on the enhancement of these features. The concept originated in the 1980s from concerns about the detrimental impact of more intensive agricultural practices in the countryside, and conversely the need to support the continuation of traditional farming practices in areas where these have contributed to a distinctive landscape or wildlife habitat, or have led to the preservation of archaeological or historical features.

ESAs are designated under Section 18 of the Agriculture Act 1986, although the concept is also reflected in European Community law. The South Downs ESA was initiated in the first round of designations in 1987. The second round of designations, in 1988, included the western extension of the South Downs.

The objective of ESAs is to provide 'public good'[2] benefits, some of which are visible to both visitors and non-visitors. Different ESAs have different appeals in terms of attributes. Thus it is important that any CVM applied to an ESA is carefully designed with reference to the particular characteristics of that ESA; and that the physical effects of ESA policy are carefully described and presented to respondents to obtain contingent values.

The South Downs ESA

The South Downs ESA was designated because of its high scenic value characterized by open, rolling downland and because of its important wildlife habitats, particularly with relation to the wildflowers and insects associated with traditional chalk grassland. The river valleys which cross the Downs are an integral part of the landscape and the pastures provide breeding sites for birds such as lapwing and snipe. Many features of archaeological interest occur in the area, including the remains of extensive ancient field systems, recording human activity in the Downs since prehistoric times; however, much of the more traditional undulating pasture has been lost to arable

---

[2]A 'public good' is one which exhibits non-rivalry in consumption (i.e. one person's consumption of the good does not reduce the amount available to others), and non-excludability (i.e. consumption of the good is accessible to all: none can be excluded) (see Willis, 1980). Several common environmental resources are 'public goods': landscape, clean air, clean water and biological diversity (see Tietenberg, 1992).

cultivation. These factors have influenced the following objectives as determined for the South Downs ESA:

1. to protect the remaining areas of downland pasture;
2. to revert arable land to grassland and to encourage greater botanical diversity in the pasture created;
3. to protect and upgrade downland landscape features such as traditional barns and walls.

Prescriptions for the South Downs ESA 1987–92 comprised Tier 1 payments of £35 per hectare to preserve typical South Downs permanent pasture, and Tier 2 payments of £160 per hectare to encourage the conversion of some arable land to permanent pasture.

Revisions to ESAs in 1992 introduced new tiers and prescriptions, and revised compensation payment levels. In the South Downs ESA these prescriptions became: Tier 1 (to preserve typical downland grassland) £40 per hectare; Tier 2 (to preserve river valley grassland) £40 per hectare; and Tier 3 (a) (arable reversion to chalk downland) £240 per hectare, (b) (arable reversion to permanent grassland) £200 per hectare, (c) (conservation headlands) £60 per hectare.

In addition to preserving landscape, wildlife and archaeological features, ESAs can also produce other external benefits. Such external benefits in the South Downs, through the reversion of arable to grassland, comprise:

1. Some reduction in externalities associated with straw burning such as air pollution, prior to straw burning becoming illegal in 1993.
2. A reduction in soil erosion and flooding, which has damaged property through settlement in areas fringing the South Downs.
3. A decrease in nitrogen and other chemicals in the water table, from reduced fertilizer applications compared with previous levels on arable land. Some local authorities in Sussex have in the past purchased land in the South Downs which they have maintained in a natural state to ensure good-quality drinking water supplies from the chalk. Through reversion, the ESA is also contributing to the objectives of other authorities (Willis *et al.*, 1993).

Questionnaire Design

In order to investigate public preferences and valuations for alternative ESA landscapes, three groups whose utility might change as a result of ESA designations were identified: those who lived within the ESA boundary; those who lived outside of the ESA boundary, but who had visited the ESA within a given time period; and those who lived outside of the ESA boundary, and had not visited the ESA within the time period.

The preferred survey instrument for the investigation of public preferences for the ESA scheme was an on-site questionnaire survey. This comprised a series of one-to-one interviews covering the respondents sampled from each element of the sampling frame. Such an approach, while costly, had the best chance of conveying the necessarily detailed information which would be required by the study, and of assisting respondents to make full and appropriate responses. The one-to-one approach would be especially useful for the presentation of visual representations of the ESA policy on/policy off scenarios.

Three separate questionnaires were used, one each for on-site visitors, residents and the general public. Each of the questionnaires was designed to elicit much the same information as the others, and to do so in as similar a manner as possible in order to avoid any framing bias[3] entering into responses. Each version was piloted in the field before implementation in order to ensure its suitability, and to highlight potential problems of ambiguity and clarity.

The questions common to each group included discovering whether respondents indulged in particular recreational activities in the countryside and their preferences for various countryside features. An estimate of the amount of money which each household spent annually on the enjoyment and preservation of the countryside was also sought: this had the dual purpose of encouraging the respondents to consider their use of the countryside and their expenditure on it, and of providing some basis for examining the possibility of part-whole bias (see Kahneman and Knetsch, 1992) in later WTP responses. In addition all respondents were also asked a range of more personal questions regarding age, income, household size and education. The most important question for each group required respondents to estimate how much their household would be willing to pay on an annual basis to ensure that the ESA scheme was maintained in England. It was upon this question that annual WTP for any individual ESA would ultimately depend.

Respondents in the on-site surveys of visitors and residents were first presented with the ESA fact sheet, a one-page document with a map detailing the location of the ten English ESAs, plus a brief written description of the meaning and objectives of the ESA scheme. Respondents were then presented with a scenario in which the government no longer had sufficient funds available to finance the ESA scheme. They were then asked what was the maximum sum, over and above that which they already spent on the countryside, which their household would be willing to pay each year in the form of additional income tax in order to ensure that the ESA scheme was maintained. Income tax was chosen as the payment vehicle because it was familiar to respondents, realistic and also relatively uncontroversial (any respondents who made zero bids because of an aversion to paying more income tax were identified in a subsequent question). A payment card booklet

---

[3]Bias resulting from the way in which WTP questions are framed.

was utilized to make this exercise more straightforward. This illustrated, using individual page displays, a sequence of ten ranges of annual household income. In each display respondents were shown a table displaying a wide range of monetary values, annotated with the approximate amounts which a married couple at the mid-point of the income range would pay annually in income tax, towards a range of seven public services, chosen both to represent a range of spending levels and because they were not directly associated with the public good being investigated.

The on-site surveys of visitors and residents both used pictorial representations of the ESA policy-on and policy-off scenarios: these were presented to respondents as Scenario A – The ESA Landscape, and Scenario B – The Agricultural Landscape. Each scenario was illustrated by a colour photomontage incorporating an element of written description: Scenario A depicted the ESA as it should look after the successful implementation of the ESA scheme, while Scenario B showed how the ESA could look if there was a greater emphasis placed on agricultural production, leading to a more intensively farmed landscape. For each area the photo-montages were introduced by a sheet illustrating the boundaries of the ESA and briefly outlining some of the issues involved in the comparison of the two agricultural policy scenarios. Respondents were handed this material in the form of a five-page booklet directly after their ESA tax budget had been elicited. When respondents had spent all the time they wanted reading the booklet and examining the photographs, they were asked among other things to rank the two landscape scenarios in order of preference.

If respondents chose Scenario A, they were asked what was the maximum amount from their household's ESA tax budget which they would be willing to pay each year in order to maintain the ESA scheme in the ESA, and by so doing ensure that the landscape of the future would look like that depicted in Scenario A rather than the more intensive agricultural landscape shown in Scenario B. If respondents chose Scenario B, they were asked what was the maximum amount of extra tax over and above their normal tax burden and any additional amount which they may have allocated to the maintenance of ESAs, which their households would be willing to pay each year in order to ensure that the landscape of the future would look like that depicted in Scenario B and not like the ESA landscape shown in Scenario A.

If respondents were not willing to pay for their preferred landscape this was investigated in a subsequent question. In addition, if respondents named a very high amount (over £50) their motivation for doing so was also investigated. All respondents who named non-zero sums were asked what was the maximum number of years over which they would be willing to pay this sum.

The majority of people in England were likely to have no recent first-hand knowledge of the South Downs. Without such knowledge the full implications of the information contained in the landscape booklet might not have been clear; because of this it was decided not to use the booklet approach in the general-public survey. Instead, the landscape booklet was replaced by an enlarged ESA factsheet, which included two extra sides briefly giving details of the importance of each of the ten English ESAs. To ensure accuracy all the material used in the ESA surveys was compiled in conjunction with MAFF experts.

Having read this material, respondents were asked if they had visited any of the ten ESAs and if they had, how often they had visited during the last year. Respondents were then asked to imagine that they had 100 points which they could use to express their preferences for ESAs; they were then asked to divide up their 100 points between the ten English ESAs in order to express their preferences for maintaining the ESA environment in each of them. This procedure was designed to enable ESA tax budgets to be allocated between the English ESAs, without asking respondents to perform the offputting mental arithmetic which would be necessary if the tax budget itself was to be allocated between the ten ESAs.

From this point the general-public survey diverged into two different methodological formats. The first followed the payment-card-based CVM approach used in the on-site surveys, while the second adopted a discrete or dichotomous choice (DC) CVM approach (see Garrod and Willis, 1992b). Thus, the first format asked respondents to estimate their ESA tax budget in an identical manner to that in the on-site surveys, again employing the payment-card booklet and investigating extreme responses. By contrast, the second format began the tax-budget question in a similar fashion, presenting the same scenario as in the other versions but, rather than eliciting a particular maximum WTP figure, merely asked whether the respondent's household would in fact be willing to pay additional taxes each year in order to ensure that the ESA scheme was maintained. If respondents were unwilling to pay extra tax then their reasons were elicited in a later question. If, however, respondents were willing to pay extra tax then they were asked to consider carefully whether their households would be willing to pay £X in additional taxes each year in order to maintain the ESA scheme. Twelve different values of X were used in this application ranging from £1 to £1000.

Sampling Design

The sample of residents used in the survey was drawn from within the ESA and from those areas adjacent to it, in an effort to include all local people whose close proximity to the ESA brings them into regular contact with it. This contact may be merely visual, or it may involve physical movement within the ESA boundary; either way it is an everyday, commonplace contact and in no way akin to the experience of the visitor. The sample population under these assumptions was estimated to be in the region of 13,600 households based on 1981 census Enumeration Districts (EDs) (see Willis et al., 1993). A total of 300 households within the ESA were targeted for sampling at an ED level.

The sampling frame for visitors to the ESA was defined more simply as those households who visited the ESA between August 1992 and February 1993. It was intended that up to 300 visitors to the ESA would be sampled on a next-to-pass basis at a range of sites. These would be chosen from the best known and most frequented sites within or near the ESA, in order to both cover the ESA geographically and to capture a wide range of visitor types.

Remote or off-site interviews captured that part of the population which chose not to visit a particular ESA in 1992. These non-visitors required the largest sampling frame, one which could potentially stretch the length and breadth of Great Britain and beyond. To rationalize this problem and to reduce costs, the sampling frame for non-visitors was defined as the population of non-visiting households living within England. Larger sample sizes were required to reflect the greater diversity of the sampling frame. Thus, for the payment-card format a target of 750 questionnaires was specified, and for the DC format the target was 1250 questionnaires. Both questionnaire formats were applied at each survey location and were rotated to ensure that each was applied to the same sample population. To ensure that a representative sample was drawn, interviews were carried out at over 80 locations spread across the country, and covering a wide range of settlement types and sizes. Respondents were drawn according to their household characteristics in order to ensure that a demographically representative sample was taken.

Perception of the South Downs ESA by Residents, Visitors and the General Public

Awareness of ESA designation by residents and visitors was low in the South Downs: only 76.5% of residents and 57.0% of visitors to the South Downs were aware that the area was an ESA. Despite this, the attractiveness of the ESA scenery was high to visitors and residents of the South Downs: 85% of both visitors and residents rated the South Downs ESA scenery as superb or very attractive, compared with only 14% of visitors and residents who regarded it as only moderately attractive, and less than 1% who regarded it as unattractive. The overwhelming majority of respondents, both residents (97%) and visitors (98%) preferred the ESA landscape to a more intensive agricultural one.

Over 83% of all visitors and residents in the South Downs preferred to see more wildflowers and butterflies; 69% more wildlife; 57% more hedgerows; and over 50% more broadleaved woodland. Thirty-seven per cent of visitors and residents wanted to see more chalk downland, a preference consistent with the objectives of the South Downs ESA, although 59% were content with the existing quantity (Table 9.1). By contrast, less importance was placed on increasing access to archaeological sites in the South Downs. There was concern amongst visitors and residents about scrub invasion;

Table 9.1. Landscape feature preferences in the South Downs.*

Feature	Visitors (%)			Residents (%)		
	Less	Same	More	Less	Same	More
Wildlife	0.0	30.4	69.6	0.0	30.2	69.2
Broadleaved woodland	1.5	48.5	50.0	2.0	29.5	68.5
Coniferous woodland	33.3	53.7	13.0	37.6	49.7	12.8
Chalk downland	4.1	59.3	36.7	3.4	59.1	37.6
Grazing animals	5.6	54.8	39.6	4.7	48.0	47.3
Ponds	0.7	39.6	59.6	1.3	34.7	64.0
Access to archaeological sites	5.9	64.1	30.0	3.0	71.8	25.2
Hedgerows	2.2	42.0	55.8	2.7	30.9	66.4
Scrub	23.7	56.3	20.0	26.5	46.6	26.8
Fields of crops	27.8	58.9	13.3	29.5	62.4	8.1
Hay meadows	5.6	48.5	45.9	2.3	49.0	48.7
Wildflowers	0.0	14.1	85.9	0.3	13.1	86.6
Butterflies	0.4	16.7	82.9	0.0	16.4	83.6

*Please note that percentages may not sum exactly to 100.0 because of rounding.

whilst increasing proportions of respondents wanted to see fewer fields of crops and less coniferous woodland.

Frequency of Visits to the South Downs

Approximately 77% of visitors to the South Downs ESA had made previous visits to the area. For 75.1% of day-trip visitors, the main purpose of their current trip was specifically to visit the ESA area.

Visitors' and residents' perception of the impact of the ESA on visit rates, however, was not especially strong with respect to the South Downs. Table 9.2 records visitors' estimates of how often they would visit the area under an ESA landscape compared to a more intensive agricultural production (IAP) landscape; and for residents how often they thought other people would visit

Table 9.2. Respondents' estimates of how often they thought they (visitors) or other people (for residents) would visit the area under an ESA landscape and an intensive agricultural landscape (IAP).

	Percentage response South Downs			
	Visitors		Residents	
	ESA	IAP	ESA	IAP
a. More than today	46.5	2.2	52.9	2.4
b. Same as today	52.8	49.3	45.8	52.7
c. Less than today but at least half as often	0.0	27.6	0.3	25.2
d. Half as often as today	0.7	8.2	1.0	11.2
e. Less than half as often as today		8.6		6.8
f. Not at all		4.1		1.7
N	269	268	295	294

Table 9.3. Respondents' estimates of their enjoyment of living in/or visiting alternative landscapes.*

	Percentage response South Downs			
	Visitors		Residents	
	ESA	IAP	ESA	IAP
a. More than today	69.1	0.4	59.0	2.4
b. Same as today	29.7	25.7	39.3	31.3
c. Between half as much and as much as today	0.4	36.2	0.3	28.9
d. Half as much as today	0.7	19.4	0.7	21.1
e. Less than half as much as today		14.6	0.7	12.9
f. Not at all		3.7		3.4
N	269	268	295	294

*Please note that percentages may not sum exactly to 100.0 because of rounding.

the area under the alternative landscape scenarios. Most respondents believed that under an ESA their visit rate to the area would remain much as it was today, although 47% thought they would visit more often. Again most respondents (49%) thought that under the IAP landscape their visit rate would remain the same as today, but 28% thought they would visit less often. Residents believed that many more visitors would come to the South Downs under an ESA landscape.

Most respondents also thought that under the ESA scheme their enjoyment of landscape would be greater than their enjoyment without the ESA. However, 26% of visitors and 31% of residents thought that their enjoyment of the area would be the same as it is today under the intensive agricultural landscape (Table 9.3). Of course this may merely reflect the fact that substantial areas of the South Downs still retain an intensive arable landscape.

Willingness to Pay for the South Downs ESA

Zero willingness to pay for the South Downs ESA

When calculating sample mean willingness to pay for the maintenance of the ESA, the inclusion of all zero WTP bids could bias the results. This would occur if some of the zero bids were the result of other factors which did not relate to WTP for the ESA scheme, but rather were a response to other factors such as political or moral beliefs or a dislike of the way in which the WTP bid was elicited.

Of the reasons given for zero WTP summarized in Table 9.4, only those described in the first three categories were considered to be legitimate in the context of the calculation of mean WTP. Those respondents who gave their

Table 9.4. Respondents' reasons for zero WTP to maintain the ESA scheme in England.

		Residents	Visitors	General public
1.	Gave no reason for zero WTP	9	3	32
2.	Could not afford to pay	22	32	112
3.	Zero value for the ESA scheme	3	2	2
4.	Did not wish to pay more tax	26	17	82
5.	Other protest bids	15	11	36
6.	Free-riding	7	2	4
7.	Other given reasons	7	2	1

reason as not wishing to pay extra tax were deemed to be expressing a dislike of the payment vehicle rather than an unwillingness to pay to maintain the ESA scheme. Other responses were rejected on the basis that the respondent's motive was free-riding or a more ethically or politically based protest. The responses of a further small number of respondents were excluded because they could not understand the question, did not wish to answer the question or did not feel that this sort of questioning was appropriate. Those respondents who gave no reason for their unwillingness to pay for the ESA scheme were not excluded from the calculation of mean WTP, as there was no evidence to warrant such an exclusion.

Residents

When respondents were asked to recall how much their household spent each year on enjoyment and preservation of the countryside, average expenditure was estimated to be £179.86 per household, with a standard deviation of £278.50. The 95% confidence interval for residents gave an upper bound to mean expenditure of £212.14, and a lower bound of £147.58. However, both the median and modal countryside budgets were found to be considerably lower at £100, giving a forceful demonstration of the effect of the higher estimates which some residents made. Of the 298 ESA residents interviewed a total of 89 were not willing to pay any additional taxes for the ESA. These were classified into a number of categories as shown above.

In summary, of the 298 residents in the sample, 203 named a non-zero sum as their maximum household WTP to maintain the ESA scheme, 89 were unwilling to pay – 34 for legitimate reasons (see Table 9.4) – and there were six non-responses. Thus, mean WTP to maintain the ESA scheme in England was based on 237 (i.e. 203 + 34) observations and came to £67.46 with a standard deviation of £137.79. This translated into a 95% confidence interval for the mean WTP of residents of the South Downs ESA which demonstrated that there was a 95% probability that the residents' mean WTP for the ESA scheme lay between the limits £49.92 and £85.00. When compared to their countryside budget, respondents' ESA tax budget was significantly different at any reasonable statistical significance level, suggesting no problem with part-whole bias.

Of the 203 respondents who were willing to pay to maintain the ESA scheme a total of 197 also preferred the ESA landscape to the agricultural landscape in the South Downs. All of these were then asked how much of their annual household ESA tax budget they would be willing to pay towards maintaining the South Downs ESA. Those who bid zero at this stage were asked for their reasons, as were those who made high bids, defined as £50 or over. Any of the 34 respondents who made legitimate zero bids for the English ESA scheme as a whole, and who preferred the ESA landscape were imputed as making zero bids for the South Downs ESA.

There was a single illegitimate zero bid for the South Downs ESA (the respondent did not feel that the line of questioning was appropriate and made a zero bid in protest), but there were ten bids of over £50 which were rejected because the respondents were either making a high bid for strategic reasons or were making a high bid as a general statement about their strength of feeling about the area and about green issues in general.

The usable sample size to calculate mean WTP for the South Downs ESA was 218, producing a mean value of £27.52 per household per year, with a standard deviation of £74.49. This translated into a confidence interval which revealed that there was a 95% probability that the residents' annual household mean WTP for the South Downs ESA lay between £17.63 and £37.41. However, median WTP at £6 and modal WTP at £0 were found to be well below these limits. Mean ESA WTP for the South Downs was found to be statistically different from the mean ESA tax budget at any reasonable significance level, again suggesting that there were no real problems with part-whole bias in the sample.

If a range of the highest and lowest bids is removed from a data set a truncated sample is obtained: this demonstrates the level of influence which the more extreme observations have on mean WTP. For the survey of residents the six highest and six lowest observations were removed from the data set (i.e. truncating by around 2.5% of the sample at either end of the distribution). The mean WTP from the truncated sample was £18.44, which while within the 95% confidence interval, demonstrated the strong effects on mean WTP of the higher legitimate bids (removing only the highest legitimate bid from the sample, i.e. removing the one £750 bid, would have reduced mean WTP to £24.08).

A total of eight residents stated a preference for Landscape B, the agricultural landscape; four of these had previously stated that their household would be willing to pay a non-zero sum to maintain the ESA scheme in England. However, only one resident made a legitimate non-zero bid, albeit a high one at £250.

Regression analysis was used to model WTP. Several functional forms were fitted to the data to predict WTP: linear, semi-log (dependent), semi-log (independent), double-log, and certain variations including quadratic transformations of variables. The preferred model was based on the semi-log (dependent) form and is reported in Table 9.5.

It was apparent that the R^2 value for this model at nearly 22.58% was acceptable for a CVM application. The signs and size of the coefficients on the variables in the model were evidence of the consistency between the WTP responses of respondents and the theoretical expectation of factors determining these WTP estimates. Income was a positive, highly significant determinant of WTP, as expected, the HIGHINC variable entered the model with a positive coefficient value and the LOWINC variable with a negative coefficient. Other positive determinants of WTP included the weekly average number of

Table 9.5. Model of South Downs residents' WTP bids.

Dependent variable: ln(WTP)

| $R^2 = 0.2258$ | DF: model 9 | F value: 6.612 |
| Adj $R^2 = 0.1917$ | DF: error 204 | Prob>F: 0.0001 |

Variable	Coefficient	t-value	Label
INTERCEPT	1.4567	4.21	Intercept term
WWFN	0.7644	2.54	Member of WWFN (0–1)
RIDING	0.6044	1.88	Visits Downs for horse riding (0–1)
HIST	0.6782	3.09	Visits historic sites or buildings on Downs (0–1)
HIGHINC	0.7909	2.30	Income ≥ £30,000 (0-1)
LOWINC	−0.9089	−3.89	Income < £7500 (0-1)
HSIZE	−0.1386	−1.80	Household size
ECON1	−1.2235	−2.25	Econ. concerns generally more imp. to respondent than env. concerns (0–1)
CREC	0.0289	2.17	Av. weekly hrs in countryside
MPONDS	0.5304	2.60	Respondent would like more ponds in the South Downs (0–1)

hours spent by the respondent recreating in the countryside, and whether the respondent engaged in horse riding or visited historic sites and buildings in the area. Factors having a negative effect on WTP were household size and the respondents belief that economic considerations were generally more important than environmental ones.

Visitors

The mean countryside budget for the South Downs ESA visitor sample was found to be £236.99 (based on 260 visitors, standard deviation = £334.73). This figure is over £50 higher than that of ESA residents, which seemed reasonable if the latter group had already invested a large sum to live in the rural South Downs to satisfy their environmental preferences. The 95% confidence interval for the mean countryside budget of the visitor population had an upper limit of £277.68 and a lower limit of £196.30. The modal budget was £100 and the median budget was found to be £104.

Of the 270 ESA visitors interviewed on site, 69 were not willing to pay any additional tax for the ESA: these responses are detailed in Table 9.4. A total of 200 respondents named a non-zero sum as their maximum household WTP to maintain the ESA scheme, 69 were unwilling to pay, 37 for legitimate reasons, and there was one non-response. Thus, mean visitor WTP to maintain the ESA scheme in England was based on 237 observations and came to £94.29 with a standard deviation of £234.65. This translates into a 95% confidence interval for the mean WTP of on-site visitors of the South Downs ESA which revealed that there was a 95% probability that visitors' mean WTP for the ESA scheme lay between the limits £64.42 and £124.17. The median bid was £20 and the modal bid £0. Mean ESA tax budget and mean countryside budget were found to be different at any reasonable statistical significance level.

After being shown a version of the ESA landscape booklet, a total of 259 respondents preferred the ESA landscape to the agricultural landscape in the South Downs. A total of 200 respondents were willing to pay a non-zero sum towards the maintenance of the English ESAs: these respondents were then asked how much of their annual household ESA tax budget they would be willing to pay towards maintaining the South Downs ESA. Those respondents who bid zero at this stage were asked for their reasons, as were those who made high bids, defined as £50 or over. Again, any of the 37 respondents who made legitimate zero bids for the English ESA scheme as a whole, and who preferred the ESA landscape were imputed as making zero bids for the South Downs ESA. This analysis showed that in the visitor sample there was only one illegitimate zero bid for the South Downs ESA (a protest bid). In addition to this there were eight bids of over £50 which were rejected.

The usable sample size to calculate visitors' mean WTP for the South Downs ESA was 220, producing a mean value of £24.26 per household per year, with a standard deviation of £64.87. This translated into a confidence interval which demonstrated that there was a 95% probability that the visitors' annual household mean WTP for the South Downs ESA lay between £15.69 and £32.83. This figure was different from visitors' mean ESA tax budget at any reasonable statistical significance level, so again there did not appear to be a problem with part-whole bias. The modal bid was £0 and the median bid was £5. The mean WTP from a sample truncated by approximately 2.5% at either end (i.e. by removing the six highest and the six lowest observations) was £15.66, which lay just beyond the lower reaches of the 95% confidence interval, indicating the major influence that the higher legitimate bids have on raising mean WTP. The mean WTP corrected for sample selection bias was £19.47, i.e. a reduction of £4.79, but still well within the 95% confidence interval.

A total of five visitors stated a preference for Landscape B, agricultural

Table 9.6. Model of visitors' WTP bids for the South Downs ESA.

Dependent variable: ln(WTP)

$R^2 = 0.2989$	DF: model 9	F value: 9.617
Adj $R^2 = 0.2678$	DF: error 203	Prob>F: 0.0001

Variable	Coefficient	t-value	Label
INTERCEPT	−1.3202	−0.85	Intercept term
RSPB	0.6226	2.09	Member of RSPB (0–1)
HIGHINC	1.0902	4.61	Respondent's income ≥ £30,000 (0–1)
LOWINC	−0.9401	−2.97	Respondent's income < £7500 (0-1)
OLDER	−0.4618	−1.58	Respondents over 65 (0-1)
LNEDUC	0.9739	1.81	Log of respondent's age when leaving full-time education
MHEDGE	0.3969	2.08	Respondent would like to see more hedgerows in the Downs (0–1)
LGRAZ	0.6691	1.73	Respondent would like to see less grazing animals in the Downs (0–1)
MBROAD	−0.3361	−1.77	Respondent would like to see more broadleaved trees in the Downs (0–1)
LNVISITS	0.1555	2.32	Log of respondent's no. of visits to South Downs in last 12 mths

landscape; one of these had previously stated that their household would be willing to pay a non-zero sum to maintain the ESA scheme in England. Only one visitor stated a legitimate non-zero WTP for this landscape.

A double-log model was chosen from a number of alternatives to model visitors' WTP for the ESA landscape (Table 9.6). The explanatory variables explained nearly 30% of the variation in the dependent variable. As expected income was found to be a positive and significant determinant of visitor WTP: in addition, older respondents were found to be willing to pay less than younger ones for the ESA landscape. Other logical positive determinants of WTP were the respondent's age when leaving full-time education, the

Table 9.7. Summary of results for the South Downs ESA (£: 1992).

	N	Mean	SD	Median	Mode
Residents:					
Countryside budget	286	179.86	278.50	100.00	100.00
ESA tax budget	237	67.46	137.79	20.00	0.00
ESA landscape WTP	218	27.52	74.49	6.00	0.00
Visitors:					
Countryside budget	260	236.99	334.73	104.00	100.00
ESA tax budget	237	94.29	234.65	20.00	0.00
ESA landscape WTP	220	24.26*	64.87	5.00	0.00

*Mean visitor WTP for the South Downs ESA landscape was reduced to £19.47 after correcting for sample selection bias.

number of visits made to the South Downs over the last 12 months and membership of the Royal Society for the Protection of Birds (RSPB). More interesting were the coefficient signs of variables reflecting respondents' desire to see more or less of various features in the Downs. If respondents wished to see more hedgerows then their WTP increased (though it seems doubtful if the ESA scheme would really achieve their desire) and if they wished to see more broadleaved trees their WTP decreased. This latter result may be attributed to the fact that broadleaved woodland would be encouraged to a greater extent by other schemes to which respondents could wish to allocate spending.

Table 9. 7 summarizes the results for both the visitor and resident samples in the South Downs ESA.

Non-users: payment-card format

The first version of the remote survey employed the payment-card format used in the on-site surveys to elicit respondents' WTP for the ESA scheme in England. This version was applied to a total of 762 respondents, which represented 41.3% of the total sample. Mean WTP for the remaining 1083 respondents was elicited through a discrete-choice question in which each respondent was confronted with a potential tax increase which he or she had either to reject or accept.

However, the mean countryside budget for the remote sample was elicited by an identical open-ended question in both versions of the questionnaire. The overall mean based on 1567 responses was £144.50 (standard deviation = £255.43): the 95% confidence interval for the mean countryside budget of the general public had an upper limit of £157.14 and a lower limit of £131.85. The mean countryside budget for the payment-card sample was found to be £142.03 (based on 644 responses, standard deviation =

Table 9.8. Mean WTP by visitor category.

Category	N	Mean WTP (£)	SD (£)
Have never visited an ESA site	98	21.16	52.42
Visited an ESA site before 1992	140	28.91	50.18
Visited an ESA site in 1992	296	45.45	85.29
Total sample	534	36.35	72.71

£253.48); this figure compares with £146.22 for the discrete-choice sample (based on 923 responses, standard deviation = £256.91). The modal and median budgets for all samples were both found to be £50. Clearly, the similarity of the mean values is a good indication of the success of the sampling strategy in obtaining samples for both versions of the questionnaire from the same population. These figures were substantially lower than those derived from the on-site surveys. This may in part be explained by the fact that the on-site surveys captured respondents who had either already demonstrated a propensity to spend money visiting the countryside, or who by living there had more opportunity to spend their money on enjoying it.

Of the 762 respondents interviewed using the payment-card format, 269 were not willing to pay any additional tax for the ESA (see Table 9.4 for a summary of responses). In all, 426 respondents named a non-zero sum as their maximum household WTP to maintain the ESA scheme, 269 were unwilling to pay, 146 for legitimate reasons, and there were 67 non-responses. Of the 426 non-zero bids, 38 bids of £100 or over were rejected as being non-legitimate: this procedure followed that used in the on-site surveys for specific ESA WTP amounts. Thus, mean annual household WTP to maintain the ESA scheme in England was based on 534 observations and came to £36.65 with a standard deviation of £72.71. This translates into a 95% confidence interval for the general public's mean annual household WTP for the English ESA scheme which revealed that there was a 95% probability that respondents' mean WTP for the ESA scheme lay between the limits £30.49 and £42.82. The median bid was £10 and the modal bid £0. Mean annual household ESA tax budget and mean annual household countryside budget were found to be different at any reasonable statistical significance level.

Again, this value was far lower than comparable estimates from the on-site survey. However, this seemed reasonable given that overall this sample used the ESAs much less than the other on-site samples. This prompted separate mean annual household WTP estimates to be derived for various use groups. The results of this analysis are shown in Table 9.8: these

Table 9.9. Model of respondents' WTP bids.

Dependent variable: ln(WTP)

| R^2 = 0.3961 | DF: model 20 | F value: 16.264 |
| Adj R^2 = 0.3717 | DF: error 496 | Prob>F: 0.0001 |

Variable	Coefficient	t-value	Label
INTERCEPT	2.9877	8.99	Intercept
VHIGHINC	0.9088	3.04	Respondent's income > £50,000
LOWINC	−1.0068	−6.74	Respondent's income < £10,000
NCARS	0.2441	2.64	Number of cars in household
HSIZE	−0.2275	−2.83	Household size
AGE	−0.0117	−2.76	Respondent's age
GROUPS	0.1999	2.39	No. of named conservation grps represented in resp's household
WT	−0.9463	−2.57	Member of local wildlife trust
NTHEAST	−0.4707	−1.80	Respondent from NE England
NTHWEST	−1.0368	−5.36	Respondent from NW England
EMIDS	−0.2319	−2.00	Respondent from East Midlands
WMIDS	−0.3292	−1.53	Respondent from West Midlands
OCCUP10	−0.3272	−1.93	Respondent or partner a student
ROCC9	−0.5583	−2.83	Respondent was a homemaker
CYCLE	0.3093	1.98	Respondent cycles in countryside
LCROPS	0.4435	2.11	Respondent wants to see less crops in countryside
LCON	0.5789	3.00	Respondent wants to see less conifers in countryside
LGRAZ	0.8189	1.81	Respondent wants to see less grazing animals in countryside
MHEATH	0.3518	2.74	Respondent wants to see more heather moorland in countryside
HIST	0.4366	2.62	Respondent visits historic sites or buildings in countryside
WILD	0.3102	2.13	Respondent visits countryside to look at wildlife

Table 9.10. Summary of results for the payment-card format (£: 1992).

	N	Mean	SD	Median	Mode
Countryside budget	644	142.03	253.48	50.00	50
ESA tax budget	534	36.65	72.71	10.00	0

figures seemed logical in that those respondents who had visited an ESA most recently valued the scheme most highly, with those respondents who had never visited an ESA valuing it less than half as much, and respondents who had visited an ESA site, but not recently, somewhere between the two. Even so, mean annual household WTP for the ESA scheme for non-users was still relatively high suggesting that the general aims of the scheme meet the approval of even those who do not choose to visit the areas in question, but who may do so in the future.

A semi-log (dependent) functional form was chosen to model WTP for the ESA scheme in England (Table 9.9). The explanatory variables explained almost 40% of the variation in the dependent variable, and the signs of the coefficient values were all consistent with expectations. This was a relatively high level of explanation for a model of WTP in a CVM application, compared with similar studies.

Income was found to be a positive determinant of WTP as was demonstrated by the positive and significant coefficient for the very-high-income indicator variable (VHIGHINC) and the negative and significant coefficient for the low-income indicator variable. Other positive and significant determinants of WTP for the ESA scheme were the number of cars in the respondent's household (a proxy for other income levels), the number of named conservation groups represented in the respondent's household and whether the respondent visits the countryside to cycle, look at wildlife or visit historic sites or buildings. Factors having the opposite effect on WTP included the respondent's age, household size and the respondent's location in the northern or central regions of England, which are relatively poorly served with ESAs at present (i.e. these regions only include the Pennine Dales, North Peak and Shropshire Borders ESAs).

Table 9.10 summarizes the results for the payment-card format.

Non-users: discrete-choice format

A total of 1083 individuals responded to the discrete-choice questionnaire. Each of these was asked whether their household would be willing to pay additional taxes each year in order to ensure that the ESA scheme was maintained. Responses to that question are given in Table 9.11. The 689 respondents who did not refuse to pay extra tax for the ESA scheme at this

Table 9.11. Responses of non-users to the question 'Would your household be willing to pay additional taxes each year to maintain the ESA scheme?'

Response	No.	Per cent
Yes	562	51.9
No	393	36.3
Don't know	127	11.7
Non-response	1	0.1

Table 9.12. Responses of 'Yes' and 'Don't know' respondents of Table 9.11 to the question 'Would your household be willing to pay £X in additional taxes every year to maintain the ESA scheme?'

Response	No.	Per cent
Yes	378	54.9
No	264	38.3
Don't know	47	6.8

juncture were then asked to consider carefully whether their household would be willing to pay £X in additional taxes every year in order to maintain the scheme. Their responses are given in Table 9.12.

These yes/no responses were used as the basis of the dependent variable in a logit model, described in more detail in Willis et al. (1993). Using the estimated logit model (see Table 9.13) mean WTP for the ESA scheme was estimated to be £138.37 per household. This figure is roughly 3.8 times that elicited by the open-ended format. Similar discrepancies between DC and OE mean WTP amounts have been documented in other comparative studies, e.g. Seller et al. (1986) and I. Bateman et al. (1993). It must be kept in mind that this figure applies only to the 63.7% of the sample not unwilling to pay extra taxes for the ESA scheme, so that net mean WTP across the population would be considerably lower.

Median WTP can also be derived from the logit model and was found to be £48.51. The figure can be interpreted as the maximum amount that at least half of the population would be willing to pay for the ESA scheme. In addition to estimating median WTP, point estimates of the implied Hicksian demand function for the ESA scheme can be derived from the logit model.

Table 9.13. Estimated logit model.

Dependent variable: Probability of responding 'no' to bid amount

Number of observations: 642

Number of correct predictions: 522 = 81.31%

Log-likelihood = −276.46

Variable	Coefficient	t-value	Label
ONE	−2.74915	−5.58	Intercept
LN(BID)	1.07055	11.90	Natural log of bid amount
NWEST	0.79666	2.50	Respondent from NW England (0-1)
MHEATH	−0.39387	−1.79	Respondent would like to see more heather moorland in countryside
SEX	−0.34420	−1.60	Sex of respondent (1 = female, 0 = male)
LN(GRPS)	−0.60043	−2.45	Natural log of number of named cons. grps represented in resp's household
OLDER	0.45187	1.51	Respondent aged 60 years or over
PROFMAN	−0.41293	−1.81	Respondent or partner in professional or managerial occupation
LN(KIDS)	−0.38134	−1.69	Natural log of number of children in respondent's household
MWILD	−1.22375	−3.84	Respondent would like to see more wildlife in countryside
INCOME	−0.08068	−1.76	Categorical variable (1-10) on household income of respondent
LN(VIS)	−0.13482	−1.24	Natural log of no. visits to ESAs in 1992

Table 9.14. DC mean WTP by visitor category.

Category	N	Mean WTP (£)	Correct predictions (%)
Have never visited an ESA site	91	122.10	85.71
Visited an ESA site before 1992	180	161.81	89.47
Visited an ESA site in 1992	371	171.39	77.78
Total sample	642	138.37	81.31

From these estimates the price elasticity of demand for the ESA scheme can be observed to be -1.14.

Mean annual household WTP estimates were again derived for the user groups previously defined. The results of this analysis are shown in Table 9.14. As with the payment-card version these figures seemed logical in as much as those respondents who had visited an ESA most recently valued the scheme most highly, with those respondents who had never visited an ESA valuing it less, and respondents who had visited an ESA site, but not recently, somewhere between the two. Again, mean annual household WTP for the ESA scheme for non-users was still relatively high, suggesting that the general aims of the scheme meet the approval of even those who do not choose to visit the areas in question, but who may do so in the future.

When comparing the bid amount used in the DC CVM question with the maximum sum which the same respondent had said that his or her household would be willing to pay annually for the ESA scheme, it was noted that in a few cases these amounts were the same. As well as suggesting an anchoring bias this phenomenon allowed a number of potentially invalid responses to be removed from the data set. Invalid responses were generated when a respondent agreed to pay a value of £X per year for the ESA scheme and then stated that this was also his or her maximum WTP for the scheme. If this amount was £100 or more, and the respondent subsequently answered a follow-up question in a way which indicated that the previous responses had not been truthful, then the bid was declared invalid. In all only eight invalid bids were discovered using this procedure: however, if the logit model was run based on the remaining 634 observations mean WTP was found to fall to £128.36, with a median value of £44.93.

Table 9.15. Visits to tourist attractions in or near the South Downs ESA.

Site	1988	1989	1990	1991
Historic properties:				
Alfriston Clergy House	33,943	33,597	29,181	38,728
Arundel Castle	182,773	178,654	170,184	153,727
Bignor Roman Villa	33,530		27,052	31,720
Charleston Farmhouse	10,839	15,756	18,000	14,057
Lewes Castle	34,494	38,500*		38,000
Parham House	29,067	21,609		37,824
Gardens:				
Denmans, Arundel	15,000*	15,000*	20,000*	
West Dean	13,644	11,913	10,618	8820
Museums and galleries:				
Anne of Cleaves Museum, Lewes	13,244	13,471		15,000*
Chalk Pits Museum, Amberley	74,536	85,000	76,006	75,613
Ditchling Museum	6592	11,127	10,000*	7500*
Filching Manor & Motor Museum	10,000*	20,000*		35,000*
House of Pipes, Steyning	85,979			
Weald & Downland Open Air Museum	179,000	186,112	163,500	172,000
Wildlife attractions:				
Arundel Wildfowl Trust	133,909	128,164	120,000	124,133
Other attractions:				
English Wine Centre, Alfriston			15,000*	
Seven Sisters Sheep Centre		12,000		
Country Park, Ditchling				18,000*

Source: English Tourist Board (1992).
*Estimated number of visitors.

Numbers of Residents, Visitors and Non-Users of the South Downs ESA

The random sample survey of residents, visitors and the rest of the general public, produced estimates of benefits, through a Hicksian WTP measure, per household per annum. The total benefits produced by the ESA requires these annual WTP values by households to be aggregated across all households in their respective groups.

Compared to residents in ESAs, the total number of visitors is extremely difficult to measure, and is subject to a greater degree of error. No surveys have been initiated by local authorities, or other bodies such as the Countryside Commission or MAFF, to enumerate the annual number of visits or visitors to ESA areas. Visitor surveys have been undertaken of broader areas than those encompassed by ESAs; for example, to the Yorkshire Dales National Park as a whole, but ESAs often form only part of such areas.

Alternative sources of information relate to specific recreation sites within, or close to, ESAs. Table 9.15 shows actual and estimated annual visitor numbers to sites within, or close to, the South Downs ESA. These estimates were derived from returns to English Tourist Board questionnaires sent out to owners and managers or operators of recreational sites. The estimates indicate that substantial numbers of purposeful visitors are attracted to recreational sites within or near to the ESA. However, many more visitors are likely to visit the ESA than those paying to gain access to recreational sites within them or those attracted to specific types of recreational experience, even where entry is free of charge – many people visit the countryside simply to walk, for example. Indeed, the South Downs Way stretches throughout the length of the South Downs ESA, while many more visitors are probably attracted to the plethora of local footpaths in the ESA. Other types of open access non-priced recreation exist within ESAs such as cycling, observing wildlife, visiting non-priced historical and archaeological sites, and photography.

Visitors to some of the recreational sites in Table 9.15 may also visit other recreational sites on the list. Hence total visit and visitor numbers cannot be determined by aggregating across all the recreational sites in Table 9.15: some element of double counting would be inherent in adopting such a method to estimate the number of visits and visitors to the ESA. In addition the number of visitors needs to be translated into numbers of households, since it is the latter quantity against which WTP estimates from the random sample surveys have to be applied.

Hence, the estimate of the number of households who had visited the South Downs ESA was derived from the random sample survey of the general public in which respondents were asked if they had visited the South Downs ESA during the year (1992). Thus a probability distribution of visiting the South Downs ESA was derived. From this the number of households who visit the South Downs each year was estimated to be approximately 3,062,000. Since no alternative estimates from any other official or authoritative source are available, this estimate of visitor numbers is taken to be the best available, and hence employed to aggregate WTP of visitors to preserve the ESA.

The 1991 Census of Population enumerated 18,765,582 households in England. By definition, non-users are the number of households who had not visited the South Downs ESA during the year (1992).

Total Economic Value of the South Downs ESA

The total economic value (TEV) of the ESA comprises use values of visitors and residents, and non-use or preservation values of the ESA landscapes by the

Table 9.16. Aggregate benefits of the South Downs ESA (£ per year, third quarter 1992 prices).

	LB	Mean	UB	Median	Mean corrected for SSB
Gross benefits:					
Residents	175,929	274,621	373,313	59,873	–
Visitors	39,155,672	60,542,804	81,929,937	12,477,907	48,588,970
Net benefits:					
Residents		263,177		48,429	
Visitors		60,372,650		12,307,753	48,418,816
General public		31,153,996			

LB = lower bound estimate; UB = upper bound estimate; SSB = sample selection bias.

general public. These estimates are reported in Table 9.16. Clearly, gross benefits to residents varying from £175,000 to £373,000 per year, with a mean of £274,000, are relatively low. The median WTP value produces an even lower aggregate estimate of £59,000.

Median and lower bound (LB) estimates are calculated so that they can be compared with cost estimates if necessary: if the benefits of a policy at the lower bound, or the lowest benefit estimates of a policy, still exceed its costs, then the decision-maker can be more confident about the efficiency of the public expenditure.

The benefits to visitors are high, reflecting the greater number of visitors compared to residents. The majority of the economic benefits (utility) of the ESA are clearly generated by visitors.

The gross benefit estimates in Table 9.16 do not take into account the negative utility suffered by households who prefer the intensive agricultural production (IAP) landscape. The *net* benefit estimates in Table 9.16 therefore estimate the benefits of ESA landscapes to households who prefer them minus the negative utility suffered by those who prefer the IAP landscapes, with respect to both residents and visitors. Net benefits of ESA landscapes are only slightly smaller than the gross benefits without the loss of utility attached to the IAP alternative landscapes.

The general public survey measured the net contribution of the ESA landscapes directly, and hence is only included in this element of the Table. Aggregate general public benefits of the ESA, whilst large, are only half those accruing to visitors.

Table 9.17. Summary of the net benefits and costs of the South Downs ESA landscape and the efficiency of public expenditure (£000s per annum).

Population group	Net benefits			Costs		B/C ratio						Minimum visitor number required*
						ESA			PE			
	Mean	Mean LB	Median	ESA	PE	Mean	Mean LB	Median	Mean	Mean LB	Median	
User	48,682	41,025	12,356	2160	970	22.5	19.0	5.7	50.2	42.3	12.7	35,715
Non-user	31,153			2160	970	14.4			32.1			
Total	79,835			2160	970	37.0			82.3			

Mean LB = mean lower bound WTP estimates; ESA = financial payments to farmers; PE = net public exchequer impact of ESA.
*Minimum number of visitors required to justify net exchequer impact of ESA; excluding (i.e. ignoring) non-use values.

Public Exchequer Costs of the South Downs ESA

The costs of the ESA were estimated based upon the prescription payments and a forecast of the uptake rate on the basis of the revised scheme and payment levels.

The study by Gould (1990) of the eastern section of the ESA, estimated the eligible area for agreement to be 85% of the total area designated. If this rate is applied to the extended area it would imply an eligible area of 52,228 hectares. The actual uptake in 1991 was 8310 hectares, with 5070 in Tier 1 and 3240 in Tier 2 (MAFF, 1992d). MAFF predicts that the uptake will rise, given the expanded area, to 14,000 hectares by the turn of the century, of which 6000 hectares will be in Tiers 1 and 2 and 8000 in Tier 3.

Financial payments to farmers with respect to the ESA scheme amount to £2,160,000. The actual cost to the UK public exchequer is lower than these financial payments after EC contributions and rebates under the CAP are included. Further reductions in agricultural subsidies will occur as a consequence of changes in agricultural output resulting from the ESA prescriptions. The financial payments to farmers and the ultimate net public exchequer costs of each scheme after EC contributions and reductions in subsidies following changes in agricultural output as a consequence of ESA prescriptions have been accounted for, are summarized in Table 9.17. Overall, the net estimated cost to the public exchequer of the ESA scheme (at £970,000) is less than half the financial payments to farmers

Conclusions

Public expenditure on the South Downs ESA appears to be efficient, and to be extremely good value for money, when measured against the benefits generated by the policy. Table 9.17 shows the B/C ratios for user and non-user groups and for total benefits.

Benefits in relation to costs are high in the South Downs, whether measured in terms of user benefits, or non-user benefits, or in terms of Total Economic Value. Even on very restrictive assumptions of judging on the basis of median values instead of cardinal values for users only, benefits are 5.7 times costs in terms of payments to farmers. B/C ratios are even higher when benefits are measured in relation to *net* public exchequer costs, taking into account subsidy savings to the exchequer from changes in agricultural output, rather than in relation to direct payments to farmers under the ESA scheme.

The benefits to visitor households contribute substantially towards the total benefits of ESAs. There is considerable uncertainty about the number of households who visit the South Downs ESA. Failure of respondents to distinguish whether they visited the South Downs or the smaller South Downs ESA within the South Downs area; what constituted a visit, as distinct from passing through the area; as well as errors in response, such as memory bias, 'yea' saying, etc., may have contributed to an overestimate of visitor numbers. An alternative measure to judge the efficacy of public expenditure on the ESA is, therefore, to use a cost-effectiveness criterion: the minimum number of visitors required to justify the net exchequer cost impact of the ESAs. Total exchequer cost of the ESA can be justified if 35,700 households visit the ESA. On this criterion the South Downs ESA appears to provide good value for money in relation to the number of visitors it receives.

Expenditure on some recreational goods has been shown to be relatively income inelastic; for example, in the USA, for swimming (0.31), boating (0.34), camping (0.42), fishing trips (0.47), although all recreation expenditure is elastic (1.4) (Walsh, 1986). Income elasticity of expenditures on recreation varies at different income levels: for low-income households recreation demand is inelastic (0.8), but elastic for middle-income households (1.3), highest (2.0) for upper-middle-income households, before declining (at 1.4) for upper income households. Expenditure on environmental goods is more income elastic than expenditure on staples such as food and housing in household budgets. Garrod and Willis (1992a), for example, found that income elasticity with respect to the amenity value of trees (broadleaved, not spruce) was 0.82, compared with an income elasticity of demand for housing *per se* of 0.6 (Nicholson and Willis, 1991). Other research has shown that the income elasticity of demand for recreational goods in the UK is strongly elastic at 1.99 (Deayton, 1975), which suggests that environmental goods may in general be income elastic. If this was the case, then as real income and prosperity increased, households would devote an increasing proportion of their budget to environmental goods and protection measures, including expenditure on ESAs. Thus, even for those ESAs which may currently be marginal in terms of B/C ratios, benefits would be likely to rise in the future. Hence, expenditure decisions should be based upon these expected future benefits, discounted, of course, back to present values.

The South Downs ESA study was an *ex post* evaluation of the costs and benefits of that ESA. There still remains the issue of the value of ESAs as a whole. First, although the benefits of the South Downs ESA exceeded its costs, this may not necessarily be true for all existing ESAs. The net value of different ESAs to residents, visitors and the general public will vary: for instance different ESAs may attract a variety of WTP values not necessarily as large as the ones described in this study[4], and a number of ESAs including Breckland, West Penwith and the Test Valley attract substantially fewer visitors than the South Downs. Second, government policy is to designate other areas as ESAs. No *ex ante* appraisal has been published on this extension of ESA policy to assess whether benefits are likely to exceed costs. However, as additional ESAs

---

[4]For example the Somerset Levels and Moors ESA, where on the basis of median values user-benefits are only 1.8 times costs (Willis *et al.*, 1993).

are designated, the marginal utility of each additional unit of ESA, in terms of landscape and wildlife interest, will decrease.

Acknowledgement

The authors would like to thank Dr Caroline Saunders for her work in estimating the public exchequer costs of the South Downs ESA.

10

COMPARATIVE EVALUATION OF ENVIRONMENTAL POLICIES
ESAs in a Policy Context

David Colman

Introduction

Several policy instruments are available for delivering environmental goods in the countryside, among which Environmentally Sensitive Area (ESA) designation is one of the most recent. Some measures, such as public land ownership and management, legal covenants placed on land use, and management by voluntary (or charitable) bodies such as the National Trust, have been around for decades. Others have been introduced more recently, such as designating Sites of Special Scientific Interest and allowances against Inheritance and Capital Gains taxes for landowners entering into heritage agreements; also since 1987 new instruments such as new standard land-use management contracts, land set aside as a (cross-compliance) condition for arable production support payments in the EC, and ESAs themselves have been created. The ESA mechanism is thus one which has been grafted on to a set of previously existing measures designed to try to protect some areas of countryside under agricultural and forest management from the pressures for change which have generally reduced the wildlife, landscape and recreational values of the countryside.

Although this will not receive much attention in what follows, it is important to recognize that the existence, where they still occur, of highly valued public goods characteristics of the countryside is due largely to the history of private land ownership and management which has preserved and created those external benefits. In many places hedgerows, woodlands, meadow flowers and wetlands have disappeared, and also insect, animal and bird species have declined. This decreased supply coupled with increased demand, as rising incomes have fed into leisure demand, has caused a higher social valuation to be placed on those areas where the history of land management has, for whatever reason (purposeful or neglectful), resulted in the continued survival of wildlife and traditional rural features. As it has become clear that the number of landowners prepared to retain systems of traditional management has declined, this increased social valuation has called forth the series of measures referred to.

Issues for current public policy include:

1. How much of the countryside which has high scientific, aesthetic, historical and amenity value should be targeted for conservation?
2. How can the appropriate management of such areas be secured? This raises questions of which instruments (if any) are required, and who should the managers be.
3. How should the cost-to-benefit calculus of conservation be performed?
4. To what extent should previous damage be repaired or new features be created in the countryside, and by what means?

From the narrower perspective of the ESA instrument itself there are a number of issues to explore, bearing in mind that there is considerable diversity between the ESAs which have been established in the UK; some are devoted to wetlands, some to uplands, others to mixed arable and grazing areas. It is therefore appropriate to address questions such as (i) what are the policy characteristics which distinguish ESAs from other instruments?; (ii) have ESAs been equally effective in all the different areas to which they have been applied?; (iii) how do they interact with the other instruments and is there a measure of instrument redundancy in some circumstances?; (iv) what modifications have been made to ESA prescriptions to improve their effectiveness, in the light of experience and criticism of their first five years of operation?; and (v) can anything be said about their cost-effectiveness?

Before addressing these specific issues it is worth setting out briefly the basic economic principles of environmental policy to enable an assessment of how ESAs and other related instruments fit into the policy framework.

General Economic Principles of Environmental Policy

Both public and private management of land has generated sizeable positive and negative externalities. In the case of private management these external benefits and costs are additional to any private benefits created and costs incurred. However, the generally accepted perception of recent agricultural development is that the output of external benefits has declined by 'volume' and that of external costs has increased.

The key to conservation is management and changes in management, and in order to maintain the output of positive externalities policy needs to support the economic viability of those who are operating systems responsible for production of these externalities and where necessary to provide incentives for the generation of additional public goods (e.g. footpaths, restored traditional buildings and walls). It is also obviously desirable to have policies to restrict the generation of additional external costs by land users. This use of disincentives for negative management, as we shall see, has not been as successfully pursued by policy in the UK as the provision of incentives for positive management.

The Issue of Property Rights

The ability of producers to force external costs (of say water pollution) onto others, or the inability of an industry to capture all the returns from benefits it produces (such as leisure access, or higher house values from an enhanced view over farmland), are perceived by economists as instances of market failure. This failure is, following Coase (1960), often attributed by economists to the absence of an appropriate set of property rights. If all water courses which ran through farms were owned by other private owners they and the farmers could in theory bargain so that any use made of each water course was fully paid for, including compensation for any pollution damage. In reality such a solution is impractical – water course owners would possess local monopoly, transactions costs would be high, information is imperfect and there is a chain of knock-on effects downstream. Nevertheless a good deal of light is shed onto issues of land-related conservation policy by placing it in the context of property rights issues.

Landowners and tenants (subject to their leases) typically have complete control of the agricultural use made of their land. They are not free to build houses or non-farm commercial premises, but there has been little to prevent them from removing hedgerows and walls, draining land, or felling trees. Society has no property rights in these matters even though many members of society have a strongly felt interest and express a sense of loss when such changes are caused by farmers or foresters.

Through the various types of statutory management agreements (MAs) public authorities may attempt to *rent* certain property rights for the public for a limited period of time. A management agreement with English Nature and other bodies, entered into to prevent 'potentially damaging operations' (PDOs) to a Site of Special Scientific Interest (SSSI), is intended to guarantee the provision of certain external benefits for the duration of a contractual period

---

[1]This was acknowledged in a report by the NCC (1990, para. 5.1.5), which states:

> The Wildlife and Countryside Act has proved inadequate to fully maintain a SSSI series. The Act does not protect sites completely from activities subject to planning control, nor does it make them available for the functional uses of nature conservation resource outlined earlier. Additionally sites often require specialised management which an owner may not wish to contemplate. SSSIs are also potentially at risk when ownership changes, despite being registered as a land charge. Thus nature reserve acquisition through purchase or long lease remains as important as ever within a strategy to maintain our heritage of nature and to develop those functions associated with it.

– although it does not always succeed.[1] Many landowners and farmers have, however, been resentful of the statutory mechanism of SSSI designation leading to management agreements since some of them see in it an implied threat (backed as it is by the remote possibility of compulsory purchase, and by the immediate cessation of PDOs for a period of negotiation), despite the fact that entering into a management agreement is voluntary.

In Environmentally Sensitive Areas, standard medium-term contracts are offered by MAFF in return (i) for the restriction of certain use rights (e.g. on the use of herbicides or on ploughing) or (ii) for the undertaking of certain agreed work to produce public benefits.[2]

As an alternative to hiring rights, public policy can involve the *direct purchase* of land and the rights to use it, or can *grant-aid the purchase* of rights by conservation bodies; that is policy may aim at transferring land-use rights to new owners with a commitment to the conservation objectives of policy. This option is discussed more fully below, as is the use of exemptions from inheritance and capital gains taxes for owners prepared to enter into conservation agreements for heritage sites. Another alternative is use of covenants whereby one generation of owners or statutory bodies attempt to place legal restrictions on the use rights of subsequent landowners and operators. Only through land purchase or covenants can land rights be appropriated by the public and quasi-public sectors. No attempt at statutory control of rights has been initiated to prevent draining of marshlands, altering of field boundaries and vegetative cover. Only over the question of water pollution have statutory powers been invoked to control emission standards. In relation to other forms of environmental, landscape and wildlife interest, 'pollution' policy is limited to control effected through the offer of MA and ESA contracts for the temporary surrender of certain rights.

How Much Conservation is Optimal?

A central aspect of answering the question as to how effective a conservation instrument is would ideally involve assessing whether the optimal level of conservation has taken place in relation to all the different environmental and wildlife characteristics towards which policy is directed.

It may be assumed (following Pearce, 1988):

1. That a certain level of land-using activity can occur without generating any external costs (i.e. that at low levels of output there are no social costs, only private ones).
2. Beyond that level of commercial activity marginal external costs progressively increase.

---

[2]In fact where walls and barns are rebuilt or repaired there is a mixture of private and public benefits, the private benefits being related to management of livestock, storage of hay, etc.

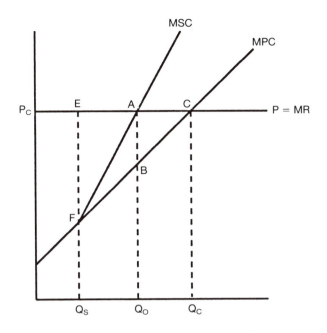

Fig. 10.1. Optimal tax on a competitive farm generating external costs.

3. That marginal social benefits decline as production intensity and commercial output increase.

These assumptions are reflected in Figs 10.1 and 10.2. For the polluting production process represented in Fig. 10.1 no external costs (i.e. costs not borne by producers) are generated at production levels below Q_s, where the subscript s invokes a technical notion of a sustainable output level. Beyond Q_s production generates increasing external costs so that the marginal social costs, denoted by the MSC curve, rise faster than the marginal private costs incurred by producers, shown by the curve MPC. For simplicity it is assumed that producers are price takers, unable to influence the price they receive, so that marginal revenue equals output price, MR = P; for farmers this is certainly an acceptable assumption.

Figure 10.2 represents the case where there are social benefits associated with production for which the producer receives no financial reward from the buyers of the product or from those who 'consume' the associated external benefits. Thus there is a positive marginal external benefit (MEB) which leads to the overall marginal social benefit (MSB) being higher than the price paid (P) by purchasers of the output.

Applying the most basic economic principle leads to the result that the

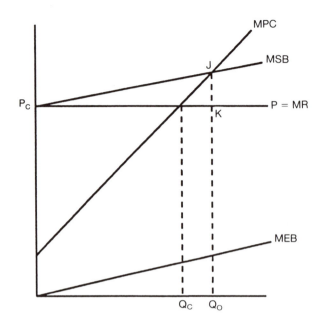

Fig. 10.2. Optimal subsidy where commercial production is linked to external benefits.

socially optimal level of output, and hence of environmental damage or public goods outputs, will be where marginal social cost equals marginal social benefit. However, according to the same principles it is deduced that, in the absence of environmental policy, actual output will tend to be around the private profit-maximizing optimum, where marginal private cost equals marginal revenue, MPC = MR. In both Figs 10.1 and 10.2 the private competitive optimum can be seen to differ from the social optimum. According to economic theory, where there are external costs adjustment closer to the social optimum can be achieved by taxing polluting activities. In Fig. 10.1 an optimal (Pigovian) tax AB levied on the producer would reduce equilibrium output from a competitive equilibrium Q_c to Q_o, at which level buyers would pay the full social cost of production P_c but producer revenue per unit would be taxed by AB to eliminate incentives to produce more than Q_o. Alternatively, if policy was to restrict output to Q_o the producer could be offered compensation for the profit which would be forgone (ABC)[3] by producing less than Q_c. It is essentially this second, 'compensation' alternative

---

[3]Strictly speaking, rather than profit forgone this is the loss of producer surplus when output is reduced to Q_o.

that is embodied in restrictive management agreements and ESA contracts, with their emphasis on incentives (rather than taxes) to encourage voluntary compliance with environmental guidelines.

However, it might be argued that an outcome at Q_o was inadequate in terms of conservation policy, that no further degradation of the environment is acceptable, and that a complete halt to species and landscape loss is desired. That is, following Pearce (1988), that a sustainability criterion should be imposed. In that case output from land-using activities would have to be cut to Q_s and could be achieved if taxation per unit of output was raised to EF, with the producer bearing the full cost of achieving sustainability. EF is the so-called sustainability tax. Alternatively if policy objectives are to be met by incentives rather than taxes, the compensation to be paid to the producer for any profit forgone by cutting production to Q_s would need to equal area ECF in Fig. 10.1.

In the opposite case (Fig. 10.2), where the commercial market equilibrium is suboptimal because of the inability of producers to capture payment for external benefits, a production subsidy of JK per unit of output would increase output to the social optimum Q_o with producers receiving, in addition to the market price P_c, a subsidy equal to the marginal social benefit conferred by the last unit of output. This type of policy is reflected in positive MA and ESA contracts, and in conservation grant policy.

While policy does follow the broad principles of theory in offering payments to secure extra conservation outputs and to compensate for reductions in output to minimize external costs, our knowledge of external costs and benefits is not sufficient to enable reliable estimates of what socially optimal levels and patterns of land use are at the national level, or of what scale and rates of payment are appropriate. This greatly limits what can be said and what is known about the effectiveness of conservation policy. Are there too many SSSIs, and is the marginal cost of extra MAs in excess of the social benefits achieved? Similarly with ESAs, do we have too few or too many, and what social return is generated by an annual cost which is projected to rise to £63 million in 1995/96 for the UK (MAFF, 1993a). Attempts are being made currently to answer this last question, as outlined in Chapter 9, and this may enable a clearer view to emerge as to where the social optimum lies. Willis *et al.* (1993a) have already applied the travel cost method (TCM), hedonic pricing method (HPM) and contingent valuation method (CVM) to value a number of environmental benefits. At present, given the reservations about these methods (Anderson and Bishop, 1986; Schulze *et al.*, 1981; Coursey *et al.*, 1987; Hanley, 1989; Hutchinson and Chilton, 1993), it would be unwise to form very strong conclusions from cost/benefit comparisons based upon them. However, there is some prospect that the methods for these valuations can be strengthened to the point where they are so widely accepted they may provide the sort of economic data required to evaluate the efficiency of conservation policy. In the meantime a more *ad hoc* approach must be employed. In what follows the assessment will draw upon a mixture of cost comparisons and subjective evaluations.

Main Characteristics of ESAs and Alternative Conservation Instruments

The comparative evaluation of ESAs will be conducted against the following alternative instruments, for which only key characteristics will be described:

1. Management agreements.
2. Public sector land purchase and ownership.
3. Grant-aid for land purchase by voluntary bodies.
4. Grants to undertake conservation work.
5. Capital gains and inheritance tax relief for heritage management.
6. Covenants.
7. Cross-compliance – making agricultural price support conditional upon conservation and environmentally sensitive management.

Environmentally Sensitive Areas

Although prescriptions for ESAs have evolved to become more flexible, their basic provision may be considered as offering standard payments for standard contracts to landowners and tenants farming within a given boundary. That is, for each of a number of tiers paying a fixed sum per hectare, there is a fixed contract controlling farming actions. Limited scope for the introduction of supplementary payments for conservation plans has now introduced a flexible element similar to a management agreement – the scope is limited by the annual payment ceiling. In the first round of ESAs contracts were for five years, but, with the extension of these to a second phase, ten-year contracts are available, as is the case with new ESAs.

Acceptance of an ESA contract is entirely voluntary on the part of landowners and tenants operating eligible land within the ESA boundary. The proportion of eligible land entered into such contracts thus varies from a low of 27% in the Test Valley to a high of 89% in the Broads.

Management Agreements

English Nature and the other national successors of the NCC, along with the National Parks Authorities and Local Planning Authorities, all have statutory powers to enter into individual management agreements with individual landowners and tenants.[4] The most important category of these are those

---

[4]A summary of the different types of MA and their authorizing statutes is presented in Colman *et al.* (1992, pp. 24, 25).

operated by English Nature, etc. to protect the system of SSSIs from potentially damaging operations, but there is also a range of options for discretionary MAs by various authorities to promote access, to protect woodland, or to maintain stone walls, ponds, etc. That is, while MAs may be contracts and payments individually negotiated for work to enhance the countryside, the dominant and most studied[5] type is the MA operating to protect the designated system of SSSIs from damage.

Where an SSSI is notified the owner/manager is given a list of operations (PDOs) which would be considered potentially damaging to the site's status and which if contemplated by the owner/manager should be notified to the appropriate authority. If that authority wishes to prevent the operation it has the power (in theory) to halt it for a fixed period while negotiations proceed to try to obtain an MA under which the farmer would be compensated for the 'profit forgone' as a result of stopping the operation. In the case of SSSIs, if the farmer refuses the terms offered he/she can ultimately proceed with the operation. However, if the site is designated a National Nature Reserve compulsory purchase powers can be applied by the authority.

In the main, therefore, MAs are one-off contracts tailored to specific circumstances. However, where there are concentrations of SSSIs in similar circumstances, such as in Exmoor National Park, the terms and conditions have converged towards standard payments and contracts of the ESA type.

Public Ownership and Purchase of Land[6]

The successor bodies to the NCC, as well as the National Parks Authorities (NPAs) and Local Authorities (LAs) all have legislative powers to hold and purchase land in order to protect access or landscape, amenity and wildlife values. Only sparing use has been made of these powers so that by 1989 the NCC and NPAs owned between them a modest total of around 92,000 hectares, with an unknown area in LA ownership. Ownership and management by statutory state bodies with good track records is the most secure way of pursuing state land conservation policy, and as argued elsewhere (Colman, 1989, 1991) it is not necessarily the costliest.

Other public bodies such as the Ministry of Defence and the Forestry Commission are substantial owners of land of conservation value. Although this land is owned for purposes essentially unrelated to conservation, this objective has assumed more importance in recent years and, as in the Breckland ESA, it is of considerable importance for conservation (see Chapter 4).

---

[5]See particularly Whitby *et al.* (1990).
[6]For a fuller description of the scale of public and voluntary body land ownership for conservation purposes see O'Carroll (1993) and Colman *et al.* (1992, pp. 13–20).

Grant-Aided Land Purchase

With the privatization of what were the public Regional Water Authorities and the mooted privatization of the Forestry Commission, plus instructions to local authorities to sell off surplus land, government policy has become less favourable to pursuit of conservation policy through public ownership. Instead it is more supportive of the idea that conservation land should be managed by dedicated voluntary bodies (VBs) with charitable status such as the County Wildlife Trusts, Royal Society for the Protection of Birds and the National Trust. Such bodies owned around 300,000 hectares of land in 1990 and leased and managed an additional 142,000 hectares; since 1990 they have increased these holdings. Much of the owned land has been bequeathed or bought with money given to the VBs, but a smallish proportion of it has been purchased with partial grants from the state, channelled through statutory bodies. This is a particularly attractive option for public policy. Often only a modest proportion of the purchase price has to be grant-aided and the burdens of management then fall upon the VB concerned and are financed in one form or another by visitors and members who are prepared to demonstrate their willingness to pay for the conservation benefits.

Grants for Conservation Works

There exist various systems for providing grants to farmers to enhance the countryside by planting small broadleaved woodlands, repairing walls and buildings, laying hedges, restoring ponds and providing footpaths. These systems may involve standard payments of so much per metre of wall, or may be on the basis of meeting a fixed percentage of the cost incurred, and support may in some cases be conditional upon drawing up a conservation plan.

From the standpoint of evaluating ESAs, the significance of grants is that as the ESA policy has evolved it has incorporated more grant elements for specific works. In the latest ESA prescriptions there are, for example, 80% grants towards the cost of protecting historical and archaeological features, 50% grants for the restoration of ponds and 30% grants for creating or reinstating dykes or their equivalent. It is significant that the rate of grant declines as the farming benefits from the work increase, the principle being that if there are significant private benefits the costs should be met by farmers themselves.

Thus the policy for ESAs has become progressively more concerned with creating new features and reshaping the countryside and less concerned with simply holding the line against further deterioration. In part this change of emphasis reflects the success of most of the early ESAs in signing up a high proportion of eligible land, but it also reflects criticisms which have been made, namely that scope existed to tighten up the contract prescriptions and to demand more for the payments made.

Tax Relief

Conditional exemption from Inheritance Tax (IHT) and Capital Gains Tax (CGT) is available on heritage land of scenic, historic or scientific interest in return for a Management Agreement. Tax exemption is dependent not only upon observing the conditions of the MA but also ensuring that the MA is transferred to new owners if a sale is made or the land is passed to inheritors. This may be interpreted as entailing acceptance of a restrictive covenant on the land (see below).

In comparison with ESAs this option is probably of minor importance, although Whitby (1993) estimates that between 50,000 and 125,000 hectares of heritage land may be IHT and CGT exempt. To the extent that there are large estates lying inside ESAs it does mean that those particular properties might be conserved by alternative means, but it is not an alternative relevant to the majority of landowners in such areas. In passing, it may be noted that a disquieting feature of the MAs qualifying for tax relief is that there is little or no publicity for them so that the public at large may be unable to benefit fully from aspects of agreements designed to provide public goods.

Covenants

In the context of farmed land a covenant is a legally binding undertaking on the use of land, which is accepted by the farmer (the covenantor) for the benefit of another party (the covenantee). The covenantee may be an adjacent farmer or property owner, who then acts as the 'watchdog' to see that the covenant is observed. In the UK the National Trusts (as well as County and District Councils and NPAs) are in the special position of being legally empowered to act as covenantee for land on behalf of society, and they are thus in the position of holding responsibility for over 31,000 hectares of covenants, without necessarily having to hold adjacent land.

Covenants may be of two types. Restrictive covenants prevent the covenantor from engaging in certain actions, while positive ones commit him/her to undertaking particular actions in regard to the property. Whereas restrictive covenants are generally binding on successive owners so long as the nominated covenantee (adjacent property owner or NT) is still there to monitor compliance, the burden of positive covenants cannot readily be transmitted to future owners. From the standpoint of conservation in the countryside, restrictive covenants are the most important.

Where a covenant agreement is broken, the covenantee may sue for damages or seek an injunction restraining violations, as with any legal contract.

Covenants do provide a rather clumsy alternative to other policy instruments for achieving conservation. Land may be purchased by a statutory body, a covenant imposed to protect its environmental value or access, and the land resold. While a loss is typically made on resale, that may be preferable to incurring annual compensation costs for an MA or ESA contract. This option is, however, only capable of sparing application because the opportunity to buy the land targeted by policy arises infrequently.

Cross-Compliance

One of the underlying ironies of land conservation policy is that the payments associated with such instruments as ESAs and MAs are increased by the levels of agricultural price supports, which have been a major stimulus to the process of farming intensification which conservation policy seeks to redress. This is a situation where the conservation policy fights against the effects of price support policy. Rather than persist with this situation, the option exists to link the right of farmers to price support to their observance of conditions ensuring beneficial public goods protection or output. This option, originating in the USA,[7] has now been introduced into the Common Agricultural Policy: livestock subsidies are now dependent upon observing stocking density restrictions; subsidies for cereals and oilseeds for larger farms are conditional upon setting land aside. While the conservation benefits of set-aside are limited, the cross-compliance conditions on stocking rates are an integral element of ESA contracts; thus there is an element of overlap. However, whereas the cross-compliance conditions for livestock payments are general to all areas, those for the ESAs can be tailored more specifically to the particular ecology of each ESA.

Conservation Objectives and the Policy Framework

The notion of countryside conservation effectiveness in relation to public policy is an elusive one which is difficult, indeed impossible, to tie down to any single measure. The reason for this lies partly in the heterogeneity of the 'conservation interest', the diversity of public and voluntary bodies with direct conservation objectives or objectives that indirectly impact on the conservation interest, and the legislative framework determining the mechanisms whereby conservation of objectives may be attained.

In the countryside, conservation policy aims to conserve valued species, habitats, landscapes and landscape features. What is valued in the countryside may reflect its intrinsic qualities ('existence' or 'heritage' value), its use by visitors for access and recreation, and the socioeconomic role it offers to those who live and work there. Not only do different agencies place different

---

[7]See Furness *et al.* (1990) for a further explanation of this type of policy.

emphases on these components of conservation, but at the same time the Agriculture Departments[8] (ADs) and Forestry Commission are implementing policies which have a dominating influence over land use in rural areas. In addition, conservation objectives may relate to the maintenance of a valued conservation interest, but they may also focus on improving that interest or creating new interest.

While the various conservation agencies do cooperate to a considerable degree, their different remits lead to different conservation objectives which imply alternative criteria for effectiveness. The Countryside Commission embraces the concept of multiple-use countryside with concern for natural beauty, heritage, public access and use, and local economies. These objectives pay regard to users and visitors, not just at prime sites but throughout the countryside, and lead to a focus on access, recreation and creative landscape conservation. Such broad objectives also apply to the National Park Authorities (NPAs) where maintenance of landscapes, whole rural communities and visitor-based activities are important objectives.

In contrast, the ESA policy administered by MAFF and the Agricultural Departments operates specifically upon the management of farms in selected, larger areas of special landscape and wildlife interest, and has in the past exhibited little or no concern for recreational use or access. (The provision of access is to be given more weight in future rounds of ESA schemes.) Under this policy there are contracts for farm management which are specifically tailored to the conservation objectives of each designated ESA area. There is a common thread to these contracts insofar as the prescriptions for grassland management all call for limited fertilizer and other chemical use, and for controls over forage making and stock levels. But other requirements or options are specific to a restricted number of ESAs, such as requirements for heather regeneration in the uplands, raising the water table in the wetlands, wall building or stone barn repair where those are key landscape features, and conversion of arable land to grassland in several cases. The objectives of all this add up to (i) prevention of further deterioration of environmental quality, and (ii) selective improvement in the landscape and wildlife quality and content of ESAs. At the inception of the ESA policy the emphasis was on the first of these, but in the second round of ESAs, and in the ten-year extension to the original five-year schemes, the commitment to the second has increased, and there is a heightened emphasis on payments linked to conservation plans which include repairs to and investment in assets which have public goods elements.

The policy for Sites of Special Scientific Interest has different objectives again, and SSSIs were selected by the Nature Conservancy Council according to the following criteria:

---

[8]Ministry of Agriculture, Fisheries and Food; Scottish Office Agriculture and Fisheries Department; Welsh Office for Agricultural Development; Department of Agriculture for Northern Ireland.

- best examples of defined habitat;
- outstanding assemblages of animal populations;
- sites containing rare/threatened and unusual species or outstanding assemblages of rare species.

There is a supplementary criterion that there should be a mosaic of such habitats throughout the country. For the most part English Nature, the Countryside Commission for Wales and Scottish Natural Heritage (the institutions into which the NCC was split in 1991) rely upon existing managers to safeguard sites but have to compensate them in cases where this reduces the profitability of their operations. In the case of National Nature Reserves, however, the statutory agencies themselves assume the role of managers.

The criteria of conservation effectiveness thus vary according to the policy instrument and managing agency under consideration. Since the spheres of influence of policies and agencies overlap, such as in the Peak Park Authority's area, which includes numerous SSSIs as well as the North Peak ESA, this inevitably poses problems for analysis. Nevertheless it is possible to identify partial, operational criteria of effectiveness which can be assessed for particular cases.

The Effectiveness of ESAs

Criteria for Assessment

There are a number of criteria which can be used in evaluating the effectiveness of ESAs and other conservation instruments. The list of these, as set out below, demonstrates both overlap and interrelatedness; for example, ease of monitoring, i.e. monitorability, is a factor in cost efficiency, and flexibility of operation may be associated with greater inherent capacity to conserve and enhance wildlife and landscape features. Nevertheless all the factors in the following list appear worthy of individual emphasis; Appendix 10.1 provides an assessment of the instruments considered above, in terms of the characteristics listed below.

Capacity to protect and enhance

Measures which guarantee long-term agreed management are likely to be more effective than short-term measures. All other things (such as cost) being equal, an instrument which guarantees the desired form of management for a long time is preferable to one with a short contract life.

Other criteria such as *adaptability* and *flexibility* to cope with individual transactions are also important in strengthening protective capacity, and are equally of relevance where environmental enhancement is the objective. Irrespective of these properties, however, the measures required for enhancement and creation of new features are those which support investment and productive works rather than those which entail possession of regulatory and control capacities.

Timeliness

The speed with which a class of instruments can be mobilized, to meet some new environmental threat or to achieve some new policy objective, is important in reviewing efficient policy options for future action. Having a policy of protection by public land purchase is of little help when land comes on the market infrequently and where there are no powers of compulsory purchase or other means of intervention.

Targetability

Some instruments can be, and are, more narrowly targeted than others; for example SSSIs are much more clearly focused than ESAs. Also instruments operate in relation to targets in different ways, e.g. by coercion as opposed to incentive. Are the chosen instruments efficient in terms of the targets?

Monitorability

In the case of activities to enhance environmental outputs, the capacity for monitoring to ensure that intended and contracted outcomes do occur is generally easier than with conservation measures. With the latter there are cases where the practices agreed under the policy are inherently difficult to monitor and hence police; that is true of limitations on stock levels, on insecticide and herbicide application, and on inorganic fertilizer application, among others. In conjunction with this is the issue of how effectively monitoring is actually carried out. Economy in monitoring for budgetary reasons could result in evasions which reduce conservation effectiveness.

Cost efficiency

This criterion is of crucial importance to policy-makers and analysts, but is only capable of application in limited ways. As previously stated, ideally the economist would like to be able to undertake a full cost-benefit analysis, weighing the social value of conservation benefits against the costs of alternative policy instruments. In the absence of adequate measures of the value of conservation outputs this is generally impractical. Where extremely high values are attached to conserving specific habitats and sites monetary cost becomes less important, and instruments which guarantee conservation are more efficient.

In more general conditions, however, analysis will typically be limited to asking whether the chosen instrument is the most cost-effective in protecting an individual site or achieving a given standard of management of a target area, and are there alternatives which might do the job more cheaply? Answering this question subsumes several others since the overall cost of any instrument will include administrative and monitoring costs in addition to transfer payments made to those undertaking conservation works or systems of land management.

For areas as large as many ESAs the notion of a single site may be unhelpful. It may be preferable to view such an area as being composed of a large number of sites, possibly coinciding with different ownerships. Then as we shall see below, it is possible to consider (i) whether the ESA payment is necessary on all those subsites contracted into the scheme, or whether some are adequately protected without the necessity of payment, and (ii) whether some of the sites would be better under some other form of conservation management contract than that provided by the ESA. Alternative ways of phrasing these questions in economic terms are to ask: (i) are all the policy costs actually necessary?; and (ii) could the same or even greater conservation benefits be achieved at lower cost?

Political acceptability and transparency

It is clear that some policy mechanisms are more acceptable to either or both the policy-makers and the landowners/farmers who are involved. From the standpoint of the latter, voluntary measures which permit farmers to opt out if it is in their best interests are clearly preferred, and the National Farmers Union strongly argues for them. Voluntarism may also be preferred by the Ministry or agency managing the policy as it breeds a more harmonious working relationship; however, other interested parties, particularly con-servation bodies and possibly the Treasury, might incline more to compulsion or at least to tightly defined compliance. In recent years in the UK the balance of political support has been in favour of a voluntary approach to countryside conservation, although in some quarters that might be interpreted as reflecting the political power of the farm lobby. Clearly linked to political acceptability is the concept of transparency. Instruments which are clearly defined in terms of function, eligibility, payment arrangements and verifica-tion (highly transparent) are likely to be more acceptable both to the farming community and as mechanisms for the delivery of EC environmental policy.

Promotion of conservation-mindedness

There is a clear relationship between this criterion and political acceptability at the farm level. That which is acceptable may be more likely to promote positive attitudes to conservation, while that which is more unacceptable may well lead to antagonism towards conservation policies. This links clearly to the political acceptability of measures to farmers. To the extent that they perceive MAFF as working to help farmers, they appear to be more positively disposed to measures operated by MAFF. The former NCC and the NPAs, however, are often seen as having a more antagonistic, regulatory relationship with farmers which is sometimes a cause of resistance.

Some Political Considerations

At the political level there is little doubt that the creation and introduction of the ESA instrument has been a success. It was pioneered in the UK in the form of the Broads Grazing Marshes Conservation Scheme (BGMCS), which was initiated in 1985 and subsequently developed into the Broads ESA. The UK government persuaded other EC member states to accept the type of policy measures embodied in the BGMCS (the halting of agricultural intensification and the support for conservation-friendly farming) as being acceptable under the Common Agricultural Policy and hence eligible in selected areas for partial funding from Brussels. This acceptance was enshrined in Article 19 of the EC Structures Regulation (797/85;[9] EC, 1985a), which authorized the payment of national aids in ESAs 'in order to contribute towards the introduction or continued use of production practices compatible with the requirements of conserving the natural habitat and ensuring an adequate income for farmers.' The process of designating ESAs in the UK has proceeded through implementation of the Regulation in the 1986 Act (as explained in Chapter 1) and has also been adopted in other member states of the EC.

For a large variety of reasons the ESA mechanism has also proved attractive, or at least acceptable, to a wide range of interest groups. From the standpoint of MAFF and the Agricultural Departments of Scotland, Wales and Northern Ireland (SOAFD, WOAD and DANI respectively) it has provided a flagship means of developing the image of a more environmentally sensitive agricultural policy and has done so at only very modest cost to the Treasury. Applied in the form of schemes which offer fixed payments for standard contracts, acceptance of which is entirely voluntary by farmers with eligible land, it has proved attractive to farmers who have generally found it a means of enhancing their incomes, however modestly. The fact that there has been high take-up in most ESAs, because the terms have proved sufficiently attractive, has in turn added to the political attractiveness to policy-makers, who have seen the objectives, as they defined them, being met.

Not all conservationists have been pleased with all aspects of the ESA

---

[9]This regulation is now consolidated in 2328/91 and is to be found in Article 21.

schemes. In some areas the prescriptions were seen as being too blunt and as having been too hastily developed to address some of the important conservation needs of their areas. However, some of the early criticisms have been met in the form of revised management prescriptions in the latest ESA schemes, and there is less unease about the true environmental colours of the scheme. Earlier perceptions by some, that they were simply a new way of channelling financial aid to some farmers, have been dampened by the increased emphasis on paying for new and positive environmental outputs rather than just making payment to ensure that unwanted changes were avoided. Nevertheless reservations still exist among conservationists about the efficacy of the ESA programme.

From the standpoint of MAFF, European policy-makers, farmers' representatives and farmers themselves the ESAs scheme has been judged successful. ESAs appear to be here to stay and have proved responsive in various ways to informed criticism. A number of reservations and qualifications relating to their cost and efficiency are raised in the next section, which can be set against the currently dominant political view that ESAs are a success.

Cost and Economic Efficiency of ESAs

A hypothetical exploration

The simplest way of exploring certain general issues about the cost-effectiveness of ESAs is to consider a hypothetical case. Suppose there was a hypothetical ESA of 1000 hectares, made up of ten farms of equal size (100 ha) but under different ownership and management. All land within the area is eligible for a single tier ESA payment and contract. The land is under traditional extensive grazing management with an interesting flora and fauna. The ESA payments are (for simplicity) £100 per hectare per annum over the ten-year contract life. Given the fact that the first-round ESAs in the UK have been given ten-year extensions with revised management prescriptions, it may be assumed that the life of the hypothetical ESA will be extended beyond the current ten-year life and is likely to continue for the foreseeable future.

Using this simple structure it is possible to construct a number of alternative policy scenarios in which the budgetary cost of the ESA policy is compared to alternative policies in which (i) only individualized management agreements are negotiated in response to the threat of a PDO, or (ii) only purchase of threatened land is contemplated, or (iii) where an opportunistic mix of policy instruments is employed with the objective of minimizing the cost of executing the policy. The criterion used to compare the costs of the policy alternatives is the net present value (NPV) of the stream of net costs, i.e. the present value of discounted future costs and benefits.

Table 10.1. Net present value of £100 per annum.

Years of life	Interest rate	
	6%	10%
10	736	615
20	1147	851
25	1278	908
30	1377	943

Because it is difficult to decide what is the most appropriate annual discount rate to employ in calculating NPV it is often helpful to consider a range of alternatives. In this case we will consider only the current Treasury discount rate for public works projects producing environmental goods of 6%, and a 10% rate for comparison (Table 10.1).

Case 1 – all 1000 hectares are enrolled in the ESA scheme The NPV for 10 years would be £736,000 at 6% per annum and for 20 years would be £1,147,000. If the administration cost, which includes monitoring, were to average as little as 10% of the transfer costs that would add an extra £73,600 NPV over 10 years and £114,700 over 20. Note that if the ESA prescriptions can be complied with at such little cost that the profit forgone annually is less than £100 per hectare, all farmers benefit from joining the scheme.

Case 2 – 200 acres are threatened by potentially damaging operations; a policy of negotiating management agreements on these is pursued If it is assumed no payments are needed to protect the remaining 800 acres, then it is obvious that provided the annual MA payments per hectare average less than £500 the NPV of the payments to farmers will be less than if all 1000 hectares receive £100 per year under the ESA. If the negotiation and administration costs are higher than those associated with an ESA scheme, even after allowing for the smaller area over which contracts have to be implemented, the 'break-even' average MA payment will be less than £500 per hectare.

An average figure of £500 per hectare per year is a very high one for management agreements, particularly in non-arable areas, whereas a £100 per hectare ESA payment is not out of line with those for lowland grassland areas in England. Whitby *et al.* (1990) calculated that, in 1988, the NCC paid an average of £141 per hectare under annual payment MAs for non-woodland SSSIs, with total administrative costs to the NCC over all types of MAs running at around 28% of the estimated total compensation payments to landowners; thus the overall average cost of an MA was around £180 per hectare.

What this case is intended to do is to raise the question of whether, from the narrow standpoint of budgetary cost, it is necessary to offer all owners and managers of eligible land within an ESA the standard payments and contracts. Other instruments might provide a cheaper alternative to providing the same level of *protection* from detrimental change. The matter of how to induce improvements and positive action is clearly a different one.

Case 3 – the possibility of purchasing land to safeguard its management and thus avoid annual payments   According to the ADAS/AMC/CLA series the average price for all sales of farmland (with buildings) in England was approximately £3750 per hectare in 1992. The Oxford/Savills series for auction transactions between July and December 1992 gives figures of £5510 per hectare with farmhouse and buildings and £3971 for 'bareland'. Suppose that within the ESA any farm which came up for sale would fetch £3500 per 'hectare' because of the 'unimproved' nature of the farmland. The NPV at 6% discount of the cost of implementing the ESA over 20 years, at £1,147,000, could be used to purchase just over 328 hectares of land; this is before considering any difference in administration costs. The lower the price of land the more that could be purchased for the equivalent NPV, and the higher the interest rate the smaller the amount which could be purchased.

This calculation of equivalence of cost is before making allowance for the fact that the public sector as owner of the land could obtain an annual rental income from it, which itself has an NPV, and also that any land owned is an asset which could be sold later to recoup most if not all of the purchase price in real terms. Suppose for example that land in the ESA is capable of generating a net rental income to a public sector body of £80 per hectare per year; current average land rentals are approximately £100 per hectare per year. The NPV of an annual income stream of £80 per year at 6% discount is £918 over 20 years and £1101 over 30 years and increasing. In other words existence of a rental income can be counted as a partial offset to the cost of purchasing land and justify the purchase of a larger area when equating the NPV of the cost of land purchase with that of operating the ESA scheme: alternatively the income could be used to purchase more land. Again, if only a small proportion of land within the ESA actually requires action to hire or buy land use rights, the land purchase option could prove attractive, particularly if (i) land prices are low, (ii) the appropriate discount rate is low and (iii) the ESA contract payments are set at relatively high levels.

Cost efficiency of ESAs in practice

There has been little systematic attempt to apply the methodology implied by the hypothetical exploration above to test whether individual ESAs could have been replaced more cheaply by a mix of other instruments without sacrificing either the degree of protection afforded by the ESA or the degree of environmental enhancement achieved. Also, given the diversity of ESA types in relation to their contract costs and the wide range of possible purchase prices of land or management agreement costs, no general conclusion is likely to apply across the board. Nevertheless there are a number of relevant observations and a limited number of results to present.

As a number of preceding chapters (particularly Chapters 2, 4 and 5) make clear, there are significant areas of eligible land in some ESAs which were already protected by other means prior to the designation of ESAs. Land owned by the National Trust (NT), the RSPB, the Woodland Trust and County Wildlife Trusts is present in varying degrees in most ESAs, and much of that land is also designated SSSI. Although these areas are eligible for ESA contracts, and the NT certainly ensures that it and its tenants enrol in the ESA, there can be little doubt that they would have continued to be farmed, for the most part, within the management guidelines, even if no ESA payment had been available. It is striking, but not surprising, that voluntary conservation bodies do not threaten PDOs on SSSI land under their control. Indeed they are continuously acquiring more SSSI land, both within and outside the ESAs, in order to protect it and where possible enhance its wildlife, access or landscape value.

In addition there are other purely private landowners and farmers with SSSI land which they have been prepared to manage without threatening PDOs and without demanding a management agreement. In fact, the surprise is that more landowners have not taken advantage of SSSI status on their land to threaten PDOs simply to obtain the extra income an MA would generate. Of the 915,000 hectares of agricultural SSSI covered by the study of Whitby *et al.* (1990) only 77,000 (or 8.4%) were under Section 15 MAs. While a substantial proportion of the remainder could not plausibly be threatened by a PDO, given remoteness and low agricultural potential, there is marked evidence within these figures for the notion of countryside stewardship by farmers. That exercise of stewardship is, however, not confined to SSSI land in particular but applies in some degree to all non-arable land which has been managed in such a way that it has merited classification as eligible for inclusion in an ESA. To the extent that much land within ESAs has been farmed extensively in a way which would not breach the ESA contract prescriptions, it must be judged that some of it would have continued to be farmed in that way even had the relevant ESA not been created.

What this all adds up to is the judgement that some, possibly substantial, areas of eligible land in ESAs on which contract payments are now being made would not have been farmed differently had the contracts not been offered. One study which did attempt to explore the possibility that protection might have been secured more cheaply than by offering a standard contract was that of the prototype ESA, the Broads Marshes Conservation Scheme (Colman and Lee, 1988). Data were available in that area relating to land prices, management agreement costs, the Tier 1 ESA payments, as well as

Table 10.2. Net present value of the net budgetary costs of conserving grazing land by alternative policy instruments (£ per ha). (From Colman, 1991.)

Years	BGMCS/ESA* fixed payment	Management agreement	Public purchase
20	1545	3115	1565
25	1748	3523	1443
30	1906	3843	1347

*BGMCS = Broads Grazing Marshes Conservation Scheme.

rental income for grazing land, and there was some information on administrative costs. In fact the values used were: (i) a flat-rate ESA payment at £124 per hectare per year; (ii) an MA costing £250 per hectare per year; and (iii) land purchase at £2500 per hectare with subsequent annual net rental income for grazing at £75 per hectare.[10] Using these figures, and a 5% discount rate (as used in the original calculations), the NPV for *any* hectare of land covered by each of the three policy alternatives is shown in Table 10.2.

What is very striking is that land purchase was estimated to be a very competitive alternative to the ESA, being only marginally more expensive on the basis of a 20-year horizon and cheaper thereafter – for while ESA payments continue to increase, the costs of the rental accruing to owned land reduces the NPV of public purchase with every passing year. Thus in the specific case of what was to become the Broads ESA, the recommendation was for the public sector to buy land whenever the opportunity arose at costs of around £2500 per hectare or less, and to thereby save the annual ESA payment. From a Treasury standpoint even more efficient would have been purchase by a voluntary conservation body with grant-aid for only a proportion of the purchase price paid for by the public sector.

In fact, the results called into question whether the ESA was needed at all. For even a management agreement of £250 per hectare per year was only twice as expensive as the ESA per hectare; thus, if less than half the eligible land in the ESA was under threat it would have been cheaper to negotiate MAs on that land than to operate the ESA. There were conflicting views as to how much land in the ESA was actually under threat, although Colman and Lee (1988) argued that it was less than the 50% of the total, which would have potentially rendered one of the alternative instruments operating selectively to be more cost effective.

---

[10]Full details of the underlying assumptions are presented in Colman and Lee (1988).

Impact of ESAs on farm incomes[11]

Through the monitoring programme of ESAs undertaken by MAFF, estimates of the policy impact on participating farmers' incomes are available, some of which have been reported in earlier chapters in depth. Overall, what is striking is the high proportion of the payments transferred to farmers which have not been offset by the costs involved in complying with the contracts and have thus been reflected in the incomes of farmers. In general, the simpler the scheme, as reflected in the number of tiers of prescription – higher tiers typically reflect higher costs of compliance – the greater the proportion of the transfer payments retained as farm income. For example, in the Shropshire Borders ESA it is estimated for 1988/89 that the £554,900 paid to farmers resulted in increased farm incomes totalling £471,000, which was equivalent to an average of £2507 per farm or £35 per hectare enrolled in the scheme. Similarly in the Somerset Levels and Moors in 1988/89 the net incomes of surveyed participating farmers increased by an estimated £97,300 as a result of ESA payments of £108,400, i.e. 90% of payments went directly to income and only 10% was required to cover costs.

Where higher tiers of the ESA involve converting arable land back to grassland larger costs are involved. In the Suffolk River Valleys ESA, over the first five years 1988 to 1992 farm incomes are estimated to have increased by £2,901,000 or 61% of the total £4,723,000 paid to farmers, but for farmers enrolling land only in Tier I there were few costs of compliance and a higher proportion of their payments was reflected in net income. In the South Downs ESA the income of surveyed farms in 1988/89 was estimated to have increased by only £70,000, which is only 30% of payments received. In the Broads ESA in 1988/89, payments of £410,100 to surveyed farms translated into an estimated £274,400 increase in income, equivalent to £3475 per farm or £96 per hectare.

It is perhaps understandable, given the sort of estimates presented above, that a criticism which arose of many of the ESA management prescriptions was that they demanded too little change and action from farmers, that there were few costs, and that farmers were being paid to do what they would have done in any case. This was not true of all ESAs and all tiers of prescription, but it certainly was the case that the farming restrictions imposed in many of the lower tier contracts appear to have been designed to demand the minimum of change. One justification that could be put forward for this was that in the first stage it was important to entice high enrolment in the schemes, to heighten environmental awareness, and to provide a platform for more demanding prescriptions in extension phases of ESAs. To some extent this has happened as later ESA guidelines stress conservation plans and

---

[11]The details in this section are taken from the monitoring reports published by MAFF for the ESAs referred to.

payments for investment in walls, ponds, hedgerows and so on, all of which call for definite expenditure.

Nevertheless, the high proportion of total ESA payments which have been estimated to pass into increased incomes does reinforce doubts about the necessity for such payments. With a standard payment instrument it is virtually inevitable that those who can qualify while incurring costs less than the payments will do so. At the margin there will be some landlords and farmers for whom the payments only just meet the costs, and in a minority of cases losses may have been made. But for the majority of those enrolled in ESAs it appears clear that the costs have been substantially less than the income and in some (possibly many) cases that the costs have been virtually zero. Inevitably that does raise questions about the need for, and the productivity of these schemes. It is of course always difficult to know what would happen had the ESAs not been created; estimating the so-called 'counterfactual' situation is usually fraught with problems. However, doubts will continue to be raised about the necessity for making payments on all the land declared eligible in some ESAs and about the amount of 'conservation' bought in certain of them. In others where arable land has been converted back to grassland, water tables raised, and physical works undertaken, the positive results are more clear-cut.

Other economic impacts

As the detailed reports about individual ESAs have revealed, ESA schemes have caused reductions in stocking levels in every case, and reductions in arable areas, particularly of cereals, in others. This reduced output associated with these changes has meant some modest reductions in agricultural commodity price support costs and expenditures by the UK government, which can be treated as benefits which partially offset the budgetary costs of the ESA payments to farmers. In the case of the South Downs ESA for 1988/89 it was estimated that the reduction in Treasury cost of agricultural support payments was £180,000 as against the UK cost of transfers to farmers/landlords of £578,900. For the Suffolk River Valleys, support cost reduction for 1988 to 1992 was estimated to be in the range £402,000 to £1,566,000 as against the UK cost of transfers of £3,960,000. In other cases such as the Somerset Levels and Moors, support cost savings were estimated to be less than 1% of the cost of payments to farmers.

It has also been revealed that the ESAs have had some small positive employment effects in their local areas. In the Suffolk River Valleys (SRV) the total employment effect in the area, including off-farm jobs, was estimated at 85 to 125 full-time jobs, while in the North Peak the comparable figure was put at 30 to 50 jobs. These employment effects were also paralleled by income effects in the local economies. After allowing for so-called multiplier effects these were estimated at between £1.4 and £6.1 million per year in the North

Peak and between £3.5 and £8.5 million in the SRV. This underlines that the effects of the ESA policy extend to rural development more generally and are not confined to agricultural practice and environmental outputs.

Additional Considerations

In several respects the cost efficiency arguments set out above might be criticized as being too narrow. One view which has been argued is that ESA payments should not be perceived as compensation for restrictions imposed and should not therefore be assessed on whether the results would be achieved more cheaply by some other instrument, by reducing ESA payments, or by abandoning the standard contract in favour of contracts tailor-made for each case. Rather it has been argued that ESAs provide positive rewards for environmentally friendly land management and should be used to raise the incomes of those providing the particular mix of public goods found in ESAs. However, that raises the question of why such rewards should only be available to landowners and farmers within ESA boundaries. The only answer to this could be that the ESAs are special areas, that resources are finite, and that a degree of arbitrariness is inevitable in determining eligibility.

These are not arguments that have convinced everybody, and several bodies have called for a 'menu' system of payments for all types of public goods outputs from land management (Countryside Commission, 1989). Under these proposals there might be a payment to manage the water level in water meadows irrespective of where they occur, or to adopt grassland management practices to maintain and improve all plant-rich unimproved grassland throughout the UK. In MAFF's Farm Conservation Grant Scheme, in which grants are available to repair traditional buildings, repair walls and re-lay hedges everywhere, elements of the menu approach have been adopted nationwide. It is perhaps ironic that the newer ESA prescriptions also adopt these grant-aid features. From one standpoint that is excellent insofar as it reflects a move to paying farmers in ESAs for positive actions and away from the earlier practice of paying them if certain things did not happen. But the fact that similar, although less comprehensive, 'menu'-type grant-aid schemes are now available nationally diminishes the distinctiveness of ESA schemes and has generated new elements of policy overlap.

It must also be acknowledged that the preceding cost efficiency analysis of ESAs is narrow in other ways. While in theory it might be cheaper to negotiate individual MAs as required after identifying all eligible areas in ESAs as SSSIs, or to purchase the same land, or grant-aid a voluntary body to do so whenever the opportunity arises, it is simpler to declare the area an ESA and to provide all landowners and farmers of eligible land with a standard contract on terms sufficiently attractive to the majority of them. The political disturbance is less, administration is easier, and there is little resistance from farmers. Also in national budgetary terms the costs are relatively small,

although that is not a justification for overlooking the fact that a distributional injustice may be committed in transferring tax revenues to a population
of farmers who may be better off than many taxpayers.

Conclusions

There is considerable diversity among the ESAs which have been created, in
both character and policy objectives. While there is an underlying common
objective of maintaining a traditional, wildlife and environmentally rich form
of farming, and where possible to help re-create it, the means and requirements for doing so differ greatly from one ESA to another. Policy has been
effected by means of a basic set of standard management contracts in which
a range of standard elements have been permutated to fit the requirements of
each case. Thus there are elements relating to grassland management which
are common to virtually all the ESAs, while others relating to water-table
management, to reversion of arable land to grass, and to the restoration and
management of traditional features are only appropriate in a subset of ESAs.
Broadly speaking this formula has been successful as the basis for an ever-
expanding programme of achieving more environmentally sensitive farming
in key areas. It has proved politically acceptable to farmers, landowners and
government. Moreover, it is accepted that for the ESAs in which monitoring
and evaluation has been completed, the schemes have slowed down the rate
of damage to existing landscapes, habitats and existing features, but that the
extent to which they have achieved a positive increase in these qualities has
been limited to a few cases, and has been most obvious where there has been
conversion of arable land back to grass (e.g. South Downs, Suffolk River
Valleys).

The changes to the basic ESA format had greater effects in certain circumstances
than others, but in some (particularly the Test Valley) it must be judged to
have achieved comparatively little. A possible index of the extent to which
individual ESAs have been effective is the ratio of the estimated increase in
farming net income to the total payment made to farmers and landowners for
agreeing a contract. The higher this ratio the less change farmers have had
to make to comply with the contract and the lower the effectiveness of the
contract. Implicit recognition of this has been reflected in the changes made
to management prescriptions for later waves of ESAs and for the second phase
of earlier ones. Incorporation of the need for whole farm conservation plans
and greater emphasis on payments for specific investments to enhance
landscape quality require more investment by farmers to qualify for the
contract payments.

The changes to the basic ESA format have, however, reduced the
distinctiveness of policy in the ESA from that applicable more widely to
farming areas. As an unpublished document from the Countryside Commis-

sion states in relation to another initiative to provide grant-aid for a wide range of improving investments, 'The Commission views both Countryside Stewardship and the revised ESA system as part of an inexorable progression towards a unified national support system for enlightened land management.' It is not only the Countryside Stewardship Scheme run by the Countryside Commission which is duplicated in some of the grant aid elements of the ESA policy but also MAFF's Farm and Conservation Grant Scheme, which provides grant aid for the restoration and repair of traditional buildings and walls, to give just one further example. Thus, some of the changes made to the ESA policy to make it more cost effective have incorporated grant-aid elements available under policy initiatives which are not restricted to particular boundaries. What ESA schemes can do, and the general policies cannot, is to tailor the rates of grant aid more specifically to each particular area's circumstances.

Another major factor which impinges on views about the role of ESA policy is the important changes made to the Common Agricultural Policy of the EC in 1992. In the case of cereals and oilseeds significant reductions in price supports have been compensated for by direct payments per hectare; farmers with more than 40 acres of cereals in 1992/93 had to qualify for these by setting-aside (taking out of production) 15% of their area. While the environmental benefits of set-aside are in themselves small, or even negative in some respects, this does mean that there is now virtually no likelihood of a loss of further grassland to arable production, and the opportunity exists to develop policies to exploit set-aside land for environmental enhancement along the lines of the Countryside Premium Scheme. In the case of beef the increased headage payments are limited to 90 animals and require compliance with certain maximum stocking rates, while the ewe premium is likewise to be restricted below a maximum number of animals per farmer, which will in the UK also have the effect of creating pressure for reduced stocking rates by large operators. Since restrictions on stocking rates are a central feature of ESA schemes, here is a convergence of general agricultural and ESA policy which at the margin reduces the need for the latter.

This chapter has attempted to assess the effectiveness of the ESA mechanism against alternative instruments for achieving the same environmental objectives. It has been argued that there is an element of overkill in ESA schemes whereby some farmers and landowners can comply with the contractual terms of the ESA by making no changes to existing or planned practice. In effect they are being rewarded for doing what they would in any case do, and such rewards may be seen to be unnecessary. To the extent that this is true, there are in principle cheaper ways of achieving the policy outcome by targeting one of a number of alternative instruments on only those farmers who might contemplate changes viewed as socially undesirable. These alternatives might not succeed in halting all undesirable change, but ESAs cannot achieve that either. Entry into an ESA scheme is voluntary, and not all farmers agree to join, as evidenced by the varying proportions of eligible land in different ESAs which are enrolled in the schemes.

The comparative simplicity of the standard contract system embodied in ESA schemes is attractive and it may be that the potential budgetary savings from employing alternative instruments are insufficient to justify change to what is perceived as a successful policy. Of more significance to the future role of ESAs are the questions raised about the need to single out these chosen areas against a background of an agricultural policy which generates much less pressure for agricultural intensification and where the costs of promoting more environmentally friendly farming are likely to fall.

Appendix 10.1
Comparative analysis of
conservation instruments

APPENDIX 10.1. Comparative analysis of conservation instruments.
(Modified from Colman *et al.*, 1992.)

Criteria of effectiveness	Management agreements		Standard payments: ESA type	Public sector land purchase/ ownership
	Regulatory (e.g. s15 and s41)*	Incentive (e.g. s39)*		
Protection of wildlife sites	Tailor-made for this purpose. Some instances of wilful damage in notification period. Negotiations almost invariably produce an agreement. Fair degree of long-term protection	May aid conservation indirectly by improving the quality of an area	Cannot guarantee to elicit voluntary agreement on key individual sites. Prescriptions too general to hit specific targets. 10-year contracts offer medium-term protection	Ideally suited to long-term conservation. Provides very strong guarantee of protection, subject to continued political will
Protection of large-scale land-use designations or landscapes	Is employed on relatively large areas, e.g. Leek Moors/Goyt Valley. No obvious reason why it cannot be successful	May aid conservation indirectly by improving the quality of an area	Developed for large relatively homogeneous habitat types within larger boundaries. Could be extended to apply nationally to specific land-use systems	Not ideal for large-scale, rapid applications. Opportunities for land purchase are limited. Supporting or supplementary role
Enhancement and creation of new interest	Not applicable	These are specifically designed to promote enhancement and access subject to opportunity	Incorporate standard contracts for enhancement, e.g. arable to grass, dyke rebuilding, heather regeneration, etc. Capable of widespread application, e.g. as through CPS†	Public ownership can be used for enhancement
Timeliness	Designating SSSIs has been a slow process, and creation of National Parks even slower	Opportunities may take time to mature. Budgetary constraints may relegate incentive agreements to a lower priority level	Rapid once ESA or special area has been designated	Has to be activated quickly when land comes up for sale
Targetability	Can be focused very precisely	Can be focused very precisely	Voluntary take-up, cannot target individual sites as opposed to larger areas	Can be targeted precisely, but lack of opportunities may prevent use

Grant-aided land purchase	Grants (e.g. FCGS,‡ s39 WCA)	Capital tax relief (e.g. from IHT and CGT)	Cross-compliance	Covenants
Voluntary bodies play a vital role in conservation of key sites. May be some conflict between VB objectives (e.g. access) and conservation. Quality of management high to fair	Not designed for protection in a continuous manner	Linked to individual holdings that successfully apply for tax exemption. Reactive instrument, therefore haphazard. Entails imposing individual management (effectively covenant) agreements. Can apply to special smaller sites and larger areas. Provides long-term protection. Use could be expanded	Not suited to individual agreements. Few direct conservation benefits	Provides for range of restrictions and positive requirements on individual sites. Not clear how effective they are
VBs may not be interested in all land supported by ESAs. As for public sector purchase, opportunities are limited	Not applicable		Is envisaged as tied to support regimes rather than designated areas. There are possibilities for controlling stock levels in upland areas qualifying for payments	Not ideally suited as covenants arise property by property
Grant aid can be made conditional upon investment in improvements by the VB	One-off standard grants used specifically to promote enhancement. Where only grant aid is available, encouragement biased to more commercial investments	Could encourage enhancement agreements and conservation investment. But Treasury secrecy has meant public unaware of use values	Not ideal for this purpose. Difficult to devise annual investment programmes of right size. Where set-aside is cross-complying condition, could supplement by grants for special works	Limited impact in the absence of complementary grants
Has to be activated quickly when land comes up for sale	Capacity for rapid response	Not timely because driven by tax planning of landowners	Applies across the board immediately legislation is passed	Can be rapidly imposed by existing owners
As with public purchase	Are transparent. Targetable on types of work and/or specific areas	Not targetable insofar as triggered by holding owner. Targetable insofar as applications may be rejected	A blunt instrument, difficult to target	Target specific

Table 10.1. *continued*

Criteria of effectiveness	Management agreements		Standard payments: ESA type	Public sector land purchase/ ownership
	Regulatory (e.g. s15 and s41)*	Incentive (e.g. s39)*		
Monitorability	SSSIs requiring sensitive management may be costly and difficult to monitor	Ready monitoring of works undertaken	Many negative restrictions are difficult to monitor fully	Makes monitoring easy
Payment system	Annual (individualized or standard) and lump sum. Latter carries fewer restrictions	Lump sum or annual payments. Negotiable	Annual, 10-year period. Subject to periodic revision	Purchase cost plus annual management costs partially offset by farming revenue
Cost efficiency	On a per ha basis, profit forgone payments for s15s likely to exceed standard ESA payments, but this more than offset by larger scale uptake of standard payments. Total cost probably lower than for equivalent ESA	Efficient, as payments individually negotiated in relation to costs incurred	Total budgetary cost relatively high. Stimulates uptake on land not under threat. Useful income support instrument	For individual sites this can be more cost efficient than ESA or s15 management agreements. Is the one case where budgetary cost buys an asset
Political acceptability and transparency	Sound principle but engenders element of conflict between NCC and farmers. Not transparent	No obvious barriers to acceptability	Has become highly politically acceptable to farmers and MAFF	Acceptable on low-profile, small-scale basis. Would be political resistance to widespread use. Indeed, govt. pressure to sell public land
Promotes conservation-mindedness	Held to have negative impact	Positive	Positive or uncertain effects	Possibly neutral for farmers

*s15, Section 15 of the Countryside Act, 1968; s39 and s41, Sections 39 and 41 of the Wildlife and Countryside Act, 1981.
†Country Premium Scheme.
‡Farm Conservation Grant Scheme.

Grant-aided land purchase	Grants (e.g. FCGS, s39 WCA)	Capital tax relief (e.g. from IHT and CGT)	Cross-compliance	Covenants
Rely on committed VB to undertake monitoring	Monitoring easy with capital works, but costly with small grant-aid works	Responsibility for monitoring lies with various public bodies. Effectiveness may depend upon type of agreement	As for ESAs	Monitoring variable. Depends upon resources and interest of covenantee
Part of purchase cost. But, land may be eligible for ESA-type payments or MAs with payments	Variety of systems, but dominated by one-off payments. Current policy seems to make only limited provision for maintenance	Cost is forgone revenue to Treasury plus administrative set-up cost to CC, NCC	No additional budgetary cost	Donated free, or covenants may be purchased by buying land and selling subject to covenant
Given low proportion of purchase cost typically granted, this is likely to be the cheapest option, provided VB management is of good standard	Efficient in sense that grants are based on cost of work done, or on average cost. Can provide some labour income to small farmers	Not possible to assess. Information is confidential. Treasury method of assessment not publicly available	Switch from old support system to new one which is cross-complied may be very efficient. New transfer costs offset by lower surplus management costs	Little evidence. Should be cost effective. Lower budgetary cost than land purchase
Most studies rank this option at the top. No political resistance	No inherent political resistance. Conservation grants favoured above farm investment grants. Transparent	Useful way of protecting heritage. Capable of expansion. Confidentiality restricts transparency	Makes continuance of direct agricultural subsidies more acceptable. Needs to be transparent	No obvious barriers to acceptability
Possibly neutral for farmers	Positive	Weak – main stimulus is tax reduction	Can be positive	Neutral buyer or tenant accepts covenant

11

WHAT FUTURE FOR ESAs?

Martin Whitby

This chapter draws together the evidence from previous chapters in summary form before turning to extract the main issues which have arisen in preparing this book. Finally a brief prognosis for ESAs is presented.

The Evidence So Far

The opening chapter reviewed the economic and political forces which culminated in the introduction of the administrative framework for ESAs in 1985 and 1986. These included the continuing European farm policy dilemma of burgeoning output, high budgetary costs and falling farm incomes, as well as consistent pressures arising in the field of international trade. The persistent pressure from an increasingly well-informed and determined environmental lobby, concerned at the loss of traditional agricultural landscapes and habitats, combined with the agricultural pressures to produce a rare confluence of interests between the environmental and the farm lobbies. Although the precise mechanism of ESAs, which reimburse farmers for following particular production systems that are considered environmentally friendly, was new, the sequence of policy instruments which preceded them in the UK can be clearly identified. Particularly well known are the Exmoor management agreements, which were introduced in 1979/80 to check the rate of ploughing-up of heather moorland, and the Broads Grazing Marshes Conservation Scheme, which was initiated by the Countryside Commission to sustain a traditional beef grazing system under threat from arable encroachment.

Following this sequence, the implementation of EC Regulation 797/85 in the Agriculture Act of 1986 led to the designation of two rounds of ESAs in 1987 and 1988. These were renewed in 1992 and 1993. Further new designations were added in 1993, and yet more are intended for 1994.

253

Table 11.1. The sequence of designation of ESAs.

	1987	1988	1989	1992	1993	1994	Totals operative 1994
Number of designations							
New	8	10	1		11	8	19
Redesignations				7	12		19
Total							38
Area of designations (ha)							
New	455,976	329,131	7400		801,400	392,700	1,194,100
Redesignations				416,070	595,929		1,011,999
Total							2,206,099

The speed with which these arrangements have been introduced and taken up is one of the notable features of this policy instrument, compared with very much slower growth in the area under management agreements in the longer designated Sites of Special Scientific Interest. The time sequence of this complex sequence of designations is reported in Table 1.2 and summarized in Table 11.1, where it can be seen that the 38 ESAs will cover 2.2 million hectares by 1994.

Another favourable feature of the 1986 Agriculture Act is that MAFF has interpreted it as a requirement to undertake substantial monitoring of its policies under this (and other) legislation. This must be welcomed as leading to a more informed policy debate and improved policy instruments. This evaluation policy has led to the commissioning of a substantial number of socioeconomic studies by MAFF and of an internal programme of monitoring of the physical and environmental effects of ESAs. These studies formed the basis for six of the seven ESA vignettes presented in Chapters 2 to 8. Each of these is derived from work undertaken for MAFF, or in the case of Chapter 4, partly for the Countryside Commission. Their order of presentation in the book recognizes some of the contrasts and similarities between ESAs, whilst the remaining two chapters deal in turn with benefit measurement and comparison of policy instruments.

An Overview of Earlier Chapters

The initial size of first- and second-round ESAs is reported in Table 1.2 and their location is shown in Figure 1.2. In a summary such as this only the broadest impression of the areas can be given.

Suffolk River Valleys ESA

The Suffolk River Valleys ESA (Chapter 2) encompasses seven discontinuous grassland areas located in valley bottoms along the southern and eastern Suffolk coast. Arable encroachment has been a particular problem even when compared with the Norfolk Broads; yet unlike the Brecklands (Chapter 4) a core area of grassland remains. Only 37% of participating farms had no land outside the ESA boundary and three-quarters of farmers had significant non-farm sources of income. The ESA scheme focused on conserving, enhancing and expanding the core grassland area, these three objectives corresponding with the three tiers of the scheme. This chapter reported substantial reductions in nitrogen fertilizer applications in all tiers. Compliance also brought some increases in both operating and capital costs. The response to the scheme was as expected for Tiers I and II but substantially greater than expected for the arable reconversion of Tier III.

Scheme impact was assessed in comparison with an assessed 'without scheme' situation. The balance of increased receipts (mainly from scheme payments) was greater than the associated costs and the average net impact on farm income over five years was estimated to be equivalent to some £342 per hectare of land entered into the scheme. The impact of the scheme on short-term grazing rents was noted and the sharing of scheme payments between landowners and their tenants was also estimated. The financial cost of the scheme was £4 million, against which a saving of some £2 million on other exchequer payments is to be set. The increase in livestock production to be expected from a substantial resurgence of the grassland economy of the Suffolk River Valleys has not yet fully developed and the stocking rates prescribed in the scheme are generally not restrictive. The possibility of demonstration effects in the ESA, whereby farmers learn or acquire positive attitudes to conservation, from the prior operations of conservation organizations and from the scheme itself, will both have contributed to the impact of the scheme.

Pennine Dales ESA

The Pennine Dales ESA covers some 16,000 hectares of land and is similar to the Suffolk River Valleys (but differs from most other ESAs) in that the designated area is in several separate valleys. This leads to particular problems in evaluating its impact because many farmers have holdings which cross the

ESA boundary. The area of land farmed by all farmers in the ESA dales amounted to virtually twice the area of the ESA, indicating the substantial scope for 'halo' effects, whereby farmers might use the payments received through the scheme to finance other developments on non-scheme land. The analysis therefore included the impact of the scheme on both land within and outside the ESA boundary. The agricultural systems are dominated by grazing livestock, on farms both with and without agreements, with sheep being the most important and dairy cows the least. Farming conditions vary considerably between dales and, depending upon location, within dales, with harsher conditions prevailing higher up the dales. The study attempted to establish control dales which could be used to develop the policy-off situation for establishing scheme impact. The material for the control area had to be augmented from published and other sources.

The estimated impact of the scheme on farm incomes, here based on income data collected from farmers in the ESA, showed a greater increase on agreement farms than on non-agreement farms and the controls. In aggregate it was estimated that the ESA had added to revenue and had reduced variable costs thus leaving an aggregate addition to management and investment income of some £230,000 over the first three years of the scheme, which compared with the volume of scheme payments made in a full year of some £800,000 in 1987. The full exchequer cost of scheme payments was virtually £1 million in 1991/92 or £0.73 million after allowing for the EC contribution. A small offset to this cost was the savings to the exchequer resulting from reduced support payments of £0.12 million in that year.

The response to the scheme quickly grew to cover most of the area which had been thought to be eligible by MAFF. The most frequent scheme impact reported was a reduction in fertilizer use, and it was also found that the rate of fertilizer use on agreement farms was less than one-third the rate on either non-agreement farms or the control group. The other major change noted was a substantial increase in the use of bought-in hay on agreement farms. The most controversial aspect of the management package, both with farmers and with those studying the results of these schemes, was the hay-cutting date restriction. The MAFF (1992a) monitoring report found that this constraint was fully complied with, the effect being to concentrate the making of hay within a shorter period, so that some fields were being cut earlier due to the scheme, with some reduction in biodiversity. Yields of hay and silage were reported to be lower on agreement farms inside the ESA boundary, but there was some evidence of increased yields on agreement farm land which was outside the ESA boundary. The changes in yield were not matched by changes in stock numbers, with a small increase in sheep per hectare being offset by a decline in suckler cow numbers, to give a very small decline in grazing livestock units per hectare.

Brecklands ESA

The Brecklands ESA consists of lowland heath covering nearly 100,000 hectares of Norfolk and Suffolk. Land cover is mainly of heathland, woodland and wetlands. Only half of this is agricultural land eligible for ESA agreements. Agriculturally this is marginal lowland with a threat of arable encroachment. Old shelter belts of Scots pine are now semi-derelict and the plantings of the 1920s are being felled and replanted. A major intrusion in the landscape has been military use, whilst the advent of myxomatosis and the reduction in sheep grazing have led to an invasion of scrub with a corresponding retreat of traditional Breckland plants. The remaining traditional habitat is severely fragmented. The management prescription for this ESA embodied three tiers, the first dealing with maintenance of heathland, the second with wet grassland and the third with the creation of conservation headlands on field margins.

The Brecklands study differs from the others reported here in that its evaluation was not sponsored by MAFF, but obtained some support from the Countryside Commission. A dominant feature of this ESA is the importance of conservation activities undertaken by other agencies. Ownership by public and voluntary bodies amounts to one-third of the ESA area, the major owners being the Forestry Commission and Ministry of Defence.

Whilst the ESA appears to have checked the long-term trend of conversion to arable from heath and grassland, substantial conservation effort is deployed within the ESA through other designations. The interactions between these activities have enhanced the conservation interest of significant parts of the area, for example in the success of the ESA scheme in complementing the purposes of SSSIs, especially where weaknesses of the latter have limited their effectiveness. Payment levels for arable reversion are judged low in that they have not generated a response from farmers. The exclusion of non-agricultural land from the scheme also limits its conservation impact.

North Peak ESA

The North Peak is an area of upland heather moorland covering nearly 50,000 hectares. In common with the Pennine Dales and the Cambrian Mountains, the main agricultural enterprise is the rearing of sheep; some farms also have cattle. On some estates, shooting is important and management for red grouse generally results in a reduction in sheep stocking rates. The main ecological threat to the area was the intensification of agriculture, expressed as higher stocking rates and silage production on the in-bye land on the lower pastures.

In common with the Pennine Dales, participants must enter all their eligible land into the ESA although they retain choice as to which tier to enter.

Tier I land is subject to an intensification constraint in that fertilizer and lime must not be increased, and draining and reseeding are precluded. Tier II involves further restrictions on farming activities and some positive conservation practices. Both tiers are subject to restrictive stocking constraints.

The response to the scheme has been enthusiastic: owners and their tenants, for both farming and shooting, saw themselves as gaining from scheme prescriptions. Participating farms averaged nearly 700 hectares in size, of which one-fifth is inbye. The land is held for various uses under a complex structure of property rights. One-fifth of the inbye and a small percentage of moorland farmed by participants is outside the area. Non-participating farms were much smaller than participants' farms, though more variable in size and more prone to extend outside the ESA boundary.

The impact of this ESA is slight in terms of land use. It was also reported that the reduction of animals on the moors does not automatically improve the vegetation where erosion is a significant problem; this will require many years be halted. Management practices which would lead to improvement include heather burning, which has increased on agreement land substantially more than on non-agreement land, although it remains at a less than optimal rate; and bracken spraying, which also remains below the specified level. Small reductions in the use of fertilizer and lime were found on agreement land. Some increase in stone walls was noted. Exclusion fencing of heather plots to allow regeneration has been erected on 145 hectares. A substantial increase in labour requirements, averaging 182 man-days per moor, has been identified; some of this has been supplied from slack resources on the farm whilst some farms have taken on extra employees.

The net impact of the scheme may be seen from the reduction in gross margins of £0.5 million, which with compliance costs of nearly £2.0 million was more than offset by payments and cost savings which together exceed £4.0 million. The resulting net impact is an addition to farm incomes of £1.2 million over five years. The exchequer costs of the scheme were £3.5 million. No evidence of the halo effect was found in evaluating this scheme.

Breadalbane ESA

The Breadalbane ESA Scheme in the Southern Highlands of Scotland covers 120,000 hectares. In common with several other ESAs, most of the area lies within the Less Favoured Areas. Agriculture is the main land use with forestry and shooting estates together accounting for about a quarter of the area. The area is evenly divided between rented and owner-occupied farms. The area includes two National Scenic Areas and it borders on another, whilst 21,000 hectares of its surface is designated as SSSI, in addition to other minor designations. Ancient woodlands are a significant feature of the land cover.

Entrants to the scheme were required to produce a simple Conservation Management Plan within the management guidelines specified. Farmers were paid up to £4500 per annum for the five years of the scheme, of which one-third is flat rate and the remainder is itemized by conservation activities, the amounts being based on standard costings. This approach to payments allows for more precise targeting of financial incentives.

The evaluation study used a control group to identify scheme impact. At the farm level, surveys showed that farmers had tended to adjust cropping patterns and stocking levels before, rather than after, the introduction of the scheme. The most common shift was away from arable farming. The stocking rate was set at a level which did not constrain existing practice.

Whilst some of the itemized conservation work was undertaken by farmers, the majority was done by contractors. The economic impact of the scheme was to generate an extra 33 jobs, only 15 of which were in the local economy. Its landscape impact may be seen from the greater amount of conservation work undertaken by participants than by the control group. A major share of participants claimed that the scheme had not changed their attitudes to conservation although some admitted an increased awareness of conservation.

Total uptake of the scheme amounted to half the area, which is a high response rate compared with other Scottish ESAs: younger farmers appeared more eager to participate than older ones. The highest response rate by farm size was in the range 50–100 hectares, reflecting the weakening of incentives due to financial constraints on farms above and below this size. Farm tenure appeared to have no impact on uptake. Farmers' comments on the scheme approved the opportunities it provided for repair of stone walls and the making feasible of other environmental work. Interference with the farm system was seen as a major disadvantage, as was under-funding of the itemized conservation work.

Cambrian Mountains ESA

The Cambrian Mountains ESA was designated in 1987 and 1988. It is one of the largest ESAs in the UK and, together with the Lleyn Peninsula ESA, occupies nearly 10% of the agricultural area of Wales. It is a relatively poor livestock farming area but possesses valuable landscapes and wildlife habitats that have been threatened by agricultural intensification and afforestation. The main conservation concern has been with the protection of the Cambrians' extensive area of semi-natural rough grazings (SNRG: two-thirds of the agricultural area). Also included within the scheme has been the conservation of broadleaved woodland, species-rich hay meadows, lakes, ponds, streams and archaeological sites.

The size and location of the Cambrians ESA has meant that its socioeconomic effects are of particular interest. It is almost entirely within the designated area of the Development Board for Rural Wales, it lies wholly within the Less Favoured Areas and is also part of a 'Culturally Sensitive

Area'. Agriculture is important to the local economy and changes in agricultural policy are seen to affect the region's future economic prospects.

The management prescriptions are generally restrictive, proscribing an array of farm practices on eligible land rather than the whole farm. The proportion of SNRG included in the scheme is 57%, including commons, or 75% of non-common land. The uptake for broadleaved woodland has been disappointingly low.

Scheme impact was assessed using surveys of participants and non-participants and a study of farming trends. Half the participants were surveyed revealing that the majority had not been obliged to significantly change their farming systems in order to comply with scheme. Some farmers were already farming within scheme constraints whilst others were able to compensate for restrictions on scheme land by intensifying on other parts of the farm. A notable feature of this scheme has been the specification of individual farm stocking rates on each farm reflecting the vegetation found. Use of fertilizer, lime and basic slag have been proscribed on rough grazings and restricted on hay meadows. Pesticides and herbicides are also limited.

The average value of net scheme payments to farmers was £2200 per annum, which is equivalent to 60% of the gross value of ESA payments and some 15% of net farm income. These payments provide some stability to hill farming incomes. They were, however, skewed in favour of the larger farms. No direct increase in employment related to the scheme was identified, partly due to the lack of positive payments in the scheme. But the cultural contribution of ESA payments, in sustaining farming and hence the Welsh-speaking population, was noted.

Mourne Mountains and Slieve Croob ESA

The 33,000 hectare Mourne Mountains and Slieve Croob ESA was designated later than the others discussed and the study presented here is explicitly a Baseline Study, to be followed up when the first management agreements are completed. The emphasis of the chapter is thus different from others in that its focuses much more on description of the area and the character of participants and non-participants, rather than on impact.

The topography of the area is diverse, ranging from river valleys to more mountainous areas and to the coastal plain where small fields bounded by stone walls and vernacular buildings are the main landscape features. Some scheme participants have access to common land outside the scheme areas for grazing. There are several areas of underdeveloped land, including wet areas and old pastures, which are of ecological interest. It is farmed in 1833 family-owned units. Most of the land cover is grassland and the farming is dominated by livestock systems: increased stock numbers, especially of sheep, have been an important means of agricultural intensification in recent years.

The prescription requires adherence to a general schedule of activities to be avoided and participants are required to produce a Farm Conservation Plan setting out which of the scheme tasks are to be undertaken. One-third of eligible farmers have signed agreements, accounting for 42% of eligible land. From a sophisticated statistical analysis of survey data it was found that one-fifth of the recorded variables were significantly different between participants and non-participants. Participants tended to be younger, their holdings were larger and they were more likely to be part-time farmers but worked longer hours on the holding than non-participants. Participants were predictably more enthusiastic about the scheme, had a more active approach to land management and were more likely to have past experience of environmental land management. Perhaps unexpectedly, clustering analysis identified a strong association between modern and traditional land management practices on individual farms, especially in maintenance of walls and hedges. Participants were slightly more optimistic in outlook.

To summarize, the case studies in chapters 2–8 risk overlooking both the rich diversity of ESAs themselves and of the studies reported here. Their methodological similarities derive from the importance of one major sponsor (MAFF) but the diversity of the studies is also important. Partly this arises from differences in timing of the studies as well as the inherent variability of the areas. One point on which several studies present detailed estimates is the extent to which the scheme has added to farm incomes and the extent to which farmer participants have not notably changed their management practices. These conclusions may make it difficult to 'sell' ESAs to a cost-conscious public, but are not at all unexpected given the nature of the schemes. Indeed it is argued that the additions to income reported, as long as they continue to constrain production and secure conservation, should be welcomed as a successful 'decoupling' of agricultural support.

The extent to which the benefits generated may or may not exceed the full economic costs they impose is also important. Chapter 9 therefore broadens the economic argument by introducing the vital question of *economic benefits* to the public at large, rather than those to farmers. MAFF recognized the possibility of estimating the benefits of these schemes, during the process of implementation of the 1986 Act requirement to monitor ESA schemes, and the opportunity it offered to enhance the studies of the cost-effectiveness of securing physical compliance with the management packages defined. Chapter 9 reports the study commissioned in 1992 to estimate benefits of the schemes using the South Downs ESA as a case study.

Contingent valuations of the benefits, reflecting the incremental value of ESA designation, were derived from visitors to these areas and residents in them and elsewhere. The results were aggregated to produce the first estimates of the value of benefits from the South Downs ESA. That the value of benefits obtained exceeds the value of financial costs incurred by several orders of magnitude would imply that such schemes are a thoroughly effective way of spending public money. However, application of this and other benefit measurement techniques to a number of other locations would be advisable before major increases in expenditure would be justified on these grounds. The much lower ratio of benefits to costs found on the Somerset Levels and Moors ESA is also noted in Chapter 9 and this may well be closer to a typical ratio for all ESAs, most of which are much further from London than the South Downs. Furthermore, the cost element of the benefit-cost ratio reported consists solely of the aggregate payments to farmers in the relevant ESAs. It therefore excludes administrative costs (see below) and all private transactions costs associated with these policies.

Chapter 10 further broadens the canvas of evaluation by representing a *comparative evaluation of alternative mechanisms* of environmental policy. It outlines general principles by which the optimal amount of conservation might be assessed before turning to consider the instruments currently in use. These include management agreements in an array of contexts, public purchase, grants for purchase by voluntary bodies, grants for conservation work, tax breaks for heritage management, covenants and cross-compliance. The strengths and limitations of these measures are considered from the standpoint of a number of criteria of effectiveness.

Of these, the three which are given most attention are: SSSI management agreements, ESA agreements and public purchase. The first two are the most frequently occurring arrangements, with the second covering much the larger area. The arrangements are compared using a hypothetical example of conserving a 1000-hectare block of land by the three different instruments. In terms of exchequer cost, the SSSI mechanism is cheaper to protect the whole area with 20% subject to agreements at £500 per hectare than ESA agreements covering the whole area at £100 per hectare. Comparing this with land purchase at current prices, the amount of compensation spent could be used to purchase 328 hectares of land and the ensuing rental stream would allow the area to be further extended.

The comparison is instructive but not, of course, prescriptive. It cannot allow for the important qualitative differences in performance of each instrument. For example, it would appear that public purchase would give the tightest control of land for conservation, but that assumes that legal tenure contracts can be applied which bind tenants more effectively than management agreements. A major advantage of public purchase is that, once secured, the land and its conservation values are available to society in perpetuity. Given effective management and an absence of intervention on political doctrinal grounds (e.g. an insistence on reprivatization) public purchase would seem to have much to offer. The comparison of ESA and SSSI agreements in terms of cost-effectiveness also overlooks important differences in the quality of conservation management that is achieved by each: it might be expected that SSSI agreements would achieve results better tailored to individual circumstances than ESAs but, in practice, the problems of monitoring individual agreements may well have prevented the appearance of such superiority. In the real world of actual ESAs the existence of multiple designation, with several different agencies pursuing similar goals, further clouds the issue of who is achieving what in this context.

Continuing Themes

First, the *methodology of appraisal*, which underpins so much of this volume, deserves careful consideration. The elements of the techniques used so far reflect the particular concerns with financial cost and accountability which dominate issues of public expenditure. As the number of evaluations builds up, so too will the experience of using them. It is to be hoped that this will lead to a substantial broadening of the scope of these studies towards an understanding of what determines rates of uptake (the relative importance of generous levels of payment, ease of compliance, administrative flexibility, and so on) and what effect such arrangements will have on output and the environment in the long term. Chapter 6 ends with a detailed discussion of the possibilities of a more sociological approach to scheme evaluation Other methodologies would also broaden the impact of appraisals.

For example, the size and nature of the public benefits delivered by such schemes and the social opportunity costs they impose will become key elements of appraisal if the policies are to be fully justified. The benefits estimated from various sections of the public, as in Chapter 9, still leave some important elements of benefit out of account. In particular the value of changing attitudes to conservation amongst farmers, together with the conservation skills they may acquire as a result of participating in ESA schemes, should not be overlooked. These benefits are of a capital nature, in that they will appear in future time periods, but apart from noting them we do not have any direct means of measurement.

Another methodological advance would be a switch of mode from the present *evaluation* (*ex post*) to *appraisal* (*ex ante*) which is surely called for if such work is to seriously contribute to policy design. This is not to suggest that present policies are introduced without appraisal but to point out the obvious fact that the relevant appraisals do not appear in public and are not, therefore, subject to critical comment. Promising moves towards transparency of policies have been made by MAFF in recent years; perhaps the next logical step would be to make full appraisals available more widely.

A more serious evaluation problem was in the *delayed response* of landscapes and habitats to ESA packages. This is a serious problem in that the first and second round of ESAs applied for five years and were evaluated during their period of operation. As their focus was on environmental activities and their success was to be measured in terms of improvements in farm conservation, it is not surprising that the responses to the policy detected were generally slight and were found in accessible variables, such as the use of fertilizer, rather than in the habitats and landscapes which are the ultimate target of these policies. This is less a criticism of the studies undertaken than a recognition of what can be done in a short space of time. In this respect the two-stage evaluation of the Mournes ESA (Chapter 8) starting with a baseline study and ending with an impact evaluation has much to commend it. More effective evaluations of ESAs will be possible – as long as there have been no substantive weather or other disturbances affecting them – after ten years, at the end of the designations just introduced or reintroduced, than in the rounds just ended. For the time being there is little detectable change in habitats or landscapes which can be attributed to the ESAs.

Methodologically, many of the studies attempted to apply the *policy-on/policy-off* dichotomy to identify and measure policy impact. This use of a reference situation is a necessary part of policy analysis but several of the studies found that such 'policy-off' situations could not always be identified and those who did attempt to use such controls found that they had to augment the policy-off information with data from other sources. This problem is not surprising in evaluating policies which apply in areas selected for their unique attributes and is one to which there is no obvious answer.

Despite its misleadingly appealing name, the *halo effect* has been a continuing obsession related to ESA policies and even more closely with set-aside. The notion here is that farmers being paid to abstain from particular actions may divert the payments into funding other unwanted activities. This problem may be expected particularly with policies which apply within defined boundaries which may cut through individual farms. Whilst individual ESA studies which could find evidence on this point generally found its effect to be small, the Cambrian Mountains study (Chapter 7) was forthright in its identification of halo effects. This general absence of the effect may be partly a matter of time. Perhaps when the payments have had time to work through the farm business unexpected investments will begin to appear. If farmers begin to feel pressure to boost yields they may succumb to the temptation to increase their input use where they can.

An interesting extension of the halo effect to intertemporal contexts was indicated by the events in the Suffolk River Valleys. Several of the original participants suggested that they may consider delaying entry into the revised scheme in order to top up the nutrient status of their soils, or undertake other proscribed activities, returning to the programme once the productive potential of the land has been restored. Clearly such a response implies compliance with the letter of the law whilst ignoring its spirit. In a slightly different vein, some farmers in the North Peak avoided entering all of their land due to the complicated ownership pattern. During the initial years there was no evidence of intensification on this land but the potential is nevertheless there. Halo effects may yet become important as the economic environment of farming changes.

The issue of *multiple designation* arose in several of the ESAs studied, most commonly where SSSI or National Nature Reserves exist within them, and has so far been dealt with by assigning a level of priority to the designation to receive basic payments with possible top-ups from others. Generally the existence of multiple designations has assisted the operation of ESAs by familiarizing farmers with the idea of management agreements and making them more acceptable. This may nevertheless become more important as other more general environmental codes of practice are built into regulations. For example, the introduction of requirements relating to the use of agricultural chemicals may make certain ESA prescription elements redundant and hence remove the need to reimburse farmers for following them.

A related problem of interactions between schemes occurred at several points in the book. It is well recognized that policies interact with each other, perhaps the most common being the interaction between price policy and environmental policies of all kinds. Other interactions which occur are recognized in cross-compliance. The idea of an optimal mix of policy instruments is one which underlies this issue although few studies have addressed this intricate problem (but see Drake, 1993).

An issue which has by no means been satisfactorily addressed in the studies is that of *transactions cost*. Most authors have ignored this in their individual studies for the good reason that data are sparse or non-existent. However, the advent of the MINIM series (MAFF 1992g) is to be welcomed as a start in this direction. The volume provides material as input into the Public Expenditure Survey (PES) process and the results of those discussions feed into the Department's Expenditure Plans (MAFF and the Intervention Board, 1993). The latter tell us that, for the UK, expenditure on ESA payments was planned to increase from £11 million in 1991–92 through £19 million and £42 million in successive years to stabilize at £63 million in 1994–96. This growth reflects the implementation of the Agri-Environment Regulation (EC, 1992a), which requires greater attention to environmental aspects of agricultural policy. The Government's proposed response to that Regulation

Table 11.2. Financial costs of ESAs in England: 1990/91–1992/93. (From MAFF, 1992g.)

Costs	1990/91 (£ million)	1991/92 (£ million)	1992/93 (forecast) (£ million)
Payments to farmers	7.5	8.7	14.7
Administrative costs	2.5	2.4	3.2
Total	10.0	11.1	17.9

was issued in May 1993 and the new ESAs were a part of that. An important feature of that initiative is that it doubles the rate of support from the EC budget, raising it from a maximum of 25% to 50%.

The amounts reported in the Expenditure Plans do not separate out the elements of administrative cost although they are presented in MINIM (MAFF, 1992g). They are summarized for the current period, for England, in Table 11.2, which suggests that they are declining in relative importance over time. That conclusion should be qualified, in that the decline reported here (from 25% to 18%) includes one year of forecast which may well underestimate the substantial increase in the number and area of ESAs now in existence. That expansion was not fully envisaged at the time these data were assembled, in the summer and autumn of 1992.

The importance of administrative costs in individually specified environmental policy instruments is not, however, to be overlooked. Their general significance in both public and private transactions has been recognized in advanced economies by those studying the evolution of property rights, and North (1990) estimates that the size of what he calls the transacting sector in the USA currently accounts for 45% of national income, compared with 25% a century earlier. That share includes all administrative and service sectors with a role in managing the economy and is presumably greater than in the UK, not least because of the ubiquity of the US legal system and their political system being based on the separation of powers between different parts of the nation. There will be further transactions costs additional to those reported in Table 11.2, some of which will be borne by other government departments and some by private individuals. Those taking decisions will be aware of such costs and they will influence outcomes and distort resource markets. It would be expected that transactions costs for ESAs would be smaller than those for SSSIs because the former have reduced the negotiation costs of setting up management agreements. There is limited official evidence available on this point (Whitby, 1993) which does not confirm this result, finding that the proportion of costs devoted to administration of the two schemes is roughly similar. However, Whittaker *et al.* (1991) report some evidence that individually negotiated management agreements do have higher administrative costs than more standardized systems of payment.

A final theme which remains to be seriously considered is the assignment of *public property rights in conservation goods* being created through ESAs. These agreements for five or ten years will contribute substantial public funds to the conservation and maintenance or even reinstatement of desired features. As the agreements come to an end there is no mechanism within the ESA system to protect public good assets beyond the life of the agreements. Strictly this applies because, although ESA designation is in principle perpetual, the agreements negotiated are finite and relate to quite short periods. In this they contrast substantially with SSSIs which bring with their designation important changes in the property rights of owners and cultivators of the soil. As the legal basis of ESAs now stands there is no presumption that the public has any right to the assets created through them, yet they are being generated partly by public funds. Will it then be acceptable, say in 2002, after some thousands of farmers have participated in management agreements for ten or even 15 years, for them to change their practices and revert to high farming, if that is what technical and market conditions indicate? One answer to that could be 'yes, if that is what the market indicates', but another might insist that these assets have now been produced with public funds and that the public therefore has some rights in their disposal. This argument might gain strength, for example, where access arrangements have been successfully added on to an existing ESA agreement and where they have been fully utilized. In such circumstances it is likely that there will be public opposition from environmentalists to a reversion to intensive agricultural practices, despite the technical legal position which would allow it. Clearly a rapid escalation of demand for food might encourage a return to high farming which would be acceptable to consumers of food but opposed by those with a stronger interest in public goods. Current writers on property rights (e.g. Barzel, 1989; North, 1990) convincingly stress the dynamic nature of such institutional arrangements and the importance of change in rights induced by changes in use.

The Prospects for ESAs

Doubling both the area of ESAs and the amount spent on them within a short space of time shows a remarkable level of commitment to this particular policy instrument; even more remarkable given that the new agreements are for up to ten years. The reaction of the farming community will depend on the complete structure of economic incentives it faces. What are the agricultural prospects for the next ten years? Should we expect stability in world trade? What are the prospects for another commodity crisis similar to that of the early 1970s (see Chapter 1) which helped initiate the increases in investment sufficiently to place the agricultural environment on the political agenda?

Any future prediction of world trade and policy conditions is bound to be speculative, especially since at the time of writing (September 1993) the outcome of the GATT Uruguay Round remains uncertain. However, at least some policy analysts (e.g. Harvey, 1993; Josling, 1993) have argued that the present trend towards a more market-oriented policy for European agriculture, as begun in the MacSharry 'reforms' of the CAP, are likely to continue, albeit accompanied by 'decoupled' compensation payments for the reduction in market price support. Their reasons are, whatever the outcome of the GATT negotiations, the political and moral imperatives of granting relatively free access to EC markets for the newly liberalizing Eastern European and former USSR states. This can only be achieved, they argue, through continued liberalizing of EC farm product markets.

At first sight, more liberal farm product markets will also be accompanied by more uncertainty in farm receipts, making the relatively certain ESA and environmentally related payments more attractive to farmers. However, the extent to which this feature encourages the uptake of ESA agreements in the future will depend on two important factors: first, the extent to which the ESA payments themselves are increased to take account of cost and price increases (where it is notable that the present government did not exercise the option of changing the levels of payment at the review point laid down after the first three years); second, the extent to which present compensation payments (for cereals) or headage payments (for livestock) are made more dependent on environmentally friendly farming practices in the future. So long as the present pressures on agriculture and the environment are maintained and budget appropriations continue to be a focus of policy restraint, such moves towards 'compliance' with environmentally friendly farming practice remain a strong possibility. Thus, it could be that more generally applicable packages of restraint on farm practice and associated 'compensation' payments will in time come to replace the present spatially specific ESA programmes.

It also seems likely that one outcome of the present Uruguay Round will be a commitment to open multilateral negotiations on the linkages between farm and environmental policies, perhaps including questions for market stability and food security. What the outcome of such negotiations might be is problematical, though it seems likely at present to lead to greater emphasis on support aimed at environmental improvement and further downward pressure on production-related payments. Future discontinuities in farm production or trade, as a result of nuclear accident, freak weather conditions or global warming for instance, are likely to colour these discussions and perhaps encourage at least a temporary return to more protective farm product policies. In addition, the long-predicted biotechnological revolution might lead to unexpected developments in farm production practices and land uses, which may have rather different implications for the general relationships between intensive and production-oriented agriculture and the environment. These possible developments make future prediction of the role of ESA-type programmes even more uncertain. However, so long as the returns and margins from production continue to fall, payments for environmentally friendly practices will become more attractive to farmers, implying increasing participation rates and demands for extension of eligible areas, albeit with continued debate on the environmental benefits of particular restrictions and ESA requirements.

The introduction of ESAs and their rapid acceptance has been followed by a similarly rapid extension of the designated area within which such policies will apply. The doubling of the EC budgetary contribution to policy costs, from the 1992 Agri-Environment Regulation, will ease the expansion somewhat, although the budgetary rebate system agreed at the Fontainebleau summit in

1983 effectively reduces the value of this contribution. Essentially Fontaine-bleau arranges that approximately two-thirds of the UK net contribution to the EC budget is returned to it as a rebate. Consequently, where the UK contributes to the cost of a programme and receives assistance through it, the value of that assistance is less than it would be if the UK did not participate (Northern Ireland Economic Council, 1992). The UK is nevertheless better off in financial terms by participating than by abstaining, to say nothing of the political implications of abstention.

The spread of this policy throughout the rest of Europe has not been officially documented and has by no means been adequately treated in this book. Nevertheless, articles are beginning to appear (Baldock, 1993; Primdahl and Hansen, 1993; Buller, 1991). Buller summarizes the French situation as late participators in ESAs. One hundred and fifteen thousand hectares of potential ESA land have been identified in 39 separate zones. Five of these are intended to combat agricultural pollution and 15 each to protect ecosystems and deter land abandonment whilst four are to maintain pasture in the interest of limiting forest fires. As yet only 14 of these have been given outline consent and three have been accepted by the EC for financing. The total budget allocated to these areas is similar to the initial funds allocated to ESAs in the UK first round. The Danish situation differs from the French in that there are 915 designated ESAs and a reported 3000 agreements (Primdahl and Hansen, 1993). The majority of Danish ESAs are aimed at habitat protection and landscape conservation, with a substantial number of agreements also devoted to the protection of surface waters. Article 797/85 was adopted into legislation in 1989 and the first agreements signed in 1990. To have reached 3000 agreements so rapidly suggests an enthusiasm amongst farmers similar to that in the UK.

Although the policy has been hailed as an overnight success, its longer-term outlook will depend on the factors internal and external to agriculture which have been reviewed and analysed throughout this book. It must also be acknowledged that, despite the rapid uptake, the impact of ESAs on the fragile environments where they have been applied has yet to be fully observed. Such changes will require decades for the manifestation of their full impact.

The several evaluations on which this study draws represent a welcome move towards transparency in policy. Yet the slow pace of ecological and landscape change will ensure that they will offer no more policy guidance than baseline studies for the time being. The challenge for the next decade will be to develop adequate methodologies to inform the designation of such areas and the design of management prescriptions which will be required as the third and fourth rounds of designation come to an end and the post-Uruguay round of GATT discussions get into their stride. Not only will benefit measurement be required but an *ex ante* form of policy appraisal would be much more appropriate than the *ex post* evaluations on which most of this book is based.

Guiding constraints on that process will be the nature of property rights in land and the understandable political caution in changing their assignment through direct policies. The distributional implications of the provision of public goods in this way will also bear thorough analysis, in contrast with the heavy emphasis on financial costs which rules so generally throughout the public sector. The continuing success of ESAs will also depend on the conflicting economic signals farmers receive from markets and policies. At the time of writing, changes in exchange rates have provided a short-term boost to investment which is probably small enough to have only modest environmental impacts. This does not mean that more substantial short-term events are ruled out.

What remains to be seen is whether major surges of farming profitability of the kind which convulsed world agriculture in the early 1970s and initiated the investment boom which, in turn, promoted environmental policies in agriculture, can be avoided in the future. If not, there is a significant chance that ESAs, even on the expanded scale now proposed, will not provide enough protection for the collection of public goods we now call the countryside. The most likely outcome is that ESAs will prove sufficient to meet environmental demands in the future. As long as we can retain enough flexibility in their administration, to cope with unforeseen problems, they still offer cause for optimism within the fraught overlapping fields of agricultural and environmental policy.

The introduction of ESAs in the UK may be seen as a substantial innovation in a policy context where reaction to events is the norm and stagnation too common. The challenge for this policy will be to continue to deliver incentives to farmers to manage the countryside in ways which are generally favoured. In the present economic climate of moderating agricultural support, the funds needed to persuade farmers to adhere to environmental rectitude are comparatively modest. So far the policy has worked smoothly without any change in property rights being seen as necessary. Some of the current fine-tuning of management packages, as the earliest ESAs are renewed and new ones designated, indicates movement towards greater emphasis on actual investment in countryside goods, particularly in the higher tiers of management packages. This, together with the possibility of attaching access agreements to ESA arrangements, foreshadows moves in the direction of shifting the *de facto* reassignment of property rights. In addition to that, the sheer duration of some agreements, currently up to a maximum of 15 years, would suggest that the public will increasingly expect to have the investments it has made through such public expenditure protected as such in the longer term. This will be one of the challenges for policy-makers in the next decade or so.

Attempts to adjust these and other environmental policies risk failure if they ignore the fact that the provision of public goods in the countryside will depend on the balance of advantage confronting land users. If there is a strong resurgence of demand for food at the farm gate, backed by price increases, society will then face an important choice as to whether it wishes to raise its offer price for land-based public goods through mechanisms such as ESAs. Another element in that debate will be the quest for a 'level playing field' in agricultural production and trade as environmental mechanisms are introduced across a wider front and begin to distort the pattern of incentives facing producers in different countries. Yet another will be the abiding interest of the conservation lobby in all matters to do with land use.

Policy-makers have bought themselves some time to consider their options with the introduction of ESAs. But this is not the ultimate solution to the agri-environmental policy problem, if for no other reason than that the economic environment of the farm business is far from static. Continued monitoring and fine-tuning will be needed as the kaleidoscopic pattern of incentives facing farmers and land users evolves. Their responses will occasionally call for rapid amelioration by policy-makers.

In Chapter 1 the connection between the attempt to control agricultural production and the pressure to introduce agricultural environmental policies was recognized. In summarizing and reviewing the work completed on ESAs this book has highlighted the remarkable success of the establishment of this policy in a short space of time. It has also identified many outstanding questions which need answering before a substantial further extension of the programme could be justified.

BIBLIOGRAPHY

Agar, M.H. (1980) *The Professional Stranger: An Informal Introduction to Ethnography*. Academic Press, London.

Anderson, G. and Bishop, R. (1986) The valuation problem. In: Bromley, D. (ed.) *National Resource Economics*, Kluwer Nijhoft, Boston.

Baldock, D. (1993) Agriculture et gestion de l'espace rural; questions à la recherche et à la pratique. In: Courtet, C., Berlan-Darque, M. and Demaine, Y. (ed.) *Un Point sur Agriculture et Société*. Association Descartes/INRA, Paris.

Barritt, E.E. (1983) *Loss of Grassland in Suffolk*. Report to the County Planning Officer.

Barzel, Y. (1989) *Economic Analysis of Property Rights*. Cambridge University Press, Cambridge.

Bateman, D., Chapman, N., Haines, M., Hughes, G., Jenkins, T., Lampkin, N. and Midmore, P. (1991) *Future Agricultural Prospects in Mid-Wales: A Report to the Development Board for Rural Wales*. Department of Economics & Agricultural Economics, University College of Wales, Aberystwyth.

Bateman, D., Hughes, G., Midmore, P., Lampkin, N. and Ray, C. (1993) *Pluriactivity and the Rural Economy in the Less Favoured Areas of Wales*. Countryside Change Initiative, Working Paper 36, Department of Economics and Agricultural Economics, University of Wales, Aberystwyth.

Bateman, I., Garrod, G.D. and Willis, K.G. (1992) *An Introduction to the Estimation of the Benefits of Non-Priced Recreation Using the Travel-Cost Method*. Working Paper 36, Department of Agricultural Economics and Food Marketing, University of Newcastle upon Tyne.

Bateman, I., Langford, I.H., Willis, K.G., Turner, R.K. and Garrod, G.D. (1993) *The Impacts of Changing Willingness to Pay, Question Format in Contingent Valuation Studies: An Analysis of Open-Ended, Iterative Bidding and Dichotomous Choice Formats*. CSERGE GEC Working Paper GEC 93-05, CSERGE, University of East Anglia.

Berlan Darque, M. (1988) The division of labour and decision-making in farming couples: power and negotiation. *Sociologia Ruralis* XXVIII:4, 271–292.

Brecks Study Group (1991) *Norfolk and Suffolk Brecks Study*. Brecks Study Group, Suffolk.

Buller, H. (1991) *Agricultural Structures Policy and the Environment in France; Report to the DG VI of the European Commission*. Groupe de Recherches Sociologiques, Paris;

Department of Geography, King's College, London.

Chatfield, C. and Collins, A.J. (1980) Cluster analysis. In: *Introduction to Multivariate Analysis*. Chapman & Hall, London, pp. 212–215.

Coase, R. (1960) The problem of social cost. *Journal of Law and Economics* 17, 1–44.

Colman, D.R. (1989) Economic issues from the Broads Grazing Marshes Conservation Scheme. *Journal of Agricultural Economics* 40(3), 336–360.

Colman, D. (1991) Land purchase as a means of providing external benefits from agriculture. In: Hanley, N. (ed.) *Farming and the Countryside: An Economic Analysis of External Costs and Benefits*. CAB International, Wallingford.

Colman, D. and Lee, N. (1988) *Evaluation of the Broads Grazing Marshes Conservation Scheme*. Department of Agricultural Economics, University of Manchester.

Colman, D.R., Crabtree, J.R., Froud, J. and O'Carroll, L. (1992) *Comparative Effectiveness of Conservation Mechanisms*. Department of Agricultural Economics, University of Manchester.

Countryside Commission (1974) *New Agricultural Landscapes*. Countryside Commission, Cheltenham.

Countryside Commission (1979) *Annual Report*. Countryside Commission, Cheltenham.

Countryside Commission (1989) *Incentives for a New Direction in Farming*. CCP 262, Countryside Commission, Cheltenham.

Countryside Commission (1992) *MAFF Review of Second Round Environmentally Sensitive Areas: Response by the Countryside Commission*. Countryside Commission, Cheltenham.

Countryside Review Committee (1978) *Food Production in the Countryside*. Department of the Environment, HMSO, London.

Coursey, D., Hovis, J. and Schultze, W. (1987) The disparity between willingness to accept and willingness to pay measures of value. *Quarterly Journal of Economics* August, 679–690.

Cox, G., Lowe, P. and Winter, M. (1988) Private rights and public responsibilities: the prospects for agricultural and environmental controls. *Journal of Rural Studies* 4, 232–237.

Cox, G., Lowe, P. and Winter, M. (1990) *The Voluntary Principle in Conservation*. Packard, Chichester.

Crabtree, J.R. (1991) Policy instruments for achieving conservation objectives. In: Laseby, M. (ed.) *The Environment and the Management of Natural Resources*. European Association of Agricultural Economists Environmental Economics Conference, Universita della Tuscia, Viterbo, Italy.

DANI (1987) *Mourne Mountains and Slieve Croob ESA*. Department of Agriculture for Northern Ireland, Belfast.

Deayton, A.S. (1975) The measurement of income and price elasticities. *European Economic Review* 19, 261–273.

DOE (1990) *This Common Inheritance: Britain's Environmental Strategy*. White Paper. HMSO, London.

DOE (1991a) *This Common Inheritance: Britain's Environmental Strategy*. White Paper. The First Year Report. HMSO, London.

DOE (1991b) *Policy Appraisal and the Environment: a Guide for Government Departments*. HMSO, London.

DOE (1992) *This Common Inheritance: Britain's Environmental Strategy*. White Paper. The Second Year Report. HMSO, London.

DOENI (1986) *Mourne Area of Outstanding Natural Beauty – Nature Conservation.* Department of the Environment, Northern Ireland.

Dolman, P. and Sutherland, W. (1991) Historical clues to conservation. *New Scientist* 1751, 40–43.

Drake, L. (1993) Relations among environmental effects and their implications for efficiency of policy instruments – an economic analysis applied to Swedish agriculture. Doctoral dissertation, Department of Economics, Swedish Agricultural University, Uppsala.

EC (1985a) EC Regulation 797/85 ('Structures Regulation'). *Official Journal of the European Communities* L93/10–193/11.

EC (1985b) *The Agricultural Situation in the Community.* European Community, 1985 Report, Brussels.

EC (1990) *The Agricultural Situation in the Community.* European Community, 1990 Report, Brussels.

EC (1992a) Council Regulation (EEC) 2078/92 ('The Agri-Environment Regulation'). *Official Journal of the European Communities* L215/85.

EC (1992b) Regulation on Protection of the Environment & Maintenance of the Countryside. *Official Journal of the European Communities* L215/85:2078/92.

Friends of the Earth, (1992) *Environmentally Sensitive Areas: Assessment & Recommendations.* Friends of the Earth, London.

Furness, G.W., Russell, N.P. and Colman, D. (1990) *Developing Proposals for Cross-Compliance with Particular Application to the Oilseeds Sector.* Royal Society for the Protection of Birds, Sandy, Bedfordshire.

Garrod, G.D. and Allanson, P.F. (1991) *The Choice and Functional Forms for Hedonic Price Functions.* Countryside Change Initiative, Working Paper 23, Department of Agricultural Economics and Food Marketing, University of Newcastle upon Tyne.

Garrod, G.D. and Willis, K.G. (1992a) The environmental impact of woodland: a two-stage hedonic price model of the amenity value of forestry in Britain. *Applied Economics* 24, 715–728.

Garrod, G.D. and Willis, K.G. (1992b) *Elicitation Methods in Contingent Valuation: Open Ended and Dichotomous Choice Formats, Iterative Bidding and Payment Card Methods.* Countryside Change Initiative, Working Paper 28, Department of Agricultural Economics and Food Marketing, University of Newcastle upon Tyne.

Gasson, R. and Hill, B. (1984) *Farm Tenure and Performance.* Wye College School of Rural Economics, University of London.

Gladwin, C.H. (1989) *Ethnographic Decision Tree Modelling.* Sage Publications, London.

Gladwin, H. and Murtaugh, M. (1980) The attentive-preattentive distinction in agricultural decision making. In: Barlett, P.F. (ed.) *Agricultural Decision Making: Anthropological Contributions to Rural Development.* Academic Press, London, pp. 115–136.

Gnanadesikan, R. (1977) Multidimensional classification and clustering. In: *Methods for Statistical Data Analysis of Multivariate Observations.* John Wiley, New York, p. 104.

Gould (Consultants) (1990) A low level evaluation of Environmentally Sensitive Areas in England. *Report to MAFF.* Gould Consultants, Saltisford, Warwickshire.

Hanley, N.D. (1989) Valuing non-market goods using contingent valuation. *Journal of Economic Surveys* 3(3), 235–252.

Harvey, D.R. (1993) *GATT, the CAP Reforms and the Future of British Agriculture.* Paper presented to the Newcastle Agricultural Society, Newcastle upon Tyne.

HM Treasury (1991) *Economic Appraisal in Central Government: a Technical Guide for Government Departments*. HMSO, London.

Hobhouse, S.A. (1947) *Report of the National Parks Committee England and Wales*. HMSO, London.

Hooper, A.J. (1992) Field monitoring of environmental change in the Environmentally Sensitive Areas. In: Whitby, M.C. (ed.) *Land Use Change: the Causes and Consequences*. HMSO, London.

House of Commons Select Committee on the Environment (1984) *Report on the Operation of the Wildlife and Countryside Act, 1981*. HMSO, London.

Hughes, G.O. and Jones, E. (1991) *Environmentally Sensitive Areas, Wales: Socio-Economic Aspects of Designation*. Welsh Office Agriculture Department, Cardiff.

Hughes, G.O. and Sherwood, A.M. (1993) *Socio-Economic Aspects of Designating the Cambrian Mountains and the Lleyn Peninsula as Environmentally Sensitive Areas*. Welsh Office Agriculture Department, Cardiff.

Hutchinson, W.G. and Chilton, S.M. (1993) Topical issues in the use of the contingent valuation method for valuing environmental resources. Paper presented to the Agricultural Economics Society Conference, Oxford, 1993.

Johnson, D. (1991) *Farm Incomes in the North of England*. Department of Agricultural Economics and Food Marketing, University of Newcastle upon Tyne. Various 1991 issues.

Jones, M.E. (1989) The linguistic implications of agricultural change in Wales. Unpublished MSc thesis, Department of Economics and Agricultural Economics, University College of Wales, Aberystwyth.

Josling, T. (1993) The reformed CAP and the Industrialised World. Proceedings of the VIIth Conference of the European Association of Agricultural Economists, Stresa, Italy. *European Review of Agricultural Economists* 21, 3–4.

Kahneman, D. and Knetsch, J.L. (1992) Valuing public goods: The purchase of moral satisfaction. *Journal of Environmental Economics and Management* 22, 57–70.

Kirkham, F.W., Tallowin, J.R.B., Wilkins, R.J., Mountford, J.O. and Lakhani, K.H. (1992) *The Effects of Nitrogen on Species Diversity and Agricultural Production on the Somerset Moors*. Institute of Grassland and Environmental Research, Okehampton, Devon.

Kuhn, T.S. (1970) *The Structure of Scientific Revolutions*. University of Chicago Press, Chicago.

Leach, E.R. (1967) An anthropologist's reflections on a social survey. In: Jongman, D.G. and Gutkind, P.C.W. (ed.) *Anthropologists in the Field*. Van Gorcum and Company N.V., Assen, pp. 75–88.

Lilwall, N., Perkins, T. and Skerrat, S. (1991) *Socio-Economic Evaluation of the Breadalbane ESA Scheme, 1987–1990, Final Report*. The Edinburgh School of Agriculture, Edinburgh.

Lowe, P. and Goyder, J. (1983) *Environmental Groups in Politics*. Allen and Unwin, London.

MAFF (1987) *Environmentally Sensitive Areas*. HMSO, London.

MAFF (1988a) *The North Peak ESA: Guidelines for Farmers*. HMSO, London.

MAFF (1988b) *Breckland Environmentally Sensitive Area: Guidelines for Farmers*. HMSO, London.

MAFF (1991) *Our Farming Future*. HMSO, London.

MAFF (1992a) *The Pennine Dales: ESA Report of Monitoring 1991, Report 1*. HMSO, London.

MAFF (1992b) *The Broads: Environmentally Sensitive Area Report of Monitoring 1991, Report 2*. HMSO, London.

MAFF (1992c) *The Somerset Levels and Moors: Environmentally Sensitive Area Report of Monitoring 1991, Report 3*. HMSO, London.

MAFF (1992d) *The South Downs: Environmentally Sensitive Area Report of Monitoring 1991, Report 4*. HMSO, London.

MAFF (1992e) *West Penwith: Environmentally Sensitive Area Report of Monitoring, 1991, Report 5*. HMSO, London.

MAFF (1992f) *Review of ESA Schemes: Breckland Consultation Document*. HMSO, London.

MAFF (1992g) *Ministerial Information in MAFF (MINIM)*. HMSO, London.

MAFF (1993a) *Suffolk River Valleys: Environmentally Sensitive Area Report of Monitoring 1992, Report 6*. HMSO, London.

MAFF (1993b) *The Test Valley: Environmentally Sensitive Area Report of Monitoring 1992, Report 7*. HMSO, London.

MAFF (1993c) *Breckland: Environmentally Sensitive Area Report of Monitoring 1992, Report 8*. HMSO, London.

MAFF (1993d) *The Shropshire Borders: Environmentally Sensitive Area Report of Monitoring 1992, Report 9*. HMSO, London.

MAFF (1993e) *The North Peak: Environmentally Sensitive Area Report of Monitoring 1992, Report 10*. HMSO, London.

MAFF (1993f) *Agriculture in the UK*. HMSO, London.

MAFF (1993g) *Environmentally Sensitive Areas: Breckland – Guidelines for Farmers*. HMSO, London.

MAFF (1993h) *The North Peak ESA – Guidelines for Applicants*. HMSO, London.

MAFF (1993i) *Agriculture & England's Environment*. HMSO, London.

MAFF (various years) *Agricultural Census*. HMSO, London.

MAFF (various years) *Statistics* (various issues). HMSO, London.

MAFF and the Intervention Board (1993) *The Government's Expenditure Plans – Departmental Report*. HMSO, London.

MAFF (and the Secretaries of State for Northern Ireland and for Scotland) (1987a) *Farm Incomes in the United Kingdom*. HMSO, London.

MAFF (and the Secretaries of State for Northern Ireland and for Scotland) (1987b) *Farming and Rural Enterprise*. HMSO, London.

MAFF and the Secretaries of State for Northern Ireland, Scotland and Wales (1987) *Farming and Rural Enterprise*. HMSO, London.

Midmore, P. (1991) *Agricultural Policy Impact and Input–Output Multipliers: A Critique*. Department of Economics and Agricultural Economics, The University College of Wales, Aberystwyth.

Mitchell, R.C. and Carson, R.T. (1989) *Using Surveys to Value Public Goods: The Contingent Valuation Method*. Resources for the Future, Washington DC.

Moss, J.E. and Chilton, S.M. (1992) *The Baseline Study for Socio-Economic Evaluation of the Mourne Mountains and Slieve Croob ESA Scheme*. The Queen's University, Belfast.

NCC (1977) *Nature Conservation and Agriculture*. Nature Conservancy Council, London.

NCC (1990) *National Nature Reserves: A Provisional Report on National Nature Reserves – Their Role Within a Nature Conservation Strategy.* Nature Conservancy Council, Peterborough.

Nicholson, M. and Willis, K.G. (1991) Subsidies to owner occupiers: Some estimates from data on individual households. *Environment and Planning A,* 23, 333–348.

Nolan, A.J. and Still, M.J. (1993) Botanical monitoring of Breadalbane ESA, 1989–1991. In: Perkins, T.J. (ed.) *Proceedings of the Symposium on Land Use and the ESA Schemes.* Scottish Agricultural College, Edinburgh.

North, D.C. (1990) *Institutions, Institutional Change and Economic Performance.* Cambridge University Press, Cambridge.

Northern Ireland Economic Council (1992) *European Structural Funds in Northern Ireland.* NIEC, Belfast, 94.

O'Carroll, L. (1993) Conservation land purchase: Past, present, future? Paper presented at the Agricultural Economics Society One-Day Conference on Agri-Environmental Policy, Manchester.

Pearce, D.W. (1988) Optimal prices for sustainable development. In: Collard, C.L., Pearce, D.W. and Ulph, D. (eds) *Economic Growth and Sustainable Development.* Macmillan, London.

Phillips, J., Yalden, D. and Tallis, J. (1981) *Peak District Moorland Erosion Study, Phase One Report.* Peak Park Joint Planning Board, Bakewell.

Primdahl, J. and Hansen, B. (1993) Agriculture in Environmentally Sensitive Areas: Implementing the ESA measure in Denmark. *Journal of Environmental Planning and Management* 36, 2.

Ratcliffe, D.A. (ed.) (1977) *A Nature Conservation Review: The Selection of Biological Sites of National Importance to Nature Conservation in Britain.* Cambridge University Press, Cambridge.

Rich, R.F. (1981) *Social Science Information and Public Policy Making.* Jossey-Bass, London.

Rosen, S. (1974) Hedonic prices and implicit markets: Product differentiation in pure competition. *Journal of Political Economy* 82, 34–55.

RSPB (1991) *A Future for Environmentally Sensitive Farming: RSPB Submission to the UK Review of Environmentally Sensitive Areas.* Royal Society for the Protection of Birds, Sandy, Beds.

Russell, N.P. and Fraser, I.M. (1993) The potential impact of environmental cross-compliance on arable farming. Agricultural Economics Society One-Day Conference on Agri-Environmental Policy, Manchester.

Russell, N.P. and Froud, J. (1991) *Socio-Economic Monitoring of the North Peak and Suffolk River Valleys Environmentally Sensitive Areas Scheme.* Ministry of Agriculture, Fisheries and Food, London.

Schulze, W.D., D'Arge, R.G. and Brookshire, D.S. (1981) Valuing environmental commodities: some recent experiments. *Land Economics* 57(2), 151–172.

Seabrook, M.F. and Higgins, C.B.R. (1988) The role of the farmer's self-concept in determining farmer behaviour. *Agricultural Administration and Extension* 30, 99–108.

Secretary of State for Wales (1986) *The Environmentally Sensitive Areas (Cambrian Mountains), Statutory Instrument No. 2257.* HMSO, London.

Secretary of State for Wales (1987a) *The Environmentally Sensitive Areas (Cambrian Mountains – Extension), Statutory Instrument No. 2026.*

Secretary of State for Wales (1987b) *The Environmentally Sensitive Areas (Lleyn Peninsula), Statutory Instrument No. 2027.*

Secretary of State for Wales (1992) *The Environmentally Sensitive Areas (Cambrian Mountains), Statutory Instrument No. 1359.*

Sellar, C., Chavas, J.-P. and Stoll, J.R. (1986) Specification of the logit model: the case of the valuation of non-market goods. *Journal of Environmental Economics and Management* 13, 382–390.

Sheail, J. (1979) Documentary evidence of the changes in the use, management and appreciation of the grass heaths of Breckland. *Journal of Biogeography* 6, 277–292.

Skerratt, S.J., Perkins, T.J. and Lilwall, N.B. (1991) *Socio-economic Evaluation of Breadalbane ESA Scheme: 1987–1990. Report for the Ministry of Agriculture, Fisheries and Food.* Scottish Agricultural College, Edinburgh.

Skerratt, S.J., McGregor, M.J. and Sharma, R.A. (1992) A socio-economic evaluation of Breadalbane Environmentally Sensitive Area scheme: methodological issues. In: Loseby, M. (ed.) *The Environment and the Management of Natural Resources.* 24th Seminar of the European Association of Agricultural Economists, Viterbo, Italy.

Skerratt, S.J., Perkins, T.J. and Lilwall, N.B. (1993) Socio-economic evaluation of Breadalbane Environmentally Sensitive Area scheme: 1987–1990. In: *Symposium on Land Use and the ESA Schemes.* Countryside Commission for Scotland, Battleby, Perth.

Smith, R. and Jones, L. (1991) The phenology of mesotrophic grassland in the Pennine Dales, Northern England: historic hay cutting dates, vegetation variation and plant species phenologies. *Journal of Applied Ecology* 28, 42–59.

SOAFD (1989) *Environmentally Sensitive Areas in Scotland: A First Report.* Scottish Office Agriculture and Fisheries Department, Edinburgh.

SOAFD (1992) *Breadalbane and Loch Lomond Environmentally Sensitive Areas: Explanatory Leaflet.* Scottish Office Agriculture and Fisheries Department, Edinburgh.

Tietenberg, T. (1992) *Environmental and Natural Resource Economics.* Harper Collins, New York.

Tracy, M. (1989) *Government and Agriculture in Western Europe 1880–1988.* Harvester Wheatsheaf, Hemel Hempstead.

Walsh, R.G. (1986) *Recreation Economic Decisions: Comparing Benefits and Costs.* Venture Publishing, Pennsylvania.

Whitby, M.C. (1993) La protection des ressources naturelles et du patrimoine l'example du Royaume-Uni. In: Courtet, C., Berlan-Darqué, M. and Demarne, Y. (eds) *Un Point Sur Agriculture et Société,* Association Descartes, Paris.

Whitby, M.C., Coggins, G. and Saunders, C.M. (1990) *Alternative Payment Systems for Management Agreements.* Nature Conservancy Council, Peterborough.

Whitby, M.C., Saunders, C.M. and Walsh, M. (1992) *A Socio-Economic Evaluation of the Pennine Dales Environmentally Sensitive Area; A Report to MAFF.* Department of Agricultural Economics and Food Marketing, University of Newcastle upon Tyne.

Whittaker, J.M., O'Sullivan, P. and McInerney, J.P. (1991) An economic analysis of management agreements. In: Hanley, N. (ed.) *Farming and the Countryside: An Economic Analysis of External Costs and Benefits.* CAB International, Wallingford, UK, pp. 197–214.

Wilensky, H.I. (1967) *Organisational Intelligence.* Basic Books, New York.

Willis, K.G. (1980) *The Economics of Town and Country Planning.* Collins (Granada) London.

Willis, K.G. and Garrod, G.D. (1993) *Valuation of the South Downs and Somerset Levels and Moors Environmentally Sensitive Area Landscapes by the General Public. Appendices.* Centre for Rural Economy, Department of Agricultural Economics and Food Marketing, University of Newcastle upon Tyne.

Willis, K.G., Allanson, P.F., Garrod, G.D., Whitby, M.C., Powe, N.A., Adger, W.N. and Harvey, D.N. (1993a) *Results of Research from the Newcastle Countryside Change Programme.* Countryside Change Initiative, Working Paper 3, Department of Agricultural Economics and Food Marketing, University of Newcastle upon Tyne.

Willis, K.G., Garrod, G.D. and Saunders, C.M. (1993b) *Valuation of the South Downs and Somerset Levels and Moors Environmentally Sensitive Area Landscapes by the General Public.* Research Report to the Ministry of Agriculture, Fisheries and Food, Centre for Rural Economy, Department of Agricultural Economics and Food Marketing, University of Newcastle upon Tyne.

INDEX

Because it is so frequently referred to throughout this text, the Ministry of Agriculture Fisheries and Food (MAFF) is not separately indexed here. The many MAFF publications that are referred to are listed in the Bibliography.